MW01230554

The Integrated
Entrepreneur

Actualize Your Potential
and Fulfill Your Purpose

RAEANNE LACATENA
LCSW-R, CPC

**LANDON
HAIL
PRESS**

Paperback ISBN: 978-1-959955-38-2
Hardback ISBN: 978-1-959955-39-9
B/w hardback ISBN: 978-1-959955-47-4
Cover design by Rich Johnson, Spectacle Photo
Published by Landon Hail Press

Bennett, Beckham, and Callan:
You are my Why.
My miracles—all that I do is for you!

Advance Praise

"*The Integrated Entrepreneur* is a transformative guide that empowers readers to unlock their full potential and fulfill their life's purpose. Through a comprehensive journey across psychological, spiritual, and practical realms, the book skillfully integrates insights from neuroscience, business acumen, and personal development. From understanding basic needs to mastering emotional intelligence and embracing entrepreneurial mindset, each chapter offers practical strategies. This book not only equips entrepreneurs with essential skills but also inspires a profound shift toward personal and professional harmony. Ideal for any entrepreneur seeking to thrive in today's ever-changing business environment."

—Jim Britt, international best-selling author, life strategist

"Through Raeanne's words, her story, and experience, she supported me with illuminating areas in my own life and business that needed to shift for self-transcendence. But she didn't stop there. She has infused science, psychology, and spirituality in a way that guides you toward a life of true freedom and abundance. The book outlines simple processes and tools to support the shift in mental, emotional, and physical health to skyrocket your success. It is truly a holistic approach to having it all without sacrifice. I would highly recommend this book to any entrepreneur who wants to create a business by design and to experience self-transcendence in this lifetime."

—Vanessa Hallick, energetic business coach
best-selling author

"The work Raeanne has done paves a pathway to the new world of entrepreneurship. She does a great job of 'unboxing' the human psyche so that we can examine it from a distance. I firmly believe that *fear management* is the key to the future at a time where the pace of change can be overwhelming. This book provides a roadmap so that we can achieve it at scale, which is greatly needed in our society today. Bravo!"

—Maria Ferrante-Schepis, author
insurance-industry thought leader

"This book is a vital reminder of how uniquely individual we all are, and how necessary it is that we find what works best for our *personalized* needs. There are no cookie cutters to finding the most effective paths to personal and business development, and the author takes a very mindful approach to the guidance she provides, with the understanding that businesses are made up of perfectly imperfect humans, therefore in need of a very humanistic approach. Raeanne helps guide entrepreneurs in discovering the path that will work best for them on their business journey, while learning how to integrate that path into a purpose-driven life. A must-read for those who wish to build and live their own dreams."

—Yarona Boster, speaker coach
best-selling author, TEDx speaker

"*The Integrated Entrepreneur* is unlike any other business book I've read. Raeanne real-life experiences hit home and gave me a sense of comfort that I wasn't alone in my struggles. Her vulnerability in sharing deeply personal stories, like freezing during her high school graduation, makes the book feel raw, honest, and completely relatable. This isn't a guide full of textbook theories—it's real life with real solutions.

"What stood out most were the chapter summaries and action plans. Each chapter doesn't just explain a concept; it breaks it down in a way that made me think about my own experiences and how I can actively apply the lessons. The chapter on limiting beliefs, for example, opened my eyes to the internal barriers I hadn't even recognized, and the action steps made tackling them seem achievable. It wasn't just inspiration; it was a roadmap I could follow.

"The STEAR Clear and Anchor model in particular has been a game changer for me. The way it walks you through the process of identifying thoughts and emotions tied to a specific situation and then outlines clear actions to shift results was incredibly powerful. It gave me practical tools that I use daily to manage stress, make better decisions, and grow both personally and professionally.

"This book is a must-read for entrepreneurs looking for real-world guidance on integrating personal growth with business success. It's full of authentic, actionable wisdom."

—Jon Sheldon, RICP, CLC
owner, BelleauWood Coaching

Contents

Foreword

IT TAKES A SPECIAL KIND of courage to embrace the path of entrepreneurship.

If you ventured into this world of your own accord, it means you are more optimistic than most. You are choosing to see the world not as it is but as it *could* be. With half of businesses failing within the first five years, stepping away from the comfort of a steady paycheck is a bold act. But it's not just your financial stability you put on the line, as an entrepreneur, but also your heart and soul.

But as you know, big risks lead to big rewards. Your business is a blank canvas, and you get to decide what manifests on the page, how vivid the colors are, and what images come to life. Ultimately, your business is a unique extension of yourself, a culmination of your passions, dreams, and values. Through it, you can find profound joy, purpose, freedom, and an endless fountain of creativity. As an entrepreneur, you have taken a leap of faith in yourself and your ability to shape the world around you in your own way, to leave your mark, and to contribute something of real substance to human history.

I know this to be true through my own experience launching my own book editing and publishing business: The White Editorial. From a content, yet lonely ghostwriter to a thriving entrepreneur with dozens of books under my belt and a team of dedicated editors by my side, we have transformed our love for stories into a business that empowers authors from all corners of the globe. What began as a personal passion has evolved into a mission to help the world's leading experts in personal growth share their wisdom and insights with a broader audience, ultimately making the world a better place. I believe that books are among our greatest legacies, and it has been a profound honor to support Raeanne as she courageously stepped into her new role as an author. Her work is a beacon of hope and guidance for so many, and I only wish I had the chance to read her book before launching my editorial. Let's just say my journey would have been much smoother with Raeanne's expertise lighting the way.

The journey of entrepreneurship can be exciting, inspiring, and deeply meaningful, but, as you probably already know, it can also be a huge challenge to maintain your balance. How can we become wildly successful in our business lives while maintaining loving relationships? How can we manage full schedules, our own, as well as our teams, perhaps, while staying physically and mentally healthy? How can we overcome inevitable blocks that surface around our self-confidence, our worthiness around money, and our ability to stay afloat in challenging times? How can we uncover the true "why" behind our business that gives our day-to-day meaning?

In the pages of *The Integrated Entrepreneur*, Raeanne shows us exactly how. As Raeanne outlines, running a successful business goes a lot deeper than the typically "masculine" approach of understanding KPIs, setting prices, and managing finances. There's another side to entrepreneurship that is just as important, if not more so, and that's the forgotten "feminine."

As a business coach with decades of experience, Raeanne knows more than most that the most successful businesses strike a balance between masculine and feminine approaches; between action and reflection, between strategy and empathy, and between healing and growing. In Raeanne's words, we must find the sweet spot between "feeling safe enough and stretched enough to grow." Our businesses will stretch us for sure, and most entrepreneurs are willing to push their comfort zones to the max. Yet many entrepreneurs are blind to the importance of finding safety and security within themselves. They miss out on self-care in the name of success. Raeanne teaches us that not caring for ourselves isn't just to the detriment of our mental and physical health, but to our businesses, and to everyone around us. Inner safety, inner balance, inner clarity, and inner peace are, surprisingly, a crucial part of our business strategy.

That said, building true safety within ourselves, and consequently, within our businesses, comes slower, and it comes when we do the *real* work. "Doing the real work" means going back and healing past traumas, uncovering unhelpful beliefs about ourselves, and reprogramming our brains in a way that serves the Integrated Entrepreneur that we strive to be. By reading this book, you'll have already taken the first, and toughest step.

So, prepare yourself, reader. This book isn't for the faint-hearted, and it isn't meant to be a passive read. Raeanne will encourage you to embrace challenging inner work in the name of unlocking your true potential. Approach this journey with an open heart and an open mind. Trust me when I say that the journey will be worth it, and the rewards will be beyond what you thought was possible. As a professional editor, it's my job to understand a book's content. But I can honestly say very few have touched my heart and mind to the degree that they become part of my own story. This is one of them.

As you embark on your own journey with *The Integrated Entrepreneur*, I encourage you to trust in Raeanne to guide you toward fulfilling your purpose and taking your entrepreneurship to the next level. Even if your business is currently "doing well," I assure you, that you will reach new heights within a very short amount of time if you fully embrace this content. Think of it as a year's worth of coaching in one book, guiding us on our path to self-actualization in service to the greater good.

Welcome to *The Integrated Entrepreneur*. Your adventure begins here.

Amy White, senior editor, The White Editorial

Foreword

IN A WORLD WHERE entrepreneurship has become synonymous with burnout, overwhelm, and endless hustle, Raeanne Lacatena offers a breath of fresh air with *The Integrated Entrepreneur*. This book is not just a guide; it's a lifeline for those of us who've felt the crushing weight of building a business while neglecting our true selves.

For years, the narrative in the entrepreneurial world has been all about grit, grind, and getting ahead at any cost. We've been taught to compartmentalize our lives, to wear different masks in different settings one for business, another for family, yet another for our inner world. We've chased success like it's the Holy Grail, only to find ourselves more disconnected, more disillusioned, and more exhausted than ever.

But Raeanne challenges all of that. She turns the traditional entrepreneurial journey on its head and invites us into a new way of thinking, a new way of being. *The Integrated Entrepreneur* is a powerful manifesto for anyone who's ready to break free from the chains of outdated paradigms and step into a life where their business is not just a job or a source of income, but a true expression of their authentic self.

This book dares to ask the tough questions: What if your business could be a reflection of your soul? What if you could integrate every aspect of your life—your passions, your values, your purpose—into your entrepreneurial journey? What if success wasn't just about numbers on a spreadsheet, but about living a life of fulfillment, joy, and alignment?

Raeanne doesn't just ask these questions; she gives you the tools to answer them. With profound wisdom, practical exercises, and a no-nonsense approach, she guides you to confront the limiting beliefs that have been holding you back, to harmonize the dualities within you, and to embrace a new mindset: one of abundance, balance, and synchronicity.

As you turn these pages, prepare to be challenged. Prepare to be inspired. Raeanne will push you to dig deep, to reflect, and to take action in ways you might never have considered. But if you're willing to do the work, I promise you, the results will be transformative. You'll emerge from this journey not just as a better entrepreneur, but as a more integrated, fulfilled, and empowered human being.

The Integrated Entrepreneur is more than just a book. It's a movement. It's a call to all of us to stop playing small, to stop living fractured lives, and to step into the fullness of who we are meant to be. It's the book I wish I'd had twenty years ago and the book every entrepreneur needs today.

So, here's my advice: don't just read this book; devour it. Let it challenge you, change you, and, most importantly, guide you to create a business and a life that's truly aligned with who you are.

Baz Porter, CEO, best-selling author, and podcast host

Introduction

"We all have the extraordinary coded within us, waiting to be released."

—Jean Houston

WHEN WE LIVE INTO our purpose, it can take us on very unexpected journeys.

Some people have an internal call to write a book. They see a storyline, have an idea, dream up a set of characters, and/or have original thoughts that they become passionate about expressing.

Some people have a natural, innate ability with the written word. Their natural poetic sense is an art form; they can take the reader on a journey into another space and time, while leveraging language to express their creative genius.

Some people crave writing, journal daily, and find solace in the art of writing. They have hundreds of completely filled journals around their homes, get lost for hours in flow with their writing, or process what they are going through in life on the page.

I have never seen myself as this type of person.

Over my lifetime, I've been told many times, "You should write a book," or "Raeanne, you have at least a few books in you."

But I never believed it or even desired to make that happen.

I have even heard plenty of times that I'm not a very good writer.

And yet, here I am, sharing with you what I have come to understand, study, live through firsthand, and witness in others through the written word.

The book path chose me.

The external voices got louder, and I listened.

The universal pull grew stronger, so I let it lead me.

These voices, signs, and signals have become a part of my inner dialogue, and now, I am an author.

This book is just a metaphor for my own personal journey of self-actualization in service of supporting others to achieve their own potential through their art and creativity of business ownership. Like writing a book, starting, building, maintaining, and growing a business is an art form that requires both internal and external commitment, transformation, and a willingness to be open, curious, creative, and self-aware. There is a process to running a business, as there is to writing a book. And in order to be successful, you *get* to trust the process.

In essence, entrepreneurship is just a personal development plan brilliantly disguised as a financial opportunity. The more you do the inner work, the more outward success you'll achieve.

Who you are anywhere is who you are everywhere—you already have everything you need inside of you right now to be successful; and you are also the only major limiting factor to your own success.

By accepting these core beliefs, you are ultimately in complete control of your success, because you are taking ownership for your results as a reflection of your own internal beliefs, thoughts, emotions, and actions. Of course, there are external factors that interfere with your "plan"; however, you still maintain control over how you respond to those external factors indefinitely.

No matter what happens in life or in business, you have a choice and you have control; you can change the course of your life and your business.

There are so many coaches, consultants, or business gurus in the world who tout, "Do it this one particular way to get results." They are missing the human element of business ownership, however. There is no one particular mode of growing a business that will be successful for every single person who uses their particular method, modality, or framework.

This book offers you a path to learn who you are as a *human*, allowing that to guide the development of your right fit, aligned business plan, which will be a reflection of who you are as that human.

You are a human being who is having many human experiences. We get to borrow clues from what's working, what's not working, where we are getting in our own way, and where we can leverage our strengths and abilities in order to create the most effective path, one unique to our innate human essence.

We can look at our life from every angle to gather the evidence about what will work for us. This examination requires the willingness to go inward, to heal, to explore our inner wisdom, look at our traumas, and really understand our personality, identity, societal and cultural programming, childhood, and what coming of age was like for us; our past relationships, work experiences, and our outlook on life, money, politics, the world, and anything else that makes us who we are!

All these elements live inside of us, whether we are consciously aware of them or not. They are the sum of our neural pathways, patterns, and default networks within our brain, which gloriously and miraculously help us move through life safely and without having to relearn how to breathe, walk, drive, or navigate our everyday anew. However, they also hold deeply rooted biases and sometimes negative or false patterns; they can alter our perspectives and limit our full potential, when we simply accept them for what they are without questioning, in the face of our growth.

We are able to explore our past and present time zones. Then, we may sail into our most preferred and ideal future. We can leverage the plasticity of our brains and bodies to be what we choose and to recover with resilience from whatever cards we have been dealt in life. We get to manifest whatever destiny we desire, to feel, be, and think whatever we choose.

To receive those outer rewards requires inner work. But too many business owners are focused on the strategy, the tactics, the numbers, and the results as the starting point to their success, without pausing to acknowledge this fundamental set of truths.

By doing the inner work, the personal development work, we can access those chosen external results. You can try to lead with the results; however, inevitably, you will be faced with this work.

I have met millionaires who have everything they could possibly desire in life but nobody to share it with, because they have destroyed every relationship along the way in their efforts to collect material wealth. They are absolutely broke millionaires, often physically ill, emotionally scarred, and relationally isolated.

I have worked with some of the most amazing people on the planet, who are still doubting their inner self-worth, because they've never learned how to celebrate their success and honor their abilities; often, they are still running patterns from early childhood neglect and rejection.

I have supported Olympic-level athletes who no longer feel their life has value after retiring from their sport, because their identity has been completely wrapped into their athletic ability, habits, performance, and training.

And I have met some of the happiest, healthiest people who are doing what they love and doing that work with passion, connection, and fulfillment, whether they are a florist, baker, or homemaker.

Many entrepreneurs come to me for business coaching to help them grow their business into whatever level of success they choose, based on where they are in their business journey. Some employees come to me, ready to take the courageous leap into entrepreneurship, knowing it's been in their heart to be on their own, fulfill their dreams, and work for themselves.

Some of these aspiring entrepreneurs come to me with deeply rooted traumas from their employment experience and are leaving because they just simply can't stomach working for someone else.

Some crave financial freedom or want to work in healthier environments, while others have been dabbling in "side hustles" or part-time business ownership and understand, if they want their business to replace their corporate salary, they will need to step more fully into attention with their business. They are ready to take their business from "hobby status" to full-time CEO status.

Some entrepreneurs have been at their business for a while; they made the decision many years ago to use business as a means to an end, to put what they love to do out into the world. Perhaps they are a service professional, artist, creative, or author, and they have a business as an avenue to do what they love. However, they haven't fully adopted the business-owner identity and may even reject it.

Some have climbed the ladder of success and entered business ownership by earning equity or partnership in a company, but they haven't been taught what it means to be in business. Others have inherited a business from family or are carrying out the family legacy and have witnessed their elders run a business from the sidelines, but they have never done it on their own. Other natural-born entrepreneurs have been collecting businesses their whole lives and can't help but have ideas that they work to bring to life in the marketplace. They see an opportunity and take it; they are comfortable with risk and chasing the external reward.

No matter where my clients are on their entrepreneurial journey, they often come to business coaching with the same idea: to receive support in the process of creating financial freedom through their business. They want the financial reward to come from successful business ownership, and then to continue to scale, leverage, and grow their business. Many of them have created a business with the initial intention of taking the limits off their earning potential; they desire to have the business support their personal needs, their family's needs, and everything they could hope or dream for in life and with their business.

Financial freedom, like everything else, is subjective to everyone; it means something different for each person. One person's financial freedom is being able to afford groceries without having to think about what they buy, while another wants a private yacht or a private island and anywhere in between.

As with some of the other elements we've discussed in business, it's important to start with the awareness of what this means for you, personally. Really getting clear about what "financial freedom" looks, seems, feels, and presents for you, both linearly and nonlinearly, will make it far more likely you will achieve it. You can't achieve what you aren't aware of, so start your process by spending some time really decoding what that means for you.

For some, the word "freedom" is more important even than the "financial" side of things; and for others; the money is the real focus. Either way, there will be feelings associated with what freedom and/or money does for you, so really drill down and discover what you want to be feeling and thinking and how you plan to behave when you have that money. When you are clear about what you want to *feel* as a result of financial freedom, you can start feeling those feelings now, because that's all anyone really needs or wants anyway! Too many people wait to feel those desired feelings until they have the final result and end up pushing that result further away from actuality.

The reality is, even when business owners make a major windfall, close the biggest case of their career, hit their big audacious goals, and/or break into a new financial echelon, the excitement and celebration that comes from hitting that goal is either quite fleeting or completely absent.

More commonly, when people hit those major targets financially, they either feel relieved, neutral, or not much at all. The number is just a number. The money is just pixels on a screen and not even real to them.

Sure, some may celebrate with some external reward, however even that brings a temporary dopamine hit that doesn't sustain them for very long.

This doesn't diminish the reality that money is the chosen currency of exchange on our planet, and thus we need money to provide for our basic needs. When we have abundant financial resources, this concern is completely taken off the table. Also, money and financial freedom can afford us luxuries, experiences, and privileges.

If financial freedom is one of your top priorities, that doesn't make you wrong or bad. I just have observed that even when we hit that highly sought-after goal, the magic we imagine is often fleeting. Also, it often leads to an intense pressure to perform in our business at that same financial level year after year or we develop a new longing for something more, such as greater fulfillment, purpose, impact, and/or legacy building.

What many of those business owners have not fully come to understand is that the business is just a part of who you already are. This is what they discover when they dive into this work.

Show me an area in your life where you are struggling, and I will show you where it's affecting your business.

Show me an area of your personal life where you feel successful, and I can help you bridge an understanding and show you how to use that success to support your business, too.

Let me take a look at your business, and I can show you how it may also be affecting your wellness, relationships, or health.

So many business owners see their lives through a lens of compartmentalization. Their personal lives are affected by their business, but they are separate. They are trying to practice boundary-setting in an effort to create "work-life balance," except in many ways this is an illusion.

When we think of the word "balance," we might visualize a scale that levels when the weight is equally distributed on both sides of the scale.

Except, that is *never* how life looks.

To think we will "get it right" when we have completely separate boundaries and a perfect 50/50 balance is setting ourselves up for failure with unrealistic expectations.

You are your business. Your business is you.

You are not a series of "compartments" in your life and business. You are one human, having lots of human experiences.

Compartmentalization has its positive benefits, and it can be a useful tool in certain contexts. However, to live our lives in that way is disrespectful of the reality that we are a *whole* human going through multifaceted events.

This is what I mean when I say I am a *holistic* business coach. I believe that human beings are already whole. They already have within them what they need to be successful. They are worthy. When we take the time to learn our unique set of circumstances and integrate them as a whole being, we are able to lead a life and craft a business that is more respectful of that reality.

Instead of trying to keep our business completely separate and isolated from our family or relationships, for example, we can begin to explore how to collect evidence of our relationship success in order to create business success; we can be respectful of what we need to build healthy business relationships, healthy personal relationships, and a healthy relationship with ourselves.

We can explore and grow curious about the areas in our relationships that maybe aren't going as well as we'd hoped, to see what we have control over, what we can shift, where we can evolve, and where we can pivot to create more success. We can be one human having lots of relationships in many different elements of our full lives.

This same truth applies to our finances, our wellness, parenting, adventure, hobbies, spirituality, sexuality, future planning or goal setting, nutrition, and so on. Any one of these elements can inform or support another. They are an interconnected channel and stunning map of who you are.

Instead of resisting this natural fact, embracing it will allow us to grow into happier, healthier, and wealthier expressions of whom we choose to be. And yes, we will be better able to actualize that potential. The operative word in the pursuit of financial freedom is actually *freedom*. The freedom to be authentically you: to fully live your purpose and to impact the lives of others through your individual expression of your unique gifts and your truth.

The entrepreneurs I serve have this in common: they are bold, powerful, visionary leaders on their journey to fulfill their purpose and actualize their potential in service to a higher mission. With that higher mission comes massive responsibility. What I have observed, however, is where a leader has such a high level of responsibility, such a meaningful mission and purpose, and a deep commitment to evolve and grow, they also have an equally pervasive shadow, which needs internal personal development work and, oftentimes, a healing of great trauma.

As a trained mental health therapist and someone who has been through this herself, I see high achievers running a trauma response that stems from their earliest memories in an effort to escape inner turmoil, family or childhood trauma, some brand of imposter syndrome, and scarcity and/or not-enoughness. The bigger the purpose frequently means the bigger the shadow.

The work of becoming an Integrated Entrepreneur will help you understand your innate worth, heal your past programming, own your unique abilities, and operate your business from a place of harmony and wholeness.

It all starts with the inner work, but that doesn't preclude or dismiss the importance of the outer work or reward. It is both.

Do the inner work, and the outer reward will follow.

Where do you start?

It can be useful to float back in your own personal timeline to ask yourself: *What happened to me that made me less whole?*

Introduction Integration

Summary: Entrepreneurship is a personal development plan brilliantly disguised as a financial opportunity. The more inner work you do, the more outward results you get to enjoy!

Resources

Complimentary Workbook: Visit the link below to gain access to your completely free workbook to supplement your learning and integration of the tools and principles discussed throughout this book.

raeannelacatena.com/integrationworkbook

Journal Prompts

❖ What does financial freedom mean to you personally? Describe the emotions, events, and lifestyle that come to mind when you think about being financially free.

❖ Consider a moment in your life when you felt a sense of financial security. What happened, and how did it impact your overall well-being and mindset?

❖ Reflect on the relationship between financial freedom and the pursuit of your entrepreneurial goals. How do these aspects complement and support each other in your journey?

❖ Explore the concept of personal freedom. What does it mean to have the freedom to live life on your own terms? How does this align with your entrepreneurial ambitions?

❖ Imagine a future where you have achieved both financial and personal freedom. How does this vision inspire and motivate you in your entrepreneurial endeavors?

Prologue

Senior Song

"If you are depressed, you are living in the past. If you are anxious, you are living in the future. If you are at peace, you are living in the present."

—Lao Tzu

IT WAS GRADUATION DAY.

It was the last day my classmates and I would be together as a group before going off into the world to become whatever we were meant to be.

I had graduated third in my class, and while I wasn't going to make a valedictorian or salutatorian speech that day, I had been chosen by my graduating class to represent them in a way that was very meaningful to me.

I had just decided to go to a music conservatory to major in psychology and minor in music. At the age of seventeen, I had decided on what I wanted to be when I grew up: a music therapist.

Ever since I was a little girl, I knew I wanted to help people and I knew that music was my most favorite thing. Music was how I expressed myself. It was a deep part of my identity as an individual, in my school community, and in my family.

What better way to culminate all of this but to sing the senior song to send my classmates off!

The choir was called up to the front of the audience, which, between my graduating class, all our family members, and the local access news, was easily into the thousands, and my biggest crowd to date.

As I looked out in front of me, I vividly saw the sea of faces. I could see my family, and I knew more of my family was watching from home. I had played the lead role in music performances for my entire school career, so my classmates knew what to expect when I walked up to the front of the audience to begin.

The song was "Music of my Heart" by Gloria Estefan and 'N Sync—very nineties, I know!

The intro music began...

But I did not...

Nothing came out...

The words were not there...

The song was trapped in my throat...

I watched as the audience sat up straight in their chairs, seeming to wonder what was going on, because everybody knew the tune to that song and were waiting for the lyrics to begin.

The accompanist started the song one more time in an effort to give me a second chance.

Except by that time, I was completely frozen.

The entire first verse passed, with nothing but music accompaniment, until my choir mates came in and took over for the rest of the song.

At that moment, I had a complete identity shift, which would eventually become an identity crisis.

What should've been one of the most amazing days of my life and, as a young woman, one of my most pivotal moments of transition, had blurred in a flash into the biggest failure of my life.

I was humiliated.

I was devastated.

My family tried to tell me nobody noticed, and they tried to focus on the fact that I was graduating at the top of my class and going off to do great things.

But I couldn't stop the ringing in my ears that was telling me I was a complete failure and an embarrassment to my community and my family.

I naturally had the summer off from everything, before I went off to college to just work and play. So, I didn't really notice what was unfolding until much later.

When I arrived at the music conservatory and was assigned my first vocal performance coach, I struggled deeply with his training. I stopped practicing and started dreading all my music classes. I fell asleep in music history and hated music theory.

I bounced around from choir to choir and never raised my hand for a solo. I tried to be brave but noticed self-sabotaging tone or tune issues that inevitably allowed me to miss the opportunity and safely slink to the back of the room.

Even in the dorm, there was an awesomely fun group of my classmates who would go out into the courtyard, play drums and guitar, and sing at the top of their lungs. Typically, this would be a dream come true for me and my college experience. But I don't think many of them even know I am a singer to this day, because I never let them hear me sing.

I remember one time, when I was visiting home, a bully who clearly was just jealous about not getting the solo for a senior day (just saying) followed me around the mall with my friends, singing that song to mock me. It sent me backward.

I started to focus more on the psychology component of my degree, and then I also adopted a French minor, which took me abroad and completely away from music.

I also started to drink more regularly during college and lean into the party culture. The spiral downward continued throughout my remaining four years in college, until music was just a hobby and an afterthought.

I still graduated at the top of my class and was invited into an Ivy League graduate program, to focus on clinical studies, which all my professors encouraged me to do.

By the time I left school, music and my voice were completely silent.

I started looking to experts, professors, mentors, my parents, and what other people were doing, in order to find answers to the questions I had about what I was meant to be when I grew up. They told me what I was good at, and I listened.

I craved so deeply to be excellent again that I dug in deeply to anything anyone told me I was good at, and I refused to do anything where I was remotely second-rate.

I said yes to Columbia and goodbye to my music career.

There was still a call and attraction to music for me, so I always found myself adjacent. I was constantly going to music festivals, surrounding myself with musician friends, and dating some pretty terrible ones, which reinforced the belief that music was bad for me.

A few times during my twenties, I tried to experiment, just to see what would happen, by auditioning for *American Idol* .... twice! Both times were pretty negative experiences. The journey into the producer's room is far different than what you see on TV, and when the man in a chicken suit made it through but I didn't, I threw my hands up and walked away.

I dove into my career as a counselor with my degree in advanced generalist practice in programming, a mixture of clinical counseling and program development, and I always found myself rubbing elbows with music therapists. At least I could be next to them, if I wasn't one of them.

I share this story with you here in order to illustrate just how deeply one moment in time can change the entire trajectory of your life, your identity, and your future.

Even though this trauma wasn't a heavy loss or tragedy on the scale of what other people have had to go through in their lives, it was one of the worst things that my brain experienced in my seventeen years.

I was born on the "wrong side of the tracks" in so many ways, and, as a child, I lived through multiple acrimonious divorces and a fairly chaotic upbringing that included frequent moves, a volatile home life, and run-ins with addiction and poverty. I was given the role to protect my family and make them look good; I became an expert at hiding any chaos behind the scenes from a very young age and letting the world see only excellence on the front stage.

So, when this singular occurrence happened, this mortifying, very public setback, it became a major source of the work I needed to do to step into my full power and higher self.

I have certainly repeated patterns from other childhood traumas growing up, and there was definitely programming to unlearn and defaults to overcome, but I thought I had things fairly well in hand and was managing, even expecting, the chaos, until...

On graduation day...

I found out.

I was a loser.

I was a failure.

I was a fraud.

I was worthless.

My amygdala (more on this later!) kicked into high gear and decided on that day that it was going to protect me, from there on out, from anything that had to do with music. It created self-sabotage, fear responses, and freeze mechanisms from that day forward to help "keep me safe."

My amygdala just wanted to make sure I never had to feel that terrible again. And so, the music in my heart became silent that day.

Terrible irony, I know.

I am only able to share this with you at this point because I have done deep soul, mind, and body work to help teach my central nervous system, my fear mechanisms, my body, my mind, and my spirit that I am safe.

I am worthy.

I belong.

That I create value.

And that music isn't dangerous.

I also acknowledge this trauma lives inside of me, and so I spiral back to it at each stage of my evolution, as I move further and further toward self-actualization.

I am committed to stewarding the parts of me that were interrupted as part of my life's work. Sharing it with you here is part of my healing.

My hope is that I can share with you as many of the tools I have gathered over the years, as I have worked in service to other people and on my own self-development, in order to support you and your healing, too. As you come to understand more fully that who you are anywhere is who you are everywhere, you can start to accept how what has happened to you—past, present, and future—will impact your ability to step into your highest potential.

I'm happy to share that now, I feel like I am living out my true calling as a business coach. I love my career, and even though I had a rocky start with music when I was young, feeling lost and unsure, over the years it became apparent that this is what I was meant to do.

To grow your business, you'll need to go within and see where those deep core limiting beliefs and that collection of experiences are no longer serving you, so you can move forward.

The first step is to ask: *What is your senior song?*

- ❖ What happened to you in your formative years that interrupted or shifted your growth and trajectory?
- ❖ Who did what to you?
- ❖ And how is your brain, body, and mind trying to protect you now?
- ❖ In what way is that serving you?
- ❖ And in what way is that limiting you?

Then, as you will learn throughout the pages in this book, your newfound self-awareness coupled with a growth mindset and a commitment to actualize your potential, you can develop the resilience and courage to succeed, no matter what life throws at you, whether personally or in business.

When I lost my song, it deepened the cultural programming that all too often happens to women, which stifles our voice. As women, we are taught to make ourselves small. To be seen not heard. We're not given a place at the table. Not asked about our opinions or beliefs. Not taught to honor our strengths, wins, or accomplishments outwardly. Or even to speak up, speak out, or self-advocate.

This book is a healing of that voice, which I lost that day. By healing my voice and allowing my words to pour out in service to others, I am hopeful that my story can make a difference for someone else doing this same work for themselves.

I'm still working on finding ways to heal my song and my voice, and I'm grateful for the opening and trust that have come from the journey of writing this book.

For now, I am enjoying the journey and grateful that you've decided to dive into what this process means for you in your path, too.

Prologue Integration

Summary: Your past events, experiences, and trauma, your upbringing and childhood, your influences, models, and internal programming have all come together to make you who you are today. You get to decide how much of that comes into your present and future experiences.

Resources

Journal Prompts:

- ❖ Explore the impact of your formative years on your personal growth and life trajectory. Identify key moments or events during your formative years that either interrupted or shifted your path and how they shaped your current self?

- ❖ Consider the individuals or occurrences that played a role in those formative years. Who or what had a significant influence on your life during that time? How did their actions or influence contribute to the person you are today?

- ❖ Delve into the ways your brain, body, and mind respond to protect you from past challenges or traumas. Explore the coping mechanisms and defense mechanisms that have developed as a result of these events.

- ❖ Examine the positive aspects and limitations of these protective mechanisms. In what ways do they currently serve you? How have they helped you navigate life, relationships, or challenges? Acknowledge the strengths and resilience that have emerged from these protective strategies.

- ❖ How might certain behaviors or thought patterns developed in response to past experiences now pose challenges or hinder your personal growth? Be honest about any patterns that may be holding you back.

Chapter One

Basic Needs

"We delight in the beauty
of the butterfly,
but we rarely admit the changes
it has gone through
to achieve that beauty."

—Maya Angelou

WHEN YOU ARE EVALUATING what you've been through in the past, where you are in the present moment, and what you're trying to accomplish with your future, it's important to acknowledge real and perceived realities, fears, doubts, and worries that are either limiting you or supporting you.

In some instances, you may be experiencing very real limits in your life that need to be addressed in order for you to climb to your highest potential. There is a classic teaching by Abraham Maslow, which he calls the "Hierarchy of Needs." He developed this tool and psychological theory in the mid-twentieth century and proposed his original five-tier Hierarchy of Needs in his paper, "A Theory of Human Motivation," which was published in the journal *Psychological Review* in 1943. The hierarchy was later refined and extended in his 1954 book *Motivation and Personality*.

The concept of the sixth level, named Self-Transcendence, was introduced later in the 1970s, well after Maslow's initial development of the hierarchy. He incorporated this additional level in the later years of his career, particularly in his later works such as *The Farther Reaches of Human Nature*, published posthumously in

1971. The inclusion of self-transcendence reflects Maslow's evolving thoughts on human motivation and the idea that individuals may be motivated by a desire to transcend their individual selves and contribute to something larger than themselves.

Maslow's Hierarchy of Needs

The theory suggests that individuals generally move up the pyramid in a sequential manner, as they seek to fulfill their needs. This means people typically focus on satisfying lower-level needs before progressing to higher-level needs in each level. The hierarchy begins with our basic physiological needs, such as food, water, warmth, and rest.

The hierarchy is often depicted as a pyramid to illustrate this progression, with the lower levels forming the base and the higher levels representing the apex as illustrated in the graphic on the prior page.

I started on my own path to self-actualization at the bottom of the pyramid, where my family sometimes struggled to keep the electricity running and a roof over our heads. My mother was a hard-working single parent who did the best she could to step back into the workforce after a divorce early in my life. She often worked long hours, leaving me to tend to my brother with the help of some neighborhood kids.

My father was a visionary and a creative, a true entrepreneur at heart, always looking to create a new idea, which often led to his moving to different roles and jobs while I was young. Child support was a regular negative conversation in our home and a source of conflict; there was a lot of fighting. I learned early on what it took to run a household financially and when there were challenges to make ends meet.

At one point during my childhood, we had to move into my grandparents' home for a period of time, for financial reasons. All of this created a constant level of stress and was a burden on my parents. I witnessed firsthand what it was like to brush up against the lower modes of the Maslow Hierarchy, and this became part of my core understanding of how the world works.

Children naturally internalize those messages around money; they witness those models of relationships and take on that burden or scarcity as their own. There is a concept in neuroscience that is often associated with a critical period of brain development and early childhood development, during which many fundamental neural connections are formed. While it's not precisely a "time frame" with a set range from birth to seven years old, this period is crucial for various aspects of cognitive and emotional development, when the brain undergoes significant growth, and when a child is especially sensitive to the effects of their environment on brain development.

What we go through early in life becomes a part of our framework and way of being; it shapes our brains, and our understanding of the world as it is. If our external environment is not meeting or is challenging our lower-level needs, it can lead to a distorted or insecure relationship with other people, places, and events.

During these critical early years of development, I learned about money shortages and relationship models, and my basic needs were not always met. Even to this day, when I am triggered into my lower self for one reason or another, I notice those parts of me become active. Since I grew up in a family blended with instability and disorder, but also joy, love, and fun, I became simultaneously comfortable with chaos and more sensitive to it.

I witnessed scarcity and fear at a young age, which led me to be conflicted about what it means to be more generous, free, and potentially irresponsible with money. I learned about how we couldn't have what other people had and how we had to work hard to earn our keep. At the same time, I heard from my parents that, if we needed something, the money would come, because the universe would provide; also, that you can't take money with you when you die, so let's enjoy it while we have it.

These conflicting messages did result in a variety of valuable lessons for me. I learned the value of hard work and about being careful with my spending. I also internalized that money is energy, meant to be shared generously and used, not hoarded, when you have it.

Those opposing values became part of my money story and identity early on. As a result, I had to reconcile and integrate them at each different level of my self-actualization journey, especially as a business owner. At times, I am able to incorporate all these divergent perspectives and attitudes into a holistic view of money. For me, now, it's save *and* spend; it's work *and* enjoy; it's provide *and* receive.

However, I can become fearful around money or make financial decisions that default to a revolving door mentality, where money constantly comes and goes, which feels like a slippery slope. Some incidents send me back to my basic foundational levels on Maslow's Hierarchy, because my money and scarcity stories are deeply ingrained in my neurochemistry and pathways, as well as in my body, life, and business events.

Identity formation and the establishment of behavioral and cognitive patterns are complex processes that extend beyond early childhood. These processes continue throughout a person's life and are influenced by a wide range of factors, including genetics, social interactions, cultural influences, and personal circumstances.

Just because our identity is strongly impacted by our childhood doesn't necessarily mean it's going to be our life's story. We can change and mold the brain; and it's absolutely necessary in the process of changing our perspectives and trajectory to self-actualize and transcend into our purpose.

Of course, being a child of multiple divorces had to have some impact on my ability to form relationships, for example; for me, this clearly led to several failed and sometimes traumatic incidents while I learned how to navigate what it meant to be in relationships.

One of the most promising and empowering parts of the human brain is its neuroplasticity, which is the brain's ability to adapt, change, and reorganize itself by forming new neural connections throughout a person's life. This allows the brain to learn, recover from injuries, and adapt to new experiences and challenges. In essence, it's the brain's way of being flexible and adaptable; this is how it can evolve.

We get to teach our brains new money stories and relationship stories or even shift our perception of traumas. However, the brain is powerful. Left to its own devices, it will run those patterns that come from our childhood learnings, our cultural programming, norms, or biases, or even amplify someone else's voice that has become deeply enmeshed into how we think and feel about ourselves.

My early childhood history led me to pursue a career in the service field. I felt passionate about helping as many people as possible, specifically children and families who needed additional support. I started my career in social work, which showed me firsthand how very difficult it is to ask someone to even have conversations about self-potential, when their basic human rights are not fulfilled and their fundamental needs are not being met. Everyone deserves to have their basic needs fulfilled; and you absolutely do need those needs met in order to evolve into the higher modes on the hierarchy.

As a young social worker, I began to see the greater depths of the cruelty in the world, the vastness of the challenges, the breadth and width of the traumas, and the deep inequalities in our society. These real-world troubles weighed on my heart, and my body started to respond negatively, because I had not yet fully understood the depths of my own empathic abilities. I could feel these troubles in my own body and mind.

I would not have been able to sustain the workload necessary to make a meaningful difference without first learning how to set better boundaries and how to take care of myself, in order to serve more people.

With my helper identity deeply ingrained in me since childhood, I wanted to make a major difference, but often I felt small and insignificant in the ways I could help. I soon realized there is also value in the work that addresses the problem from a "top-down" approach, as well. With this, we invite as many change-makers and love-driven leaders who are willing to actualize their potential, supporting them to serve the mission of a more loving, equitable, and inclusive society. That work matters, too.

The essential work begins with fulfilling one's lower needs in the hierarchy, in order to provide a stable foundation for personal growth. In a business context, basic physiological needs encompass the fundamental requirements for survival and well-being. This includes a fair and competitive salary or revenue production, a safe and comfortable working environment, and access to necessary resources like breaks and rest periods.

If a business owner perceives or is actually unable to get those needs met through their business, then the opportunity to progress or, as I call it, "spiral upward" on the hierarchy becomes very, very challenging, if not impossible. It is completely out of order to speak to someone who doesn't know where their next meal is coming from about transcending the ego and self-actualization. The brain and body will put on the brakes to any evolution, in order to first keep us safe, by insisting we focus on fulfilling those basic needs.

Fear and the Amygdala

All humans have what's called an amygdala embedded in their brains. Its primary function is to keep us safe, by running everything through a filter that helps us quickly to assess whether something is going to kill us or deprive us of our basic needs; pertaining both to the physiological and safety needs on the hierarchy.

That's the job of the amygdala: to keep us safe from harm. It does everything in its power to help us focus on staying alive. Therefore, this fear center has a positive purpose.

The first step to calming our fears is to practice recognizing the possible positive reason a fearful reaction or response exists.

At the same time, we must also use our higher-thinking brains to better assess what you are going through, instead of letting the amygdala or reptilian brain decide it is going to kill you.

The amygdala draws from an information bank comprised of everything you've ever lived through to help determine what is dangerous. It identifies anything that feels dangerous in our bodies.

While many of us have had truly limiting events in our lives, many others of us have not. If you have had a life-threatening situation occur in your life, that becomes a trauma that your brain stores as information to watch out vigilantly for anything that looks, smells, or seems like it might be related to that circumstance. The brain works constantly to interpret any clues in our environment that might be similar to the original trauma; then, it fires signals for either to run, freeze, or fight your way out of that position immediately.

The major flaw with the amygdala is that it's running on the *feelings* in our body generated by our senses taking in our environment, and it doesn't always accurately interpret the environment as life-threatening. A smell that was associated with your trauma may send you into a fight, flight, or freeze response, for example, even if there is no real danger. It's just trying to protect you, based on the logged memory from your past.

Also, the amygdala cannot distinguish a *real* danger from a *perceived* danger. Again, anything that remotely looks or seems related to the danger leads this part of our brain to run our body into overdrive in an effort to protect us.

In that process, the brain sometimes ends up deeply limiting us, when left to its own devices, because it may perceive a threat that isn't real. This is where fear, becomes:

F - false
E - evidence
A - appearing
R - real

The brain will guide the body to run or fight something that isn't really going to hurt us. It may feel like a danger or look like one to our brain, but that simply isn't the case.

I see this manifest all the time in high achievers: the fear of failure, the fear of success, the fear of vulnerability, the fear of not belonging, the fear of being seen, the fear of stepping out of our comfort zone, or imposter syndrome, just to name a few.

Fear of failure is the fear of not succeeding or not achieving a goal and the potential consequences that may follow, such as embarrassment, shame, or loss of self-esteem. This fear can lead to avoidance, procrastination, or self-sabotage, as the person may become afraid to take risks, try new things, or pursue their passions. They may also set low expectations for themselves or engage in negative self-talk that reinforces their fears. This is all the amygdala at play, keeping you safe, while also limiting you.

Fear of success, on the other hand, is the fear of achieving success or reaching one's goals and the potential changes that may occur as a result, such as increased responsibilities, expectations, or pressure. This fear can lead to self-doubt, self-sabotage, or avoidance of success, as the person may be afraid of the unknown or become uncomfortable with change. They may also feel guilty or undeserving of success or worry they will lose their sense of identity or relationships, if they achieve their goals.

Both fears can be rooted in past events, beliefs, or expectations, and they can manifest in various ways in a person's life and work. Overcoming these fears requires awareness, acceptance, and action.

The brain perceives a real threat, except it cannot see that it is limiting our growth, abundance, success, happiness, fulfillment, and highest path. It's our job to use our neocortex, or higher-thinking brain, to engage tools like thought work, emotional intelligence, mindfulness, trauma processing, and reframing to show our brain that we are, in fact, safe. We can use its neuroplasticity to our advantage. We need to teach our brain and amygdala that we are safe.

Sometimes, this looks like reprocessing a memory, trigger, or trauma with a skilled professional in counseling, especially when we are aware of a known past incident when our safety, security, or wellness was in danger.

Other times, we've had instances in our lives that felt uncomfortable, unpleasant, irritating, or annoying, and they may be logged in our amygdala as threats to our safety. But are they?

Oftentimes, they are not.

The amygdala isn't evolved enough to notice a *real* threat versus simple discomfort. So, sometimes, even when we haven't had a deeply held trauma or truly life-threatening event, the amygdala starts to categorize uncomfortable occurrences as life-threatening. Then, it starts to fire signals of avoidance, ignoring, delay, procrastination, or other limiting or self-sabotaging behaviors, in order to "keep us safe" from that discomfort, when these triggers or signals are actually limiting our potential.

Making friends with our fear by deeply understanding it can show us where we need to nurture and care for those real memories stored in our minds and bodies that are keeping us safe. Then, once we are actually safe, we can practice calming our central nervous systems and teach those systems that we are, in fact, safe.

We want to keep those really important clues logged in our brains, because we don't want to replicate any of those traumatic occurrences, if possible. That is where the amygdala is useful. It is something to be grateful for; and certainly not something we want to remove as a survival mechanism.

However, we also need enough self-awareness to recognize when our brain *thinks* it's unsafe but it's actually just uncomfortable, and the very thing it's making us avoid or ignore may be exactly what we need to shift, in order to get what we truly want.

There is a delicate balance in the interpretation of these realities that deserve our careful attention.

Progressing to Safety and Security

Once the actual and/or perceived physiological needs are reasonably satisfied in the hierarchy, attention shifts to progress upward to ensure our basic needs of safety and security, including money, resources, and shelter. Professionally, we see this manifest as employees seeking job security, a safe working environment, and protection from potential physical or emotional harm. Companies can address safety needs by implementing robust health and safety policies, providing job security, and fostering a supportive workplace culture.

I will often see this particular mode manifest in the business leader, if there are ebbs and flows in their income or revenue in business. Some business owners will have emotional, mental, and even physiological responses that are vastly different during a high-revenue-producing month versus a low-producing month. If there are unhealed traumas or deeply rooted limiting beliefs around money for the business owner, we will begin to see that manifest as safety. This is when I've observed business owners move down the hierarchy, because they begin to feel, think, believe, and behave like their needs on this level are not adequately met.

Business ownership, like all things in life, is subject to ebbs and flows. We see it in all things in nature: the different seasons, the juxtaposition of light and dark, day and night, the tide, the sun, the waves, the life cycle, gravity, etc. We are beginning to understand that business is also subject to those natural laws, so it makes sense for businesses to have a rolling flow with ups and downs; the market will fluctuate, sales will ebb and flow.

In some ways, this is simply natural. However, when we carry these internal limiting beliefs inside of our brains, bodies, and hearts, the ebbs in business become particularly stressful, painful, worrisome, anxiety-provoking, or even panic-driven and wrought with scarcity. Our deep core beliefs are driving the negative thoughts, emotions, and actions that can continue to contribute to not-so-desirable results in our business.

The overarching message in this pattern of thinking, feeling, and behaving is that there is not enough. It manifests in many ways:

- ❖ Not enough time
- ❖ Not enough revenue
- ❖ Not enough ideal clients
- ❖ Not enough confidence

❖ Not enough happiness

❖ Not enough voice

❖ Not enough impact

❖ Not enough reach

❖ Not enough relationships

❖ Not enough energy

❖ Not enough sleep

The universal laws, which we will go over in more detail throughout this book, suggest, if we are thinking, feeling, and behaving from that patterning, then more of that will come back to us in our experiences. Therefore, it's critical to become self-aware of the patterns we are running, which all come from this incredibly limiting place.

This doesn't mean we don't want to be a good steward of all these categories. Time may feel scarce, but we all have the same twenty-four hours to utilize in a day.

That said, when we approach time from the highest possible expression, we understand that there is *plenty* of time. Since we are all given the same amount of time and some of us are incredibly successful, that means we can use our time to do and be the same.

So, next, we can make a series of decisions that start with believing it is possible and knowing that we do have enough time to get it all done. It's both being a steward of the time we have *and* our trust that there is plenty to go around.

If you are self-aware and notice that you are running a story about how you don't have enough money, that "money doesn't grow on trees" or that "money is the root of all evil," it is critical to do the thought, trauma, and reprogramming work to create a more abundant perspective of money for your life, business, and personal evolution. Money is an energy, a currency, and an exchange. If you are constantly feeling, thinking, and behaving as if there is never enough of it; that's the experience you will likely have with that energy. Shifting into a place of abundance around your financial receivership and expression is necessary for optimal success in your life and business.

The movement up and down this hierarchy can sometimes be linear, once one component is satisfied; when you have enough of that need met, you can continue to move up the model. However, in reality, individuals may simultaneously consider and address needs at different levels. Something like a major health issue can send someone back to basic needs very quickly. That doesn't mean they've lost all their progress on their journey of evolution; it just means this is where they currently are in their personal story, and it's time to address those very real needs now.

Conversely, sometimes the need may be satisfied, but our beliefs, past traumas, cultural programming, set of circumstances, or life events may take us up and down the hierarchy at any given moment in our own individual journey. With the business owners and entrepreneurs whom I serve, I see this movement upward and downward constantly.

As they advance to the next level in their personal development, continue to evolve or spiral upward, they will inevitably uncover some deeper work that needs to be done in order to fully shed some of the deeply held beliefs and events that continue to linger in their mind, body, and way of being. They will "spiral back" to these lessons or beliefs as a *part* of their personal development. When they do, it doesn't mean they are taking a step back, failing, or even faltering. They are just spiraling back to those core lessons and beliefs, which will show up differently on our own personal journey to deepen the learning around those major core beliefs and limits to our advancement.

It's natural to spiral back to our deep core beliefs at every stage of our evolution. So, don't be surprised or ashamed if you think you've done the work to move out of scarcity into abundance, and then, you notice those thoughts, emotions, or actions based in scarcity creep back in over time, especially as you grow, develop, or transition into higher and higher levels of actualization, success, and transcendence. I hear this all the time with the entrepreneurs I serve.

Instead of getting frustrated that you are experiencing a core pattern or limiting belief, in your personal development you can eventually begin to welcome it, accept it, or even invite it in. When you are experiencing resistance, fear, or limiting beliefs, that is just your fear brain trying to protect you from whatever level-jump you are making in your path to actualization. Of course, the brain feels fear and discomfort! It's just trying to protect you from what feels like uncharted territory. When you are on your path to transcendence, you are headed to places you've never been before, so you have to take a literal leap of faith and believe that the uncertain is safe.

When you understand the brain science, the body wisdom, and your typical patterns, you can recognize them, become aware, and even be grateful that they are just trying to protect you. Then, you can practice whatever you need to feel safe enough *and* stretched enough to grow into whatever's next on your journey. When I notice those patterns creeping in now, I say, "Oh, hey, girl! There you are again. Thanks for protecting me. What do you need to show me, teach me, or protect me from now? How can we feel safe enough *and* stretched enough to grow?"

Basic Needs Integration

Summary: In order to transcend to your purpose, make a greater impact, and actualize your potential, you will need to start by addressing your basic needs and whenever your brain and body think there is an interruption of those needs.

Resources

Making Friends with Your Fear

This exercise is designed to help you develop a healthier relationship with your fears. By acknowledging and understanding your fears, you can transform them into allies that guide and protect you, rather than obstacles that hold you back. By regularly practicing this exercise, you can foster a more compassionate and collaborative relationship with your fears, allowing them to become supportive companions on your life journey.

Instructions

Set the Scene: Find a quiet, comfortable space where you won't be interrupted. Have a journal or piece of paper and a pen ready.

Deep Breathing: Take a few deep breaths to center yourself. Inhale deeply through your nose, hold for a moment, and exhale slowly through your mouth. Repeat this several times until you feel relaxed and focused.

Identify Your Fear: Choose a specific fear that you would like to explore during this exercise. It could be related to personal goals, relationships, or any area of your life where fear has been a significant factor.

Personify Your Fear: Imagine your fear as a character, giving it a name and a form. This could be an image, an animal, or even a color. Visualize your fear standing in front of you.

Dialogue with Your Fear: Begin a written or mental dialogue with your fear. Ask it questions such as:

- ❖ "Why are you here?"
- ❖ "What are you trying to protect me from?"
- ❖ "What message do you have for me?"
- ❖ "How can we work together instead of being in opposition?"

Listen and Reflect: Allow your fear to respond. Write down or mentally note the responses you receive. Approach the conversation with curiosity and without judgment. Try to understand the underlying concerns or intentions of your fear.

Express Gratitude: Thank your fear for its presence and protection. Acknowledge that its intentions are rooted in keeping you safe, even if the methods might seem restrictive at times.

Transform Fear into Action: Consider how you can address the concerns raised by your fear in a constructive way. Are there practical steps you can take to mitigate the risks or uncertainties? Write down actionable steps that align with your growth and well-being.

Visualize Empowerment: Envision a positive outcome where you face your fear with courage and resilience. Picture yourself successfully navigating the challenges, knowing that your fear is now an ally guiding you forward.

Reflect and Journal: Take a moment to reflect on the insights gained from this exercise. Write in your journal about your newfound understanding of your fear, and any action steps you plan to take.

Closure: Conclude the exercise with another round of deep breaths. Express gratitude to yourself for engaging in this process of making friends with your fear.

Maslow's Hierarchy of Needs

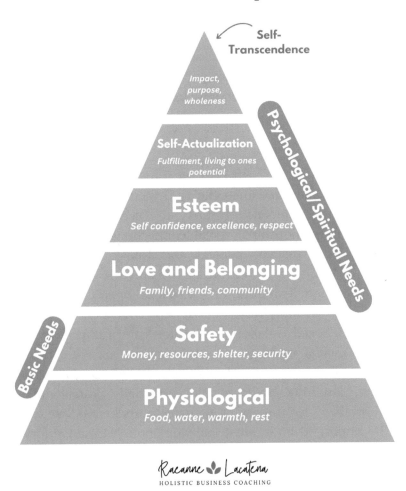

Chapter Two

Psychological and Spiritual Needs

"It is essential to our health and happiness that we dedicate ourselves to some kind of mission or purpose that transcends the mundane hustle and bustle of daily living."

—Oli Anderson

ONCE THOSE BASIC NEEDS are met in the safety and physiological categories, then the next focus becomes the social needs, where someone begins to seek companionship, interpersonal relationships, social connections, and a sense of belonging. In a business context, this translates to creating a positive work culture that encourages teamwork, communication, and collaboration. Team-building activities, open communication channels, and a supportive atmosphere contribute to fulfilling social needs. Social isolation or rejection can prompt a return to focusing on social needs.

We now better understand that the amygdala's job is to protect us from anything that seems potentially threatening or uncomfortable. One important element to understand, as well, is that the brain and body must feel safe enough to move forward through Maslow's Hierarchy of Needs.

A lot of coaches will preach, "Feel the fear and do it anyway." With some fears, this will be possible, and we don't need to completely eradicate fear to move forward. However, it is important to know that we need to create favorable conditions for success by calming enough of the fear in order to move forward.

Our bodies and brains will throw up psychological and physical stopping points, both consciously and unconsciously, in an effort to keep us safe. So, thinking we just have to power through and get to a point where we are jumping off a cliff without a net will set us up for a variety of pitfalls along our journey.

We need some elements of support and psychological safety in order for the internal and external environment to work in support of our desired outcome of success.

A great example of this, one I often see with business owners, is through the use of social media. The core original purpose of social media was social connection. Business owners turn to this medium to network with potential clients, customers, and colleagues, in order to fulfill that need. However, many entrepreneurs, especially those who are new to the use of social media, especially for business purposes, will feel a variety of possible fears in using social media.

For example, many introverted entrepreneurs will fear being the center of attention or taking the spotlight, and they'll end up avoiding the use completely. Some will fear losing their privacy or having an invasion of their personal life. Some entrepreneurs who are also parents might be concerned about protecting their children, knowing there are predators online, along with real trafficking and sometimes kidnapping. Other business owners might fear being ridiculed, judged, or misinterpreted about their content or use of social media.

Any and all of these possible fears will lead entrepreneurs either to avoid using social media to build their businesses completely; or at least to stall their progress, their visibility, or the organic growth of their personal brand.

Now, the first piece to acknowledge is that not every business owner *needs* to use social media in their business plan and development. I didn't use social media in my business until about ten years into the process, and I had a successful, multiple-six-figure-earning practice the entire time.

Part of the development of psychological safety is to remember that we have choice, which means we also have the choice not to do something.

That will often at least reduce the fear on some level. Knowing there are options and that it's not a necessity will calm the central nervous system as we explore the next step, which is to identify the aligned path for ourselves, as individuals.

Because there is no right or wrong way, no necessarily perfect path, and because we have complete autonomy and freedom to choose, we can decide to have a private personal account and a separate business account, for example. We can choose to leave our children out of our social media, or we can choose to have someone else do it for us. We can choose what we talk about, in which ways we choose to speak about it, and our preferred frequency and duration on our particular chosen platforms.

The act of creating a safe *enough* plan for our unique risk-and-reward tolerance helps us to make a decision that won't fire our fight-or-flight mechanism so deeply that it unnecessarily limits us from what we actually could do, feel good about, and that aligns to our preferences while creating choice and freedom. When goal-setting, you want to design a goal that is safe enough and stretchy enough to allow you to grow, be challenged, and feel supported.

One useful step the business owner can take is to remember their original intention for accessing a social media platform, which may be to fulfill their core social need. Doing this can take the pressure off what the platform needs to produce for you and remove the temptation to push or force your business into the process. You need not try to sell on the platform, but instead you can focus on connecting with real humans in real time. This can create a significant shift for any business owner, during this process of spiraling in their learning and evolution, while also satisfying this important need. These shifts can also keep us from spiraling down to the lower modes, when the use of social media feels out of alignment.

When we are adequately supported and connected with a network of people, we can begin to spiral upward to the next level on the hierarchy, to what Maslow calls *esteem* needs, which come into play when people look for recognition, respect, excellence, achievement, and a positive self-image, plus self-confidence and self-esteem.

In this phase of evolution, we are working on gaining a sense of accomplishment, recognition for our work, and opportunities for personal and professional development. In a business setting, this can be addressed through performance evaluations, recognition programs, promotions, and training opportunities for personal and professional development, and these can offer avenues for advancement.

Many of my clients in the financial services industry, for example, will be overtly ranked based on their performance and rewarded through a series of "clubs" or other echelons that offer them additional perks, trips, conferences, higher levels of support, or even higher-level payouts. As these individuals climb into this mode on the hierarchy, they are seeking that belongingness with other high-level advisors; they are craving the public recognition and notoriety that comes with being in that club. Sometimes, this drives them to continue to excel, and sometimes, this can become a vast source of pressure, hustle, grind, self-judgment, or even the judgment of others.

When we move into this esteem mode in the hierarchy, the needs become both psychological and spiritual in nature. We are working on building our internal self-love, self-worth, self-esteem, and self-confidence, which will increase our emotional intelligence and self-perception, while we also work toward removing self-doubt.

Self-esteem sums up an individual's overall sense of value and self-worth and involves feelings of confidence, self-respect, and self-acceptance, all of which can be influenced by external factors such as achievements, social status, and relationships. Self-confidence is more related to the belief in one's abilities, qualities, and judgment, as it involves feeling capable and competent in various areas of life and being willing to take risks and pursue goals.

Self-love involves treating oneself with kindness, compassion, and respect, and prioritizing one's own well-being and happiness. It is a foundation for healthy self-esteem and self-confidence through a deep sense of unconditional love and acceptance for oneself. When we recognize our own inherent worth or value as a human being, independent of external factors such as achievements or social status, we are building our self-worth.

Inevitably, the work in this mode is impacted by your own personal experiences related to self-doubt, which encompasses the negative thoughts and beliefs an individual may have about their abilities and self-worth. For example, those same financial advisors can carry their innate value and self-confidence into whether they receive rewards, clubs, or recognition; they can begin questioning their self-worth, their belongingness or acceptance of themselves; or they can end up leading these business results through pressure, push, force, hustle, and grind to get to the top.

Core Limiting Beliefs

All human beings, whether you are a business owner or not, will carry one of the following main core beliefs and corresponding emotions throughout your life, and it will keep triggering you to this stage on the hierarchy, if not addressed. We all have our own unique stories that anchored these beliefs within us, and certainly, we carry them with differing degrees of severity and complexity. However, there is no human exempt from feeling or from experiencing at least one of these deep limiting core beliefs, and we often suffer a series of patterned thoughts and emotions that correspond with those beliefs.

The first major core limiting belief can be described as "I am not worthy or deserving." This limiting belief manifests itself with thoughts that tell us we are not worthy of good things, that we cannot have what we desire, that we do not deserve to have anything good in our lives.

When this programming is running in your brain, body and way of being, you truly believe, whether consciously or unconsciously, that you don't deserve goodness in your life; consequently, your results start to match.

The thoughts that tend to run alongside this core belief sound like: "I am not worthy or deserving of love, happiness, money, respect, attention, a good life, peace, freedom, a promotion, having a fulfilling career, friends, health, a caring spouse, etc." Or, "I cannot have what I want."

This core belief creates feelings of shame, fear, guilt, anger and/or pain, which ultimately leads to frustration. If you continue to run that programming and operate from that belief, you will produce results that mirror not having enough, which will result in scarcity. The cycle will continue to go around and around.

This will often manifest itself in what is commonly known as "Imposter Syndrome," the psychological phenomenon in which individuals doubt their accomplishments, feel like a fraud, and fear being exposed as unqualified or inadequate, despite evidence of their competence. It is common among high-achieving individuals who have difficulty internalizing their accomplishments and who often attribute their success to luck or external factors.

Symptoms of imposter syndrome may include self-doubt, negative self-talk, perfectionism, fear of failure, and a constant need for validation from others. Individuals with imposter syndrome may also go through anxiety, depression, and a lack of confidence in their abilities.

To shift this belief, you need to know that you *are* worthy, and you *are* deserving of whatever it is you want. You wouldn't be on this Earth if you weren't worthy of all the beautiful things life has to offer, such as joy, happiness, love, freedom, health, and abundance. The art of practicing shifting those core beliefs starts with acknowledging and becoming aware of these deeply held patterns and being committed to creating a new story, in order to move through this unuseful and untrue pattern.

A related, but slightly different version of the next core limiting belief can be summarized as "I have no value." The thoughts that run with this limiting belief sound like, "No one wants to hear what I have to say, no one likes me, people will reject me, other people are better than me, people will make fun of me, I have nothing to offer, I am not special, I am not important."

Those same core limiting and frustrating feelings are produced with this belief set: shame, fear, guilt, anger, or pain. And these are actually the same core feelings that show up for each limiting belief.

The work that is necessary to break this downward spiral of belief in your lack of innate value is to remember that, by virtue of being uniquely who you are, you have unique value on this planet. Only you see the world through your eyes and your personal circumstances, and therefore, you are unique and create value through that unique lens.

By starting with that core fact, you can begin to heal and collect more evidence to support that the wisdom and knowledge you have gained, and the perspective from which you see the world, are of value and importance. And there is so much that people can learn from you.

The next limiting belief is one I commonly see at some point or another, among most entrepreneurs and most humans: "I am not enough." The list of not-enoughness runs long and can show up in many different ways: "I am not good enough, smart enough, capable enough, strong enough, young enough, pretty enough, rich enough, creative enough, athletic enough, confident enough," and any other adjective imaginable.

This belief is a major limitation, because when we don't think we are enough, we are never happy with who we are, and we can never forgive ourselves for our flaws and mistakes. We then constantly strive to be more perfect, and when we fall short of this perfect ideal, we beat ourselves up. This vicious cycle destroys our self-esteem and keeps us feeling small, powerless, and unhappy. This will often result in the development of perfectionism in high achievers.

Perfection is a fantasy.

It doesn't exist, and it's an impossible target.

So, many high-achieving individuals are stuck in the trap of pursuing perfection as a goal, which sets them up for constant failure, given that this target is unattainable.

Culturally, we are all taught that perfection is the goal, and some of us internalize this programming as if it's the only way of being. Consider the traditional educational scale, which ranges from "F" being failing to "A+" being excellent.

The rating of "F" encompasses between zero and sixty-five percent of the material tested or assessed. This is literally to say that anyone who knows sixty-five percent, which is more than half of the material, is a failure. A student who is learning and growing into understanding a subject matter, has to contend with the fact that knowing only more than half of the material will result in the assessment of "failed."

Between sixty-five and seventy-five percent is barely passing, seventy-five to eighty-five percent is viewed as just average, and eighty-five to ninety-five percent is above average. The small margin of success lands only between knowing ninety-five and hundred percent of the material, with that elusive "perfection" at the pinnacle, 100%.

Students see these judgments of their worth over and over again on a daily basis. It's no wonder high achievers are prone to high anxiety and stress, as well as a harsh assessments of self.

As a student growing up, wearing this mask of perfection was part of my personal identity. There was even a reward in my primary school called the "perfect attendance award," where a student was publicly recognized for never missing a single day of school. This ended up promoting unrealistic expectations, fed into my anxiety as a high achiever, and led me to make choices that went against my health, mental health, and wellness, in order to achieve a generally insignificant designation.

I didn't know it at the time, but this mask of perfectionism was a significant contributing factor to my Senior Song crisis. In an effort to be perfect, an unattainable goal, I cracked under the self-imposed and externally reinforced pressure.

Perfectionism has been and continues to be an internal battle for me at times, especially around my musical ability, academic performance, and physical appearance. One way this manifests for me is, if I can't be sure I can achieve mastery at something, I won't even start. I will completely avoid anything that doesn't start off with a relative level of confidence and talent.

With my own physical body, I often fall into heavily judgmental, critical, and harsh internal thoughts about myself. Society shows us images of the perfect woman and expects everyone to fit that mold. I have often struggled, along with many of the women whom I serve, with the reality that my physical form doesn't match up to that perfect Barbie image.

This is also seen in high-performing athletes. Often, their achievements are harshly criticized for what they did "wrong" in their athletic performance, as opposed to receiving positive reinforcement for what went right. More often than not, the first thing an athlete hears, when coming off the field or court, is what went poorly, said under the guise of moving them closer to perfect performance.

It's no surprise that the inner voice of the star student, athlete, and high achiever is unnecessarily critical and tends to blame self as opposed to others.

Criticism and harsh judgment of self become a source of motivation, albeit a low-fuel source. The illusion of perfection and the inevitable failure to attain that goal become the inner dialogue and the focus of our attention. This creates an internal environment of anxiety and stress, which actually makes it more difficult for us to be as successful as possible. We understand that stress creates inflammation in the body, making it more likely we will become ill. Stress fires chemicals like adrenaline and cortisol, which makes healthy sleep near impossible; that, in turn, negatively impacts our clarity of thinking, problem-solving, access to internal knowledge, and decision-making.

This response can cause an individual to feel a sense of urgency and need to perform to their maximum ability. In the case of perfectionism, this drive for excellence can lead to an unhealthy fixation on achieving perfection, as a way to cope with the perceived threat. It can become a downward spiral of self-sabotage to pursue perfection, and with the confounding addicting internal chemicals and negative self-talk, it is a very difficult pattern to break.

This is especially true because the high achiever is often positively reinforced for their behavior in pursuit of perfection. The harder they work, the more they do; the more they push, the faster they work; the more ahead they are of the pack or deadline, the more our hustle-and-grind culture praises the perfection-seeker.

To top it off, the perfectionist often does perform incredibly well. As a result, falling into these norms of push, force, avoid mistakes, and do more becomes their baseline mode of operation. Perfectionists deeply believe this is how they have to behave in order to be truly successful, even if they never hit that perfection target. It leads to constant self-criticism and the fear of making mistakes.

They are not taught how to be kind to themselves *and* strive for a growth mindset. They aren't guided with curiosity to see a "mistake" as an accelerated opportunity to learn. They aren't greeted with self or other compassion or given the grit or internal resilience to believe they are worthy and whole now, no matter their performance, with the additional knowledge that to actualize their potential can actually be quite fun, and they can truly do less to achieve more.

Natural high-achieving entrepreneurs often come to their business-building with these self-negating and limiting processes associated with perfectionism, which leads them to be constantly stressed, overwhelmed, uncertain in decision-making, hypercritical, and never feeling good enough.

To overcome perfectionism, it is essential to identify the underlying fear or anxiety that is driving the behavior. Some common fears associated with perfectionism include fear of failure, fear of being judged or criticized, and fear of not being good enough. Once these fears are identified, it is essential to challenge them and replace them with more positive and realistic beliefs.

As a starting point, to begin breaking the pattern of perfection, it may be helpful to use a mantra, which is a short word, phrase, or affirmation that encapsulates a guiding principle, belief, or intention. People may use personal mantras for motivation, affirmation, or as a tool to maintain focus and positive thinking in their daily lives, as well as a way to replace old, unhelpful, and depleting belief systems like perfectionism with more empowering beliefs. In this sense, a mantra serves as a concise and impactful expression of one's values or goals.

An example of a great mantra to shift perfectionism is simply, "I am enough." By consistently replacing the self-negating thoughts and any of those familiar, accompanying feelings, you can begin to release and reprogram whatever you decide no longer serves you.

If you want to add in the color commentary, those adjectives you would prefer to believe (e.g., thin enough, smart enough, fast enough, etc.), you certainly can. However, starting with "I am enough" is all the brain and body needs to hear to move into a more truthful representation of who you truly are at your core and essence: *enough.*

You can then begin to replace those self-negating thoughts with more supportive and loving thoughts, behaviors, and activities. For me, instead of needing to be "perfect" at everything I engage in, I am focusing on being perfectly imperfect and being willing to learn, try, and engage in activities and habits just for the sake of doing something new and having a little fun. Not everything needs to be mastery, some can just be for the joy of it!

I work at replacing those negative thoughts about myself with more loving thoughts. I see my body as powerful, and I practice being grateful for the miracle that my body has produced in the form of three beautiful babies. I get curious about what my body is capable of doing, leaning into my empathic and intuitive senses as superpowers, instead of problems. I am reclaiming the identity of a musician by allowing my musical inclinations to be for the fun and joy of expression, instead of needing to be a star or prodigy or needing to make it my soul's purpose to share music with the world.

As a business owner, breaking the perfectionism pattern allows us to embrace the necessary code to success, where every step in the process is greeted with curiosity and gratitude instead of fear, doubt, and worry. Knowing that the market is just giving feedback about our product and service, we can take that feedback as neutral, in order to move into our next step with ease and appreciation. The highest achievers enjoy the process and find it fun! They are witnessing the journey as exciting, no matter the outcome, and they don't let it affect their identity negatively when something doesn't go their way or perfectly.

They see the world as happening *for* them, not *to* them, and they seek the clues to continue to climb into the greatest expression of their potential in service of a higher mission. They understand that, even when their mission or journey isn't perfect, it is not a problem or source of angst, because they understand it's about the journey, not one particular destination. They feel fulfilled, connected, grateful, confident, happy, and excited for each new opportunity to greet the day with love in their hearts, in service to their perfectly imperfect reality as a human being who is having lots of imperfect experiences!

Another common limiting belief set is to focus on the need for approval or acceptance, where we fall prey to needing people's approval before making a big life change, like before taking on a new position, pursuing a dream, or making a move. People with this limiting belief system desperately need people to validate their choices and think it's acceptable in their eyes, before they can move forward, and they will often not take action before hearing those comforting words of approval over and over again.

I even see people waiting for that approval without their even asking for it, because they've convinced themselves that, if this next big move is important enough, other people should just know and tell them of their own volition. This internal fantasy is based on the desire to not disappoint anyone, on the fear of being judged or criticized, and on the desire to be loved and accepted under all conditions. It often stems from the beliefs that "I do not belong" or "they are better than me."

This belief system tends to result in a people-pleaser mentality, which is particularly common for female business owners. One of the key messages women are taught in their lifetimes is that they have to care for everyone else and look pretty doing it, and they have to sacrifice their dreams in order to help those around them.

This messaging, in combination with the increasingly impossible standards, makes female business owners and professional, career-driven women suffer immensely. Women are taught to prioritize other people's needs over their own and to deny their own dreams, desires, and intuition. They are taught to do more, to push and grind, and they are somehow held to an impossible standard of perfection. They develop people-pleasing tendencies and end up suffering or burning out, due to these unattainable standards, not to mention unhealthy codependent relationships with others and self-neglect, as a result.

A useful way to approach this belief system is to get in touch with the voice that is telling you that you shouldn't disappoint, that you should seek approval or don't belong, and ask yourself, "Whose voice is that in my head?"

More than likely, someone else made you believe that you need to focus on making them proud, or that you aren't smart enough to make a decision on your own, or that you don't belong. Who made you believe you need the world to agree with you, before you pursue your dreams?

Once you begin to see where this voice stems from, you can begin to separate yourself from this voice as being your own internal voice, and you can name it when it shows up. For example, if you are hearing your father's voice or that coach from grade school or that mean girl or bully at school or the boss who fired you, name that voice in your head. Remind your brain that it's not your voice. This will create some separation between you and that other person's voice, so you can begin telling yourself a more loving story.

Then, you can deepen that feeling of acceptance by finding a place where you *do* feel like you belong and start practicing making decisions for you, loving yourself as you are now, and allowing yourself to make small, simple, easily implementable decisions without checking in with the whole village of people before moving forward. It's okay if you aren't a right fit for every community; and there is a community out there for you.

The next set of belief systems is one I spend a lot of time helping my entrepreneurs overcome: "I'm not like that. I can't. I don't. I shouldn't." These negating sentence-starters are rampant and often unconscious. I hear people "should-ing all over themselves" constantly, which is not surprising, given the volume of societal pressures to do a certain set of this or that to get your outcomes.

We see coaches, health gurus, financial advisors, social media, spiritual teachers, and any number of other self-proclaimed experts constantly telling people that they have the right product, framework, service, or tool to change your life, if you'd only listen to them, buy their program, and do the work in this one particular way. You *should* drink more water, be in a calorie-depleted state, fast, work out this particular way, grow your business with this exact framework, or resolve your relationship problems using this proven tool.

This "my way or the highway" approach to life doesn't work and breeds unhealthy environments of comparison. It leads to a whole lot of unsuccessful, unhappy people who use those methods and don't find the results they are seeking, because they haven't done the work to go within and find out what works for *them*. The art of listening to your own internal wisdom is not something that is taught or even something that is spoken about, and the experts' voices are loud and enticing to follow. So, we end up following the pack and continuing to be unfilled and scarce in the results we seek.

The identity of "I'm not like that" is a very stuck belief system and completely disrespectful of that neuroplasticity of the brain and incredible healing power of the body. We *do* have the power to change our brains and bodies and thus our results and realities. To carry the belief, "Just because we always have means we always will permanently," is a huge limitation.

This often manifests in the need for deep identity work, because people with this set of beliefs have claimed their permanent parts as immovable aspects of who they are. So, first, they need to become conscious that they are consistently claiming those identity markers; this is the first line of defense to change them. This may sound like, "I am a procrastinator or a people-pleaser." "I'm an introvert, a private person, and too shy." Or, "I've always been told that I've never been very good at that…"

Spiral Upward into Maslow's Higher Modes

Instead, practicing the art of listening to your internal voice and intuition is a critical skill, and it can make all the difference when it comes to your healing.

Different people experience intuition differently. Some will be able to have a full-on conversation with their internal intuitive voice; some will have waves of emotion before they come to a decision; some will receive "gut feelings" in all different parts of their body; some will receive messages, signals, or voices; and some even have external confirmation of their intuition through synchronistic events.

Just because the intuitive voice might have been silenced for years or even decades doesn't mean it no longer exists inside of you. Think of it like peeling back an onion and working through the layers, until your true essence and internal voice are again revealed.

If you haven't already heard of the teachings in Human Design or Gene Keys, they are fascinating tools to play with during the process of learning about your internal world, decision-making, purpose, relationships, and your level of intuition. Human Design and the Gene Keys combine elements of astrology, the chakra system, and other metaphysical teachings to provide insights into an individual's personality, strengths, and challenges based on their birth details, such as date, time, and place.

The chakra system is a spiritual concept originating from ancient Indian traditions, consisting of seven main energy centers. Each chakra corresponds to specific aspects of the human experience, ranging from basic survival instincts at the root chakra to spiritual connection at the crown chakra. Practices like meditation, Reiki, and yoga aim to balance and activate these energy centers for overall well-being; this can be incredibly supportive in the process of shifting old belief systems and reprogramming the brain, body, mind, nervous system, and energy.

For example, my personal Human Design reading does confirm I am a highly empathic being and an emotional authority, which means, without active energy management, I run the risk of taking on other people's emotions, and I need to ride the waves of emotion before making an aligned decision. My voice of intuition doesn't hit me like a brick; it takes a while to settle in. Knowing that about myself helps me to honor my decision-making process, instead of making it wrong or bad that I can rarely make a big decision within about forty-eight hours.

Also, one of the readings from the Gene Keys gives insight into what is called the Life's Work Sphere, where you are given more details about how you shine brightly in the world and about a key aspect of your personality, especially how people perceive you. My particular Life's Work Sphere is Gene Key 9, known as the Gift of Determination, which holds the energy of "one foot in front of the other," as a means of getting where you want to go.

With Gene Key 9 as my gift, as it is explained in the Gene Keys, I am a master of creating forward movement in my life and goals, using a step-by-step approach. I have learned, and I am meant to share with the world, that a consistent approach to anything leads to big results and is often called the "taming power of the small."

In many of my Gene Key Gifts, I don't accept that "it is what it is." I firmly believe, instead, that what is can be shifted, no matter the circumstance. Every human being can evolve. Every context can be shifted. Every pattern, habit, or even personality trait can be altered, if you choose.

This doesn't mean that what was before is *wrong* and that you can make yourself *better*; it just means, when you notice a part of yourself or reality in your life that no longer serves where you are headed, it's possible to move into another way of being, doing, or having. Everything is changeable. Everything is malleable, one step at a time.

"It is what it is" is not my baseline. There is always a way to look at things differently and shift your perspective, results, thoughts, feelings, emotions, and realities. Always. It's just a choice you have to, or better said, *get* to make.

I put one foot in front of the other to continue to work through the areas where I fall into my lower self; I am here as a teacher to help guide others to learn how to tame the power of the small, one step at a time; one tool or resource at a time; one option or possibility at a time.

This gift is very useful in a coaching capacity, in service to my clients and their path to transcendence, because I can see clearly and quickly which areas can shift, change, and grow, what tweaks we can make, which levers to pull, and what small, simple, and easily implementable changes we can make in their business that will make a radical and impactful difference over the course of time and repeated implementation.

With this insight, I discovered that the hierarchy can be climbed one step at a time, and you can integrate and create harmony to wholeness through repeated steps in the right direction, and you can build a life and business of your dreams simply by making a one-degree shift at a time.

There is a shadow side of this gift as well, which can happen when the small tames you. For example, I have been known to overthink the details, to get too obsessed with perfection or flaws to a fault, to my detriment, which certainly sends me into my lower self. This leads me to hold patterns of negative self-judgment, fear, doubt, worry, or scarcity. However, I am aware. I know these patterns. And the good news is that all I have to do is return to putting one foot in front of the other, in order to get back on my path to transcendence. I find this incredibly empowering.

If these types of assessment and self-awareness tools are interesting to you, there is a plethora of information out there, so you can dive deeper. These types of tools can help bring awareness to where you are now and create a pathway for you to begin stepping into deeper ownership of who you choose to become.

Another helpful step is to acknowledge that you are carrying a limiting belief and then start to interrupt the old story in order to replace it with a new one. This work requires the willingness to explore who you truly want to be and also, in essence, who you truly are in your highest form. This is when we can begin to step into the next phase of self-actualization on the hierarchy, where we are striving to be the greatest expression of who we are meant to be.

The practice of crafting your ideal vision of yourself and focusing on that outcome can be very supportive in this process, especially when you incorporate the interruptions of the old pattern in the moment. Whenever possible, incorporate all five senses into your vision, to practice showing your body and brain how you prefer to be, think, and feel. This is also incredibly important.

The interesting part about manifesting your ideal outcome or identity is that you can choose to feel the way you desire to feel right now, by generating those desired feeling-states that every single human actually craves: joy, passion, love, fulfillment, and ultimately, really, to just feel better about yourself.

At first, perhaps you think external validation or an end result will get you there. But then, you learn that what you truly want is fulfillment, to be valued, to have a voice, and to contribute to the world. The manifestation work is amplified by inserting these high-level emotions into your *present* feeling states, as if those goals are already present and available to you here now.

Meditation to practice generating these emotions can be incredibly powerful in amplifying your manifestation practice, and it will send more effective, comprehensive changes to the brain during the reprogramming process. The brain can't decipher whether you are actually changed or not; but it *can* decipher a positive feeling state and goes to work on creating new neural pathways for the preferred state of being. So, feel those emotions now, and your brain will begin to replicate that in your life. Those high-level vibrations will emanate back to you, and your full desired state will be more likely to come to you now.

It's about thinking, feeling, and growing rich; not making a vision board and hoping it will happen. To believe it, you have to feel it; and to feel it now allows you to experience those outcomes as if they are here now. You'll learn in the process that all you ever wanted anyway was to feel those feelings. So, feel them now. Don't wait for the outcome or result for the feeling.

High achievers will often launch into the masculine side of success in order to get to what they want, such as setting clear goals, creating effective plans, and taking consistent action. They will model successful individuals, learn from their strategies, and apply those lessons to achieve their goals. They may even understand the principles of success and develop a mindset of resourcefulness, finding ways to overcome obstacles and challenges.

However, without understanding the feminine side of this process they are left feeling unfulfilled. That is why the art of practicing those desired feelings states *now* can support self-actualization to unfurl. By practicing the feelings of joy, passion, satisfaction, and love along the way, the journey becomes far more enjoyable throughout its entirety!

What ends up happening is that those feelings generate a different energy, and eventually, a different set of behavioral choices will match. When you match that emotion with your behavior, you start to make choices and behave in ways that are in alignment with your true desired identity and ideal vision, and thus you are more likely to receive those outcomes with greater efficiency and effectiveness. This results in making a more loving and joyful impact on others, which creates a life of significance, usually a desire to give back, along with a greater sense of meaning and purpose in life and business. Those results and the general sense of well-being, often paired with the scientific, evidence-based power of gratitude, creates that upward spiral, and the speed with which your desired outcome manifests continues to amplify.

What used to be a downward, self-negating spiral that was fueled by those limiting beliefs becomes a powerful upward spiral toward your actualization, where people embrace their personal potential, follow their passions and the pursuit of meaningful goals, engage creativity, and embark on a path of personal growth, ultimately becoming the best versions of themselves.

Finally, they reach for the pinnacle expression of personal development, self-transcendence, which is where purpose becomes the focus, and the goals shift from self-only to how their work impacts the greater good, the community, and the world at large. Self-transcendence is when someone begins to understand that they are a part of something bigger, and they move toward their peak performance in service toward the collective. Impact for others through our purpose is what characterizes this mode on Maslow's Hierarchy.

As we move more deeply into our personal development, the high achiever moves to the boundaries of their own abilities and tests the limits of themselves to gain their full potential. Eventually, that same high achiever recognizes having achieved such a high level of success for themselves, so they begin to develop a sense of responsibility, compassion for others, and a desire to move into the commitment to make a greater impact on the entire planet. They still benefit from this self-expression, as it is incredibly rewarding to give back to the greater good.

There is a theory that is based on Maslow's Hierarchy of Needs by Pamela Reed, which explains that self-transcendence is a natural and desired developmental stage that people must reach, in order to be fulfilled and to have a sense of purpose (Reed, 2003). She references a few major factors that lead a person to pursue this expression, the first being vulnerability. Her particular definition of vulnerability speaks to the understanding of one's own mortality, whether it be through age, health issues, or some other crisis, which leads a person to behave with urgency to give back, once they fully understand the fragility of life.

She also explores a sense of "wholeness" that comes with self-transcendence, which is the recognition that we are connected to so many more people, affect many different environments, and create a ripple effect in so many different ways through our actions and who we are being in the world. In Maslow's theory, he describes the process as follows:

Transcendence refers to the very highest and most inclusive or holistic levels of human consciousness, behaving and relating, as ends rather than means, to oneself, to significant others, to human beings in general, to other species, to nature, and to the cosmos.

Maslow, *Power of Strategic Synchronicity*

That holistic picture of a human being's experience is when we are stepping into the highest realm; it's where we can truly step into the strongest positive emotions, such as joy, peace, and awareness or perspective. When we can grasp that we are whole, not just beyond the categories in our lives, such as finances, relationships, our business, parenting, health, well-being, etc., but that, further, we are whole in relationship to the greater good, it generates a new, higher sense of self, a greater fulfillment of our purpose, and a commitment to uphold our highest potential in service to that full collective.

With transcendence, there is an accompanying certainty that there is some higher purpose beyond what we can fully understand and an acceptance of the interconnectedness of all things, which manifests spiritually for many. This greater trust comes no matter how challenging the circumstances a person is going through.

This was illustrated by the work of Viktor Frankl, who survived arguably some of the most horrific conditions in human history during World War II, in concentration camps. Despite the inconceivable personal and collective suffering around him, he clung to his higher purpose during these trying times, and in essence, he attributes his survival to that core belief that his life has meaning and purpose. He witnessed those who had some connection to a part of their purpose survive longer, think more clearly, make decisions to support their survival, and also even maintain a strong immune system and body.

Only to the extent that someone is living out this self-transcendence of human existence, is he truly human or does he become his true self. He becomes so, not by concerning himself with his self-actualization, but by forgetting himself and giving himself, overlooking himself and focusing outward.

—Viktor Frankl

There is this duality in the process, where we are both striving to go outward and fulfill inwardly. During the self-actualization process, we may be more self-focused and even tend to compete with others to get there, but we are left feeling unfulfilled, even if we achieve our highest physical, mental, or financial goals. With self-transcendence, we understand that the only true goal we need to set is to continue to transcend to the highest, greatest expression of ourselves in service to the higher good. To work toward becoming our best selves and, in the process, to serve humanity and the planet. During that work, when we reach our inner best, we simultaneously feel immense inner joy and fulfillment, but we also are incredibly fulfilled in the process of improving the world around us.

There is a remarkable Japanese concept known as *ikigai*, that blends the idea of one's "reason for being" and "purpose in life." It emphasizes the intersection of four core elements:

1. What you love
2. What you're good at
3. What the world needs, and
4. What you can be paid for

Ikigai showcases how an intersection of these four elements can produce feelings of delight, fulfillment, satisfaction, comfort, and fullness, as well as wealth in all realms.

Identifying your ikigai helps you pinpoint what you love and what you're passionate about, which is deeply tied to pursuing your passions and deriving a sense of purpose and fulfillment from them. Your ability to recognize your strengths and skills to their fullest potential will contribute to your personal growth and self-realization.

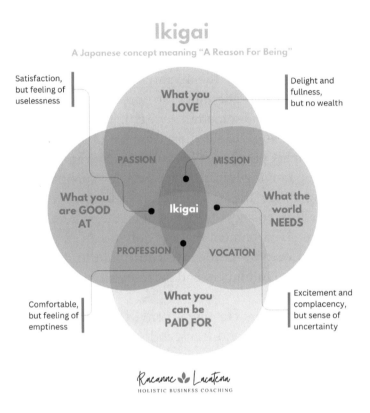

Bringing that contribution to the world in an area that the world needs will allow you to fulfill making a positive impact on the world or the people around you, aligning your actions with the greater good. Recognizing, also, what the market will pay you for helps to carve the path to financial sustainability, which allows you to support yourself and continue pursuing your passions and purpose.

Ikigai serves as a guiding principle for self-actualization by helping individuals identify their unique purpose and create a life that aligns with their passions, strengths, values, and the needs of the world. It encourages a more holistic and meaningful journey toward self-realization.

The world desperately needs individuals who are striving to reach their full potential in service to others. There are boundless problems to solve and possibilities to unearth on this planet, so this work is never "done," but this limitless potential fuels the highest achievers.

Some will fall down the hierarchy during their evolution process, because life continues to present those challenges; sometimes, we rise, and sometimes, we fall. When we are grounded in our highest mission, our steadfast values, and our vision to create the greatest impact possible, it helps high achievers to get back up again and keep moving toward that pinnacle expression.

By integrating the concept of self-transcendence into entrepreneurship, business leaders can create a more holistic and purpose-driven environment that not only meets employees' basic needs but also empowers them to contribute to a higher cause, fostering a sense of fulfillment and meaningful engagement in their work.

As business leaders creating an environment and culture that promotes actualization and transcendence, we want to recognize that different employees may be motivated by different needs; therefore, we want to adopt a flexible and individualized approach to motivation and employee engagement. This level of understanding can lead to increased job satisfaction, higher morale, improved overall employee engagement, retention, loyalty, and productivity.

The younger generations tend to understand the value of purpose and crave to work in cultures that naturally create the space for growth, development, and purpose. Not to mention, we are in a position to encourage employees to engage in activities that contribute to a greater cause, whether it's through corporate social responsibility initiatives, community involvement, or aligning the company's mission with a larger positive societal benefit and impact.

No matter where you are on the hierarchy at any given moment, I urge you not to think of your current set of circumstances as "lesser or greater." Comparing yourself harshly to other people, or even being hard on yourself internally, will only continue to send you further down the hierarchy and limit your growth.

Instead, do your best to greet yourself with self-compassion, treating yourself with kindness, care, and understanding, especially during times of difficulty, rather than be critical or judgmental. This involves acknowledging and accepting your own suffering with empathy and compassion, rather than denying or avoiding it.

Self-compassion has three key components:

1. Self-kindness

2. Common humanity, and

3. Mindfulness, which is an excellent way to practice climbing into transcendence.

Self-kindness refers to treating oneself with warmth and tenderness, like how one would treat a good friend. It involves being understanding and gentle with oneself when things go wrong, instead of being harsh and critical.

Common humanity is the art of recognizing that suffering and imperfection are a part of the shared human experience, and that everyone goes through difficult times.

Mindfulness is the practice of being present in the moment, without judgment or distraction. It involves being aware of one's thoughts and emotions and accepting them without resistance or avoidance, with an attitude of openness, curiosity, and acceptance, in order to cultivate greater awareness, clarity, and insight into one's thoughts, feelings, and circumstances.

A meditation for self-compassion can be done in the following way:

❖ Begin by finding a comfortable seated or lying position. Take a few deep breaths and allow your body to relax.

❖ Focus your attention on your heart center, the area around your chest where you feel emotions. Imagine a warm and loving light emanating from your heart center, filling your entire body with warmth and love.

❖ Repeat to yourself some self-compassionate phrases, such as:

May I be kind and gentle with myself.

May I accept myself as I am, flaws and all.

May I be patient and understanding with myself.

❖ Allow yourself to feel the emotions that arise, and continue repeating these phrases for several minutes.

❖ When you're ready, gently bring your awareness back to your surroundings, take a few deep breaths, and open your eyes.

* * *

This meditation can be practiced regularly to cultivate self-compassion and to promote a greater sense of self-love and acceptance on your road to fulfilling your spiritual and psychological needs toward actualization and transcendence.

Psychological and Spiritual Needs Integration

Summary: Overcoming the ego and limiting beliefs will allow you to climb into new heights, mentally, emotionally, spiritually, relationally, financially, personally, professionally, and collectively.

Resources

Mantras or Affirmations

Identifying Limiting Beliefs and Internal Voices

Self-Assessment Tools (Human Design, Gene Keys, Mindscan, Kolbe, DISC, etc.)

Ideal Vision Creation

Mindfulness and Self-Compassion

Ikigai Exercise

❖ Draw Four Intersecting Circles: On a blank sheet of paper, draw four circles that overlap in the center, creating a Venn diagram.

❖ Label the Circles: In each circle, write one of the following:

Top Circle (What You Love): Write down activities or things you are passionate about and genuinely enjoy.

Left Circle (What You Are Good At): List your skills, talents, and areas where you excel.

Right Circle (What the World Needs): Identify the needs of the world or community that resonate with you.

Bottom Circle (What You Can Be Paid For): Write down skills or activities that have the potential for financial compensation.

❖ Explore Overlapping Areas: Examine the intersections between the circles. Note where two or more circles overlap.

❖ Identify Ikigai Zone: In the center, where all four circles overlap, you'll find your potential ikigai. Reflect on activities, skills, or pursuits that fall into this central space.

❖ Write Down Your Ikigai: In the center, write down a statement that represents your potential ikigai. This could be a combination of your passions, skills, what the world needs, and what can provide financial stability.

❖ Reflect and Refine: Take a moment to reflect on the exercise. Consider whether the identified ikigai truly resonates with you. If not, adjust and refine your statements until you feel a sense of alignment and purpose.

Ikigai

A Japanese concept meaning "A Reason For Being"

Satisfaction, but feeling of uselessness

What you LOVE

Delight and fullness, but no wealth

PASSION

MISSION

What you are GOOD AT

Ikigai

What the world NEEDS

PROFESSION

VOCATION

Comfortable, but feeling of emptiness

What you can be PAID FOR

Excitement and complacency, but sense of uncertainty

Raeanne ❦ Lacatena
HOLISTIC BUSINESS COACHING

Chapter Three

Duality

"I do not have any set goal; my goal is self-transcendence. I always try to transcend myself. I do not compete with the rest of the world. I compete only with myself, and I try to become a better human being. This is my ultimate goal."

—Sri Chinmoy

BEYOND THE TEACHINGS of Maslow and other psychologists, there are some important universal laws that can help in the process of understanding where we are on our journey of climbing into our potential and integrating our fragmented selves back into our whole selves. These laws, such as Sir Isaac Newton's Law of Gravity, later refined by Albert Einstein's Law of Relativity, are the laws that govern the way the universe works.

There are also some lesser-known laws that are metaphysical in nature and that also help to organize what we know about how everything works, such as the Law of Polarity, which suggests that everything in the universe has its opposite or polar counterpart, that these dualities are inherent aspects of existence, and that opposites are not separate or unrelated but are instead part of a unified whole.

We see duality show up as a natural concept and be reflected in many different ways. We see it in fundamental teachings like Yin and Yang in Eastern philosophy, with Yin often being associated with feminine qualities like receptivity, darkness, and intuition, while Yang is linked to more masculine qualities like assertiveness, light, and logic.

Psychologist Carl Jung explored it heavily in his archetype exploration with what he called the anima and animus presentations of the conscious and unconscious mind, which represent the carrying out of the inner masculine and feminine in each opposite gender.

It's important to note that while the Law of Polarity has roots in ancient philosophical traditions, it is also a concept found in modern psychology and science. For instance, in physics, the concept of positive and negative charges, or the poles of a magnet, align with the idea of polarity.

We also see it in nature: day and night; rise and fall; seasons changing; ebbs and flows; high and low tide. The concept of balance is also crucial to the Law of Polarity, which asserts that the harmonious interaction between opposites maintains balance in the universe. Imbalances or extremes can lead to disharmony, sometimes referred to as the Law of Harmony. The Law of Polarity is sometimes also linked with the Law of Rhythm, which proposes that everything has a natural cycle or rhythm of ups and downs.

What we want to recognize in these fundamental truths is that it is the presence of opposing or complementary forces, qualities, or elements that allows for the existence of balance, which sometimes involves tension.

These laws come together to provide a framework that encourages individuals to recognize the interconnectedness of seemingly opposing forces and to seek balance in their understanding and approach to life. This is often used as a tool for personal and spiritual growth, encouraging individuals to navigate challenges with a broader perspective.

Masculine and Feminine Energies

To truly understand balance and harmony, we need to understand ourselves in the differing energies of masculine and feminine, and further to understand when we are carrying out distortions of those energies or more aligned harmonious manifestations. There is a spectrum of distorted and healthy manifestations of both the feminine and masculine energies, as illustrated below.

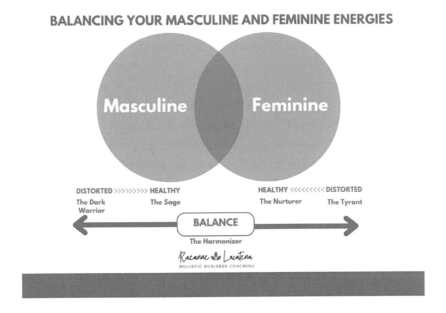

Healthy feminine energy, or what I call the Nurturer Archetype in my Entrepreneur Energy Archetype Quiz, is characterized by qualities like receptivity, nurturing, intuition, and empathy and is associated with an open and compassionate approach to others and the world. Someone with well-integrated feminine energy is emotionally balanced and in touch with their intuitive abilities.

On the opposite side of the spectrum, within the feminine energy sphere, you find what I call distorted feminine energy and the Tyrant Archetype, which may lead to excessive passivity, dependency, or emotional volatility. It can manifest as an overemphasis on emotional reactions without rationality or as an inability to assert oneself.

Healthy masculine energy, known as the Sage, includes qualities like assertiveness, rationality, and strength and is associated with taking charge of one's life, making logical decisions, and setting boundaries. A person with well-integrated masculine energy, called the Dark Warrior Archetype, is confident and self-assured. Distorted masculine energy may lead to aggression, dominance, or emotional suppression, and it can manifest as an overemphasis on control and power, leading to an inability to connect with emotions or relate empathetically to others.

By achieving a healthy balance of both worlds, individuals can avoid extreme ego manifestations and enjoy a more harmonious, authentic expression of their true selves. That is why it is called the Harmonizer in the spectrum of the different energetic archetypes. Integration is vital for personal growth, professional fulfillment, and psychological well-being; and every human being needs a different fluidity in their makeup, just as the Law of Polarity suggests.

In society, women are taught the language of the masculine, and this is especially true in business. Even the act of having the courage to step into business ownership is often handled from a masculine perspective, and over time, the approaches that are widely accepted and revered as healthy business practices can move female business owners into a highly masculinized state.

In order for women to survive and certainly for them to self-actualize in business, they are commonly faced with male-dominated board rooms, masculine business practices, gentlemen's agreements, and mano-a-mano, hierarchical, or dog-eat-dog approaches that women often have to learn how to live in and with or be left out.

So many women find themselves shedding natural parts of themselves to fit into these cultures. They are then faced with the pressures of societal norms to behave as a feminine woman and fulfill the natural feminine roles and responsibilities, but at the same time to strive for success as a masculine woman, while shedding their natural tendencies to operate in their divine feminine right.

This isn't only true for women. All humans, gender or sex aside, have the duality of both energies inside of themselves. We all have the soft and hard skills available to us as leaders, for example. We just choose how we are going to behave or adapt our natural tendencies, based on social programming, reinforcement, and what we pursue as our life's path.

For men, the societal pressures to show up as aggressors, dominant, or as providers leaves many men who want to be present parents, caring collaborative business owners, or someone who disregards financial success as their primary driver feeling lost, isolated, weak, or like they aren't doing their lives and businesses "right."

When we learn to integrate both worlds into a more harmonious whole, we can begin to skyrocket our success in life and business. A great model of this reality is Gary Vaynerchuk, an inspiring entrepreneur who, at the time of this publication, had a total net worth of $200 million, after starting his entrepreneurial experience with a lemonade stand and then bagging ice for $2 an hour at his father's wine store.

Gary is a prominent public entrepreneur, popular in the digital space, and he speaks to the importance of consistency, persistence, hustling, being competitive, and working hard to become successful in business (masculine energy), while also being self-aware, being empathetic, compassionate, and kind; of following your passion, and the importance of gratitude (feminine energy).

When any business owner leans into their divine feminine attributes more fully, they engage in being intuitive, spontaneous, playful, appreciating beauty, embracing the unknown; in being dynamic, circular, vulnerable, and nurturing; in prioritizing community, receiving, experiencing, the both/and mentality, gathering, pulling, and flow, so they are able to step into the full expression of the "feminine "It" factor and find the harmony that they seek.

The feminine business owner is selfless, reflective, grounded, supportive, trusting, expert with body language, patient, visionary, emotional, gentle, lives for joy, enthusiastic, has a zest for life, is soft, heart-centered, pleasure-driven, and remains want- and connection-focused.

Embracing the healthy feminine energy in entrepreneurship carves the path for nurturing leadership, collaboration, the use of intuition, empathy, and emotional intelligence to build relationships and trust. It is often characterized by flexibility, inclusivity, and authenticity, and it is a holistic approach.

Developing your emotional intelligence, or the ability to perceive, understand, and manage one's own emotions and the emotions of others, is a genderless, imperative responsibility of all high-level leaders. It involves a set of skills that enable individuals to recognize and regulate their emotions, communicate effectively, make effective decisions, empathize with others, and build and maintain relationships, such as self-awareness, self-regulation, motivation, empathy, and social skills. The feminine energy is meant to receive and also engage in activities, adventures, spontaneity, and pleasure for the sake of pleasure.

With that in mind, the very important neurochemical called oxytocin, which is often referred to as the hug, bonding, or love chemical, is created during so many of these more pleasure-focused experiences. We need oxytocin to feel good and calm, but we also need it to manage our insulin production and our sex hormones, to manage our stress and cortisol levels, to bond with our loved ones, and so much more.

We need pleasure to be in a healthy state, along with the oxytocin that comes in the process. We can get a dose of oxytocin released through saying, "I love you," petting your favorite animal, giving or receiving a hug, masturbation, massage, or sex, engaging in meditation, yoga, or laughing. Don't underestimate the importance of these activities in your overall well-being!

The focus on the feminine attribute of pleasure is often discredited, skipped over, disregarded, silenced, or even viewed with an air of shame, as we hear in the common adage "guilty pleasure," which limits our potential and makes those highly sought-after feeling states very difficult to attain. Learning how to get back to the simple pleasures of life as a way of healing and growing into our potential is definitely not taught in business school. However, these neurochemicals and experiences are critical to our happiness, health, mental health, and yes, even our wealth.

The most successful business owners exhibit a combination of both feminine and masculine qualities regardless of gender, as the Law of Polarity suggests. Moreover, successful business leadership often involves a balance of various traits, and the effectiveness of these qualities can vary in different business contexts.

When we integrate the masculine styles of energy, we see attributes like doing, being logical and predictable, thinking, being functional, concrete, visible, sturdy, linear, and protective, providing, individuality, giving, serving, the either/or mentality, and structure. The empowered or healthy masculine is out for the search, pushing, protecting, empowering, pleasing, observant, and decisive; it achieves, is territorial and challenging, and seeks freedom and adventure.

Each energy type can also be distorted, disempowered, and unhealthy, if not managed. With the disempowered feminine, we see controlling, manipulation, push (to figure it out; being hard), martyr, blame, stuck, helpless, chasing, hurt feelings, hidden energy ("Notice me"), demanding, fixing other people's flaws, judgment, pity, and unsatisfied longing.

The disempowered masculine is lost, withdrawn, isolating, defensive, needy, sabotaging, and destructive, defiant, rebelling, shut down, resentful, critical, nitpicking, complacent, smug ("I told you so"), and insecure.

The process of learning these different energies starts with our own models early in life. A lot is handed to us in the nurturing or modeling we receive from our parents, grandparents, and caregivers early in our childhood development.

My own family taught me healthy and distorted tendencies of both the feminine and masculine energy. I was shown the modeling of a strong work ethic, timeliness, a logical yet safe interpretation of finances, and a firm directness in delivery of feedback (healthy masculine), as well as the tendency to use guilt, blame, gossip, or be the martyr (distorted feminine).

Other family members instilled in me a zest for life, enthusiasm, adventure, trust in the universe, spontaneity, and a generosity of spirit (healthy feminine), as well as a tendency for indecisiveness, a consuming mentality, and a tendency for impatience (distorted masculine). There was a strong contradiction in these approaches, which has often led to confusion and uncertainty in my own blend and management of energy. I could adopt any one of those tendencies based on what was taught to me as a child.

When I was very young, I received the most praise and attention from my family when I was useful to them, by helping out around the house, not making too much of a mess, or generating any additional problems; this was exacerbated when my baby brother was born. I found myself consoling or caretaking and even speaking for him, when he was a little boy. It felt good to be helpful. It felt good to be a caretaker. And so, I continued to live out those roles in a variety of ways throughout my life and continue to do so. The more I learned about my own authentic blend of these energies, the more I was able to climb on the Hierarchy of Needs by shedding patterns from my old way of being, thinking, feeling, and behaving.

This was constantly confounded, because society showed me the value of the female who is emotionally intelligent, a helper, a people-pleaser, and someone who is willing to put everyone else before themselves. My past led me to believe that my voice wasn't worthy, that I didn't have an original thought, that I was better seen than heard, and I was only valuable if I was attractive and obedient.

All of these factors are related to my internalization of the balance (and imbalance) of my own natural feminine-masculine blend that, even now, often manifests itself today. I have sorted through some of these distorted energies in therapy, and I have made some conscious decisions in my life to overcome my natural programming, which is to fall into these teachings, expectations, default modes, or patterns. Some continue to rear their heads and limit me, while others, I have chosen to embrace and use to propel me.

Often, the female business owners who come to work with me have bootstrapped their business together. They have had to push or force their way into board meetings. They have had to rely on their hard skills, such as negotiation, competition, focusing on the numbers, KPIs, strategies, and other *doing* skills, to help them create a successful business. This is especially true for traditionally male-dominated businesses or industries, where, in order to get a seat at the table or a modicum of respect, they've had to shut down parts of their natural state of being in order to fit into their world.

They often become very insulated, isolating themselves to protect what they have built, and often have a difficult time trusting other people. They are running a "do more, push more, put your head down, and work harder" paradigm and are often headed in the direction of burnout.

When these female business owners are also parents, they are trying to juggle the responsibilities of the ever-increasing demands and responsibilities of parents *while* fighting tooth and nail to make their business work. They often feel a heavy burden of guilt or are pulled in too many directions or feel like they are failing everywhere, because they can't allocate their full attention in one particular area or another.

Often, through societal norms, they are expected to be the primary parent and maintain all of the inner workings of the home, health, and school requirements for their children and family. They have a tremendous mental load to carry and, as a result, aren't sleeping well, eating well, or taking time for themselves, because they are always putting others before themselves. They have a deep call and desire to actualize their potential in *both* areas, family *and* business, but can't seem to strike the balance between all of the moving parts and pieces to make it work.

I also see female business owners who are more creative in nature or those in service professions who completely reject the idea and identity that they are, in fact, business owners. Some have developed deeply held negative beliefs about what it means to be a business owner, so they have decided they are not, in fact, under that entrepreneurial umbrella, either consciously or sometimes unconsciously, which was the case for me.

For example, one prominent business owner, whom we will call Sarah, came to me as a bestselling author, actor, online business owner, real estate owner, mother, and wife, who was feeling overwhelmed with all of the moving parts of her life and business. She had already had great success in a number of different areas of her business and would soon be embarking on the journey of bringing her bestselling book to screen on Netflix.

Sarah had some support in building her online course and maintaining her social media but was otherwise on her own in her business model and feeling like she was pulled in a million directions. She continued to take on more roles as her body of work gained popularity and was feeling uncertain and frustrated with all that the business required of her.

Sarah would speak about the fact that she didn't see herself in the business-owner identity, but instead more as a creative, as an actor or writer. She was in a pattern of struggling with the harmony between the two energies, with her strong feminine creativity being her natural state, but feeling like she needed to push, grind, force, and do more in order for her business to succeed.

One of the first mindset shifts we sorted through to support her was that business ownership is inherently creative. The most successful business owners get curious in their approaches to problem-solving, decision-making, and planning, and they see their business as an extension of their art; as a blank canvas to create what feels aligned in the mediums that feel supportive and expansive. Indeed, a creative approach to business.

Instead of feeling resentment for *having* to work in the business or thinking that the business was taking away from her energy, we found ways to shift into embracing certain elements of the business, systematizing others, and delegating the rest.

This is an impactful example of embracing the feminine and masculine in business, the both/and approach, because she was able to create, be creative, and feel freer *while also* setting up systems, structures, and plans to support it all.

Sarah let the business support and provide for (masculine) her desire to create and receive (feminine).

Creativity is one of the most underrated expressions of entrepreneurship. So many business owners I encounter have a story made up about what it means to be a business owner, and it's usually very masculine in nature: focused on money, strategy, logic, metrics, tactics, goals, and the linear outcome.

However, when we are looking deeply at the marriage of the masculine and feminine world, that applies to business as well. Integrating the fact that business is inherently a creative process can be a great source of healing for many of the entrepreneurs I encounter, especially those who have built a business out of a means to an end. Many of the service professionals, artists, authors, creators, etc. struggle, at first, with the idea or identity of being a business owner, because they reject the masculine approach or have a negative story about what it means to be in business.

They wanted to be in business only to express their art, their service, their mission, or their passion for the world. The business is an afterthought to the original intention of sharing what they love with the world. This mindset about their business identity runs the risk of creating an environment to resent the business, to become overwhelmed or frustrated with the business, or to neglect the business completely, due to the thoughts and feelings they have, running on programs about business ownership.

When I offer the idea that creativity can be reflected in the process of business ownership, many of the business owners I serve feel a puzzle piece has finally locked in with that possibility. They can creatively pursue building a business plan or strategy that is authentically aligned to their vision, their mission, their purpose, the values, and their art. They feel supported by the possibility that they can take their own unique spin on its presentation in the world, and they don't have to follow one particular model or framework to be truly successful at bringing their craft to the world.

Their business can be a blank canvas, and they get to decide what colors, what medium, and what image they showcase on that canvas. This is a phenomenal example of the power of the integration of the masculine and feminine, because it is both of these two worlds, coming together. Without a doubt, finding ways to creatively express can help heal the inner divine feminine within us all. This doesn't only have to be through creatively building your business plan. It can also be through getting in touch with any given art form or creative expression that you feel called to explore.

If you are having trouble tapping into the creative expression of the business plan, perhaps you can get in touch with a medium that feels right to you and see if you can create a metaphor for that process in your own plan. Can you scrapbook a vision board? Can you write a script for your ideal outcome in life and business? Or paint the ideal vision?

For Sarah, we also needed to get clear about the overarching mission of her businesses, given how many different approaches there are to business development. When we really dug into her beliefs, her vision, and her values, one "golden thread" came through to tie them all together: she stands for *love*.

All Sarah does and all she is and all she creates is based in love and the mission to bring more love into the world. She is able to do this through the lens of grief, death, dying, disease, travel, food, art, and so much more, via her writing, producing, acting, speaking, cooking, etc. For her, it all comes back to *love*.

When her business or world feels like it is swirling out of control or like an unpredictable roller-coaster, doing the work to draw out that "golden thread" that ties everything together for her became a grounding force that helps her stay calm during whatever storm happens in life and business. Sarah is a true love-driven leader, and through this connection and mission, she is able to bring myriad details into a more loving focus, and she can approach any potential struggle through a more loving lens.

The journey of business ownership is never the same. It's always shifting and changing, and it's a constant moving target. Without the clarity in *why* we do what we do, what we stand for, our values, and our purpose, we run the risk of letting our business run us, instead of running our business. Or we get sidetracked by misaligned tasks and opportunities, and a draining feeling sets in.

Tapping into our spiritual meaning for business allows us to climb up that ladder to self-actualization with greater ease and grace, physical and emotional wellness, and spiritual growth. When I have the privilege of working with someone like Sarah, who is choosing to live their mission of love to the fullest, through harmonizing their masculine and feminine energy, it is remarkable to see what can come from the process.

In coaching, the energy of transcendence is powerful, and when we are cocreating in this space together, the ripple effect is multiplied. I can see and feel that energy expand as we both step further and further into our purpose, mission, and vision for the higher connected purpose, especially when the mission is grounded in love. Coaching calls are joyful and fulfilling, as well as impactful for those whom we serve and touch through our shared purpose and commitment to grow in service to that greater mission.

It feels like we are both simultaneously plugging into a higher force and amplifying our power in service to others. It is amazing to be able to get into such a flow in your work that it creates this level of joy, fun, and fulfillment. This feeling is in part why I love my work and want to bring this possibility of transcendence and harmony to as many people as possible. I know the world is a better place as more people step into their potential and bring it in service to others. Plus, this approach is just so much more fun and enjoyable!

That said, not every coaching call is about transcendence, nor does it always need to feel electrifying to make a significant impact and difference. Being a human can be challenging, and being a business owner can be hard at times, too! Every client comes to each of our calls together in a different place, simply because the context of their lives and businesses constantly shift and change. Part of my role as their coach is to assess where they are in the Hierarchy of Needs, how they are showing up in their energy, mindset, and approach to life and business, and then to support them in spiraling up as far as they can on any given day with any given situation at hand.

They may have been triggered into their lower selves or into a lower need due to something that occurred personally or professionally, and they really need support to sort through what they are experiencing in order to pivot their beliefs, feelings, thoughts, and energy and move forward.

When we are facing hard times in our personal life or our business, we naturally will see movement between the spectrum of feminine and masculine energies, both of the healthy and distorted varieties, just like when we are spiraling up and down the Hierarchy of Needs. Another client, whom we will call Chris, is a great example of this phenomena.

Chris has held a belief very close to his heart for his whole life that you either give with your time, talent, or treasure. When he started his career, he didn't have the money to donate to the charities that meant the most to him, so he heavily leaned into giving via his time and talent. He would spend countless hours helping his church carnival, his local fire hall, and countless other charities that called to him, in an effort to give back as much as he could. Chris did backbreaking setup and cleanup work, ran a number of food services and helped in any way he could to make the charity events he cared about come to fruition. He has an impressive blend of wanting to nurture and serve, while also giving and providing for his community, his family, his clients, and those in need.

When he built his financial advising business to an incredible level of success, he did so through that blend by creating a culture of connection *and* service, trying to continue to give as much as he could to those communities. When he attained financial success, he also started to give his treasure by making sure to donate tens of thousands of dollars to charities annually.

Within all of this blend, there also came distortion. Chris had *such* a strong passion and connection to giving back and helping others that he drives, pushes, and forces an extremely strong workload for himself and others, so his personal life and relationships suffer. He had such a difficult time slowing down that he found himself unable to connect easily on a deeper level with those he loves and cares about, and he could not stop to take care of himself, either. While he had been so selfless in providing his talent, time, *and* treasure, he had not been able to find the harmony, where he could release control or allow the space to just be or connect.

He has been practicing slowing down and is acutely aware of how it is affecting his body, relationship, and experiences. He is finding ways to step away and bring into his life people whom he can trust, in order to release control of some of the tasks. While he continues to thrive and strive for excellence, quality, and quantity in all areas of his business and service, he is beginning to explore what it means to care for himself. Eventually, he will open himself back up to what that means in terms of more deeply connected relationships.

One of the ways this manifested was in Chris's relationship with his father. He wanted desperately for his father to be proud of him, so he has spent his life going, chasing, serving, and collecting successes and responsibilities. His father developed Alzheimer's at the end of his life, which ultimately led to his death. Sadly, Chris was not able to hear from his father those words he needed so desperately: that he was proud of his son.

Since his father's death, Chris has launched headfirst into finding ways to create a remarkable event named "The Longest Day." This event honors his father's endurance of this cruel illness.

Chris organizes an entire all-day rowing event, with bands playing, food trucks, VIP client events, bounce houses, a poker run, and volleyball events. Tens of thousands of dollars are donated to the charity annually, not to mention providing additional education and awareness around the illness.

Chris's passion and drive are unwavering, and his father *must* be proud of his accomplishments. He is practicing letting this fact wash over him and allowing himself some internal personal peace and balance, in order to be as happy, healthy, and wealthy as possible, both in currency and relationships. It's about finding the harmony to *both* keep the passion and fire *and* maintain internal wellness and peace.

He also went through a divorce plus the entire implosion of his business team, because human beings need more depth of connection and they really crave *presence*, not just service or the gifts of treasure or talent. They may need quality time, words of affirmation, or physical closeness. Love is about finding what the *other* person needs and being willing to step out of what our own personal internal comfort zone of love preferences are, in order to make that other person feel fully loved and appreciated.

When we get caught up in what we naturally feel is the best way to receive love, we forget that different people need different things at different times to truly feel and experience the depth of love.

While the gifts of time, treasure, and talent that Chris brings to the table are vast, generous, and truly a part of his calling, he also deserves to receive love in return. He is working on dropping more deeply into and leaning into the feminine, in order to truly heal these parts of him.

Neuroscience of Harmony and Integration

If it feels difficult to grasp the Laws of Polarity, Harmony, and Rhythm from a metaphysical sense, perhaps looking at it from a neuroscience perspective will help. For example, an artist may see themselves as more skilled with their "right brain" activities and reject any need for the "left brain," having convinced themselves this is simply out of their skill set.

The right brain is responsible for processing information in a holistic, intuitive, and creative way. It is primarily involved in spatial awareness, visual and auditory processing, and pattern recognition. The right brain is also associated with tasks that require creativity and imagination, such as art, music, and storytelling. People who have a dominant right brain tend to be good at visualizing and conceptualizing ideas, recognizing patterns and relationships, and expressing themselves through creative means. The right brain governs the left side of the body.

The left brain is responsible for processing information in a sequential, analytical, and logical way and controls the right side of the body. It is primarily involved in language processing, mathematical calculations, and analytical reasoning. The left brain is also associated with tasks that require attention to detail and accuracy, such as reading, writing, and solving problems. People who have a dominant left brain tend to be good at following instructions, analyzing data, and solving problems in a logical and systematic way.

While the left and right brain have different functions, they work together to perform complex tasks. For example, when reading a book, the left brain is responsible for processing the language and meaning of the words, while the right brain is responsible for visualizing the scene and creating an emotional response to the story. Similarly, when solving a mathematical problem, the left brain is responsible for performing the calculations, while the right brain is responsible for recognizing patterns and developing new strategies.

The integration of the left and right brain is essential for creativity, innovation, and problem-solving. When both hemispheres are working together effectively, individuals are able to approach tasks in a more holistic and creative way. This integration can be achieved through activities that involve both analytical and creative thinking, such as playing a musical instrument, practicing mindfulness, or engaging in a team brainstorming session.

As a holistic business coach, I utilize all of my skills and abilities as a mental health practitioner and service-based business, in combination with my business acumen to support my clients. From my feminine side, I use empathy, collaboration, nurturing, caring, creativity, gratitude, vulnerability, and supportiveness, while also engaging my masculine side by being strategic, analytical, disciplined, direct, resourceful, purpose driven, focused, and tactical.

The business owners who tend to gravitate to work with me appreciate the blend of the masculine and feminine, the "both," and no matter their gender seek to find their own personal harmony to integrate both worlds. The art of learning how to balance, integrate, or better yet harmonize these energies is a life's work and a journey in and of itself.

There is an ebb and flow of these tendencies from day to day, moment to moment, and some are useful in certain contexts, while becoming unproductive in others. Becoming integrated in the healthy feminine and masculine blend will allow you to encounter more joy, grace, and ease, as well as the balance of the more outward manifestations of success in life and business, too.

To be also able to have a level of self-awareness, combined with the self-discipline, self-compassion, and commitment necessary to overcome the programming, allows you to have more control over your destiny in the future of how you allow your energy to grow over time in the new balance to support your self-actualization.

To begin, self-awareness is the art of knowing who we are being in any given circumstance. This is the first, most important step toward our self-development. We cannot change what we aren't aware of, so learning to develop self-awareness is absolutely necessary on that journey. Self-awareness is developed through formal thought work, emotional intelligence, receiving honest feedback, self-reflection, inner-child work, and other therapeutic modalities to deeply explore who we are, in our own inner and outer worlds.

Many people will derive great value from exploring assessment tools, such as the DISC, Kolbe, or Strengths Inventories, along with Human Design and the Gene Keys I mentioned earlier. Assessment tools like these can be fascinating tools for developing self-awareness. They can show you who you are naturally, where you are now, and can draw some attention to areas of opportunity for growth and development. By using these tools, you can get curious and clear about who you are and begin to identify who you'd strive to become.

A few assessments that I love to use with my clients in particular are the 5 Love Languages assessments, in order to learn more about how best they feel loved and appreciated; and the Mindscan, to assess their different ways of thinking and behaving and to highlight current areas of growth and development. I am beginning to explore the phenomena of Human Design and Gene Keys more fully as a set of tools to learn more about who we are and how we are thinking, feeling, and behaving in the world in relationship to our natural tendencies.

Specifically, the premise of the wonderful 5 Love Languages teaching by Gary Chapman helps people to understand one fundamental truth about giving and receiving love and appreciation:

Different people need different things at different times.

We all have a natural primary and secondary love language, which is the way that we are organically drawn to give and receive love. However, the person *to whom* we are trying to be loving may need something completely different than what *we* need.

Part of the process of being loving is stepping out of our own internal preferences to really settle into what the *other* person needs in order to feel loved, cared for, heard, seen, and appreciated. To nurture what someone else needs and to lead with love, gratitude, and appreciation are feminine qualities of a business owner, which can create huge shifts in the culture of a team.

The following graphic talks about the 5 Love Languages, which applies in the workplace and can be called the Languages of Appreciation.

Do you know your primary and secondary Love Languages?

Do you know your loved ones'?

How about your teammates', staff's, or even clients'?

Taking the step to learn what your key players in life and business really, truly need to feel appreciated can be a complete game changer! Some of this work can be externalized to others; however, recognize that it all starts with the internal work.

Values and Self-Direction

One of the most important measures that can unlock some major shifts in your self-actualization and self-transcendence is developing your skill set of self-direction, which refers to the ability to take charge of one's own life and make decisions based on personal values, goals, and aspirations. Self-direction involves being proactive in setting and achieving goals, rather than rely on external influences or directions. Self-direction is closely related to the concept of value, as personal values play a critical role in guiding one's decision-making and behavior. We can't know what to direct ourselves toward if we don't know what we value.

When we think about self-direction, we might consider this to be just the willingness to get things done without needing someone else to hold us accountable. However, there is much more to it. We are self-directed toward what is important to us or our values and value systems. When we have clarity about what's important to us, we are better able to stay on track for whatever we set out to accomplish and avoid getting knocked out of belief in ourselves and our mission, when we remain focused and clear about our values. This also helps us stay passionately connected, create the greatest impact, and make more effective, aligned decisions.

This involves taking ownership of our life and making choices that align with our values; it requires a high degree of self-awareness and introspection, as well as a willingness to take risks and make decisions independently. Self-directed individuals are often proactive in seeking out opportunities to learn and grow, and they are not afraid to challenge themselves or others in pursuit of their goals.

This process of aligning and directing ourselves toward our values can also involve overcoming obstacles and persevering in the face of adversity. It requires a strong sense of self-efficacy and the ability to bounce back from setbacks, because you are able to rely on your internal values and goals to guide your decision-making and behavior.

Values are the principles and beliefs that guide a person's life and define what is important to them. They provide a framework for making decisions, setting priorities, and choosing behaviors that align with one's personal goals and aspirations. Values can be influenced by a range of factors, such as family upbringing, cultural background, personal experiences, and societal expectations. However, it is ultimately up to the individual to define their own values and align their actions with them.

Without our values, we run the risk of being lost without a path. Without the guardrails that values offer, we may begin to question our next steps and all that goes into our actualization, or we may become confused about why we are even putting in the effort at all. This leaves people feeling hopeless or unfulfilled, overwhelmed or frustrated.

Identifying and articulating our values is a critical factor in business success for all of these reasons; most importantly, to help us craft and implement a business plan that is in alignment with who we are at our core, who we choose to be, what we believe, when we take a stand, and how to behave in the marketplace, with our clients, customers, and team members.

When we are operating in alignment with our values, they become an attractor factor of the right-fit clients, because our right-fit clients will believe what we believe and care about what we care about. Our messaging will help people see who we are and feel more connected to what you stand for and what you are looking to accomplish. Equally important is the repelling effect that your values will have to keep the "wrong fit" from coming into your life and business, which can be detrimental to your time, currency, and energy resources.

In my own journey of defining my values for my business, one of the major lessons I learned through my business ownership was that values adjust, shift, change, and evolve over time. One of the ways I've developed my values is to be self-aware enough and willing to pay attention, when something feels out of alignment in my business.

Instead of getting frustrated and throwing in the towel when things don't go our way in business, we can pause and say, "What is this situation trying to teach me?" or "If this doesn't feel right to me, what *does* feel right to me? What is my value set trying to show me?"

For example, when I stepped into business ownership, I started as a solopreneur and quickly decided there were some tasks that I wouldn't want to continue to use my time for on a regular basis, and I found a path to get ready to hire some support. As I stepped into "entrepreneurship," where I was working *with* people toward the common goal of running the business, I started by reaching out to interview individuals and talk about what they claimed they could do to help with my business.

I focused first on the tasks I could delegate, and I took each interviewee at their word. What I didn't do during this process was talk to them about *their* values and what was important to them, to see if we were aligned not just in *what* they could do for me, but also *why* they were motivated in business and whether we had alignment in our value system.

It took me a few different failed hiring attempts to learn that what I value is not what every business owner values. And that if I was going to find a right-fit support team, I personally needed to focus on our shared core values as a primary focus, instead of only what each potential support person could do for me. Eventually, I was able to clue into this lesson and hire, instead, the team that carried the same values.

Now, I am happily supported by an amazing team. We have similar values and are on the same page about the higher mission of my business. That creates a foundation for trust, connection, care, and collaboration toward a shared common goal. Now that I deeply understand this lesson, values are where I start with anyone I hire, including my coaches, team, support staff, mentors, publishers, PR, or anyone else who joins to support what we are building. They are the cornerstone of operation and connection.

Take the time to identify your top ten values, qualify and describe them, and then get clear about your top three to five personal and business values, to help you further climb into your potential. Below are some samples from my values list at the time of publication:

- ❖ **Love:** Everything is love. Love is everything. Striving to live a life and business in service to love through love-driven leadership.

- ❖ **Joy:** Engaging in life through curiosity, fun and adventure with a beginner's mind to create happiness in all realms.

- ❖ **Harmony:** Integrating our own unique blend, personally and professionally, internally and externally, to live a balanced life and business.

- ❖ **Health:** Self-care and wellness as a priority to ensure healthy bodies, minds, and experiences, so we can serve more people, live into our potential, and lead a life of significance.

- ❖ **Wealth:** Richness of life in all realms—relationships, financial abundance, adventures, spiritual enlightenment, and more.

- ❖ **Honoring Uniqueness:** Celebrating, respecting, and embracing each person's individual unique abilities, personality, and background and being true to our authentic selves.

❖ **Integrity**: Committing to do what we say we are going to do, when we say we are going to do it, and practicing what we teach as best possible.

❖ **Open, honest, authentic communication:** Lovingly direct communication, even when it's hard to build a foundation of trust and transparency.

❖ **Gratitude:** As the cornerstone for health, happiness, and wealth; appreciation for all that we have, all that we are, and all we encounter.

❖ **Freedom:** The flexibility to choose and the trust to know we can have it all.

If you want to have it all, you must first start with the clarity that comes from going inward to decide what that means to you. This will involve introspection, reflection, and processing to help you really understand to the core what matters to you and what drives you.

At this point, it can be helpful to slow down and do some work in identifying your mission, your true vision, your purpose, and your values for yourself, personally and professionally. Starting with clarity about why you do what you do and what you are looking to accomplish, in addition to what impact you'd like to make, will help you lead with the end in mind.

Next, craft those North Stars to help you stay focused on the deeper motivation driving you. We already understand that there are outside, external influences that will tell you to do things differently, because that is what brought you to this work. This intensifies the importance of understanding why you personally want to achieve the goals at hand, why you are building your business, and what purpose you are fulfilling in the world, as well as what impact and ripple effect is possible as a result of your efforts.

When you understand your values, you can use them as the guard rails or bumpers to keep you on track when the world tempts you to move in another direction.

Duality Integration

Summary: Learning to integrate the healthy feminine and masculine energies, personally and professionally, will help your business grow and will allow you to actualize your potential.

Resources

Entrepreneur Energy Archetype Quiz Link

Find it here: raeannelacatena.com/energyquiz

5 Love Languages

Values Exercise

Here is a comprehensive list of common values among business owners, to help you begin to explore what resonates most for you and your business. There are so many more options, so feel free to expand this list to meet your needs to make sure you've identified your core values.

You can begin by circling the ones that resonate with you the most personally and professionally and then take the time to describe what your top five mean to you:

CORE VALUES

- Integrity
- Quality
- Learning
- Honesty
- Knowledge
- Respect
- Expertise
- Accountability
- Leadership
- Perseverance
- Creativity
- Courage
- Initiative
- Innovation
- Efficiency

- Risk-taking
- Entrepreneurship
- Excellence
- Effectiveness
- Empowerment
- Customer satisfaction
- Fairness
- Teamwork
- Diversity
- Communication
- Inclusion
- Collaboration
- Social responsibility

- Environmental sustainability
- Community involvement
- Productivity
- Responsiveness
- Philanthropy
- Transparency
- Flexibility
- Openness
- Adaptability
- Authenticity
- Growth
- Humility

Racanne Lacatena
HOLISTIC BUSINESS COACHING

Chapter Four

Money Story

"Your income can grow only to the extent that you do."

—T. Harv Eker

ONE AREA OF BUSINESS THAT ALL entrepreneurs must come to face is that of money. We know now that entrepreneurship is a personal development plan disguised as a financial opportunity, and many entrepreneurs elect to undertake this journey with an original intention of finding their financial freedom. Whether money is their primary focus or not, all entrepreneurs will be faced with their money story on a consistent basis; because business is measured in the real world through the revenue it produces. They don't take love and fulfillment at the bank, so we do need to be respectful of the reality that money is a part of the process of business.

For many people, money is also one of their most triggering conversations. We all carry a money story deep inside of us that began early in our development, and that has been further solidified by cultural programming, parenting, societal stories, and pressures plus so many other messages and events that happen to us along the way. Money also interplays directly with our feminine and masculine energy through receptivity, providing, giving, and so many different exchanges along the way. For these reasons, and so many others, it is imperative for entrepreneurs to explore where we are in relation to the feminine and masculine energies in all three tenses: the past, the present and the future.

From the perspective of the past, we can look into and more deeply understand some of the ways we were taught, influenced or normalized into one manifestation or another of these dualistic energies. We've already explored some of the masculine and feminine imprinting that was given to me by my parents and how that created polarizing perspectives around what it means to be successful and hardworking, as well as what it means to have money.

Those early childhood experiences became a part of who I was and how I have behaved around money throughout my entire career. To continue to explore what it looks like to decode the timeline of our life in relationship to the development, unlearning, and reprogramming our money story, I offer you a glimpse into what I've been through during the years that have impacted my ever-evolving internal and external relationship with the money.

I've already shared a fair bit from my early childhood that affected my money story; now, let's explore how my relationship with work and life as I continued into my earning years started to take some of those combined perspectives of scarcity and abundance, masculine and feminine, distorted and healthy views of money and work, and culminated in my personal growth in life and business.

My Introduction to Employee vs. Entrepreneur

As soon as I could get my working papers, I was ready to get a job. I craved having my own money and saw it as a source of freedom and separation from my parents.

As a single mom, my mother had to work hard to keep everything afloat in our household, and she was very used to having to tell us "No" for the things we wanted as kids. Other kids were able to go on expensive trips, wear fancy clothes, or participate in outings with their friends, all of which my mother viewed as superfluous. She drilled into us, "If you want those things, you can have them when you can get a job."

Part of my money story, which became deeply embedded in my body, mind, and experience, was that work meant freedom; and hard work meant having the things I desired. I started my employment at a family-owned franchise called Auntie Anne's Pretzels™.

When I was fifteen, which was when I could begin working legally, my mother worked as the manager of a location of her cousin's franchise. I had never come in close contact with a full-time female entrepreneur prior to her, so what she had built and how she operated made a strong impression on me.

I remember being in awe of her and really thinking that her life and way of being was something I wanted to emulate. She was wealthy, impeccably dressed, well put together, happy, generous, and free to do as she pleased. My first cousin once removed became a possibility marker for me for female entrepreneurship. But to my untrained and youthful eyes, it looked like she could whisk into the store to pick up the money the business had generated and then whisk away, to carry on with her life without ever having to touch a pretzel.

I remember thinking that this is what it was like to own a business: other people doing all the things she didn't want to have to do, and just picking up the money that someone else had made for them. I have since learned there is definitely more to business ownership!

My mother was an incredibly hard worker, and she definitely prided herself on her ability to keep things spotless and organized, with a tightly run ship. So, even though I partially entered the workforce to step away from my parental oversight, I landed myself a job working under my mother. This further deepened my already strong work ethic. My place of employment was actually quite fun, and I have many good memories.

Life Lessons on Via Lacatena

I eventually moved onto college and elected a work-study throughout all my years there, to help pay for my room and board. I was footing the bulk of my own tuition bill, apart from some scholarship aid and whatever financial support my mom could provide. She did her best to offer as much as she could; even so, I left with well over $125,000 in student loan debt. This forced me to be very careful with money when I went to college. I even took on additional work as a waitress during the breaks and over summer, and I added another work study as a lab assistant later in my college career.

In college, I often felt self-conscious about my finances; knowing how much debt I was carrying to be there created a ton of pressure and shame for me during those years. I often felt "lesser than" or that I didn't belong alongside many of the students who attended the universities where I was enrolled.

One of the decisions I made to keep myself safe, as I was backing away from music and the feeling that I didn't belong during college, was to study abroad. I followed the teachings handed down from my father to live life fully right now. And even though I had to take out additional student loans to make it happen, I made the choice to invest in myself with this journey.

I had a second college minor studying French, and I very much enjoyed learning this language throughout my higher education. I poured myself into this academic pursuit and further backed away, unconsciously, from my love of music, subsequent to that trauma I went through on my final day of high school. From a fear-response standpoint, in this case, it was a flight response. And this time, it meant a literal flight: I spent five months in France, away from everything, during an immersive study abroad experience. There were no music lessons, no performances required, and nobody knew me, who I was, or what had happened to me in my past. I hid behind the mask of academics to keep myself safe.

A couple of weeks after I arrived in France, I received a call from my father to let me know that my beloved grandfather had passed away unexpectedly after a rapid decline. The family decided for me that my grandfather wouldn't have wanted me to come home for the funeral, that he would have preferred I stay in the program, instead of canceling my enrollment to come home or doing a whirlwind trip to go back and forth from the South of France to New York for a funeral. I also received the message that I had already stretched myself beyond my limits financially; so, booking a round-trip flight for a weekend funeral wasn't smart.

I was devastated and alone in my grief. I didn't know anyone or enough of the language to communicate my feelings effectively with my host mother, whom I was staying with in France, and who tried to understand why I was crying and suffering so deeply.

The next few weeks of my program were a fog, and I eventually decided that I needed to honor my grandfather somehow in my own way. I followed my intuition and went against the messages I was receiving from home. I decided to book a trip to the small village in southern Italy, outside of Bari, called Alberobello, where my Italian cousins still resided, and where my family on my grandfather's side had emigrated from, originally.

My dearest friend in the program, who was studying French with me, also spoke Spanish and English, decided to join me on this trip, but neither of us spoke Italian. And we had no plans other than to go to this place to see where my family had originated, to honor my grandfather.

When I arrived in this small, stunning, picturesque village with homes made from volcanic material and whitewashed stone, there were signs on the streets with roads labeled *Via Lacatena*, along with churches and major buildings also bearing my family's name. I had hunted down an address from some of my distant cousins, and I went to their home to introduce myself as an American Lacatena. They completely and totally embraced me as family.

They quite literally paraded me through the streets, showing me the family's landmarks and shops, homes, daily lives, attractions, and sources of pride. They made me the most decadent, delicious meal of my life, with too many courses to count, and we sat around big tables, doing our best to speak in a melting pot of languages: English, Italian, Spanish, and French, all coming together through the focused lens of love and family.

My elder cousins showed me photos of my grandfather and other family as children, and we cried together. I grieved in a way I could never have imagined possible, and I found love and closure for the deeply held loss of my grandfather as a result of making this choice. Sometimes, the best way to come out of a dark place is to exercise the value of choice and follow the breadcrumbs that the universe provides us, to take something painful and turn it into something beautiful.

While I was unconsciously escaping the trauma and a feeling that I didn't belong, I was forced to feel and grieve after this loss of a loved one. The art of feeling your feelings fully was something I had often been told to stifle. As an empath, an emotional authority, and a highly sensitive person, I had been made to believe that all of the feelings I have are "too much," unnecessary, or burdensome. While I was away in France with nobody to speak to about my grief, I let myself fully feel my feelings of grief and move through whatever came up for me on my own, at first, and then, eventually, with my newfound family.

This put everything into perspective for me, as the world became a much bigger place, and I started to see the value of listening to my own inner wisdom. I started to trust my intuition and learn what was valuable to me in my life and with money.

As a business coach who works with all different types of people, I recognize now just how many people are numbing themselves off from their own feelings, completely skipping over or denying their existence or trying to repress the way they are feeling internally, both in life and in business. Part of the work we do is to get back in touch with the reality of feeling and emotion; then we work to understand that, in order to have a full experience of life, we need and want to have a full spectrum of emotions. We cannot see light without darkness, and we cannot feel joy without pain. None of the emotions are wrong or bad, and they can actually inform and support one another for a more real, full life, if we allow ourselves to feel them fully and move through them.

This impromptu trip to Italy also gave me an extraordinary education in the truth that love is the healing force. My family grew to encompass these amazing people whom I previously hadn't even known existed. They wrapped their love around my wounded heart to allow me to heal and further understand that there was so much more out there for me to see, encounter, and explore. What started as a painful period became one of the highlights of my life.

I gained more confidence and clarity, and I healed a part of the belongingness story, as well as filled in a gap in my money story. Travel, family, adventures, and love were something not to be skimped on for the sake of money. Those parts of my money story and value system continue to be a heavy part of my life today, because now I understand that allowing the full spectrum of emotion and creating opportunities for peak experiences are essential parts of the journey to actualization and transcendence. Feeling and engaging in all that life has to offer are key ingredients in the process.

Book vs. Street Smarts

When I returned to the States, I spiraled back to my belongingness and "not enough" story in an intensified polarity. I went to Columbia University, where my student-body cohort was highly privileged and came from very wealthy families who were footing their bill for their master's programs. Few of my classmates worked during school, so they were able to engage in elaborate projects to submit for our requirements during school.

For part of her thesis project, one of my classmates brought thirty high-quality cameras to a poverty-stricken African village, to have the children document their daily lives. By contrast, I studied one child, in one program I had already been placed with, in New York City. Both of us received perfect scores, and while I felt proud of that achievement, I also felt the divide between what they had and what I did not. What I *had* to do to make it work versus what they *got* to do, while I was working to pay my fees.

When I started my master's program, I also worked at a local restaurant across from the School of Social Work. I landed the job on my first day in the city and started work immediately. The restaurant was often slow, and the management team often stood outside with the servers, inviting people in to have a meal.

While we sat out there, one male manager often commented on the appearances of people walking by; he made comments about my physical appearance, too. He would often come onto me, which I handled by ignoring his advances.

One day, while we were outside, after commenting on some woman's body, he turned to me and said, "Is she your type?" I asked him what he meant by that, and he replied, "Well, you must be gay if you aren't willing to sleep with any of the men here at the restaurant."

That was one of my last days working at that restaurant. This was only one of the many unfortunate instances when I had to fend off predatory behavior from men in the workplace. The power dynamics of any work environment are often a breeding ground for hypersexualized behavior from men with distorted masculine egos. This reality is something all women have to face at some point in their lives. The distorted egos of those in power around money and earning is an all-too-common story.

Another very well-known restaurant in the area was local to my hometown, Dinosaur BBQ. I walked in one day between shifts and asked to speak to a manager. I told him I was from Rochester, knew the restaurant well, and was looking for a waitressing job. He hired me on the spot, and I was able to quit that other terrible job.

I loved waitressing at Dinosaur BBQ. The restaurant was incredibly fast-paced, so busy and so much fun to work for, no matter what time of day. We often saw celebrities come in to eat, and we had such a long line during prime mealtimes, we servers would literally be running to keep up with the demand.

We wore biker-type server gear and put on a little sassy persona with our customers, which was part of the fun. After an evening shift, I often had between $500 and $700 in my pocket from cash tips alone, which was the most money I had ever earned at any given time. My coworkers were fun, flirty, and adventurous, and there were certainly a lot of extracurricular activities happening behind that scene.

We all came off these high-volume, heart-racing shifts and needed to relax. Because of how late we got off a shift, many of us would stay at the bar and have a few drinks to unwind. Some nights, we stayed at the bar until the sun came up the next day.

I did get quite the "street smart" education from working at Dinosaur BBQ. I had to learn how to protect myself with large sums of cash in my pocket, as I walked home alone at all hours of the night through the heart of Harlem. I had to learn how to fend off advances, deal with problem customers, and learn how to decline unwanted drug use or pressures, and I figured out who was smart to keep in my good graces, should a problem arise. I also learned how *fun* it could be to make a lot of money. I felt more at home working in this restaurant than I ever did with the people who attended my college. These were my people: hard workers and somewhat chaotic. This, I was used to.

I often say I learned more at Dinosaur than I did at Columbia University. I still believe this on some level; however, I also recognize that the juxtaposition of these two worlds was part of my healing and growth. I also learned how to be more professional, and Columbia opened my eyes to things happening in the world that I had never experienced or been aware of before. The practice of getting comfortable with all different types of people, both the student body and through my placements during my education, were critical for my growth and development. I learned that diversity is the spice of life!

My training and development as a social work student also taught me that nobody is exempt from societal pressures, programming, or norms. The work of exploring our own internal and often implicit biases can help us to see the ways we are falling into deeply held cultural programming that is forcing us into distortions in our own masculine-feminine blend. We cannot expand into our full potential if we are not aware of how we impact other people, consciously or unconsciously, through our choices. The whole idea here is that biases also exist in our money story, so unlearning societal norms and breaking through any existing stereotypes inside of us are necessary parts of the process of crafting a new story.

Social work training awakened me to be more aware of what I say and how I behave in relationships with all humans and am more comfortable and courageous about having conversations proactively, to make sure that the people of all races, ethnicities, life circumstances, and cultures whom I serve feel safe and supported, and that they understand I am aware of how my experience is different than theirs. I make space for the differences between us *and* connect as human beings.

Freeing ourselves from biases as best we possibly can will also help us to step more fully into transcendence around our money story, because we can have a more informed approach to our impact and our career, one that encompasses more of other people's experiences, needs, wants, realities, etc. By choosing to have the hard conversations and then work to unlearn what is limiting us, we can create a more robust understanding of life, business, people and money.

One of the internships during my Columbia education was a perfect fit for me and one I really loved. I worked for the CityKids Foundation, where at-risk youth could come after school and on off days to receive support, connection, and activity.

I was there as one of the in-house student counselors and care managers, to support the kids should anything challenging come up while they were there, but also to connect with them about how things were going at home, in their internal world, and at school. What unified these particular children was that they all had a love of, passion for, and connection to the arts, specifically music and dance. We coordinated elaborate performances and recitals for the kids to showcase their abilities, we organized practices, and we ran programs to help them tap into their creative sense.

Being able to be in a room with these creative musicians *and* perform my counseling and social work responsibilities was so gratifying and healing for me. I even pursued employment at this placement after I completed my program but ultimately decided that New York City on a social worker's salary was not the lifestyle I envisioned and decided to go home.

Into the Real Working World

When I returned to Rochester, my first job right out of my master's program was at the Teenage Parent Support Services program. I didn't realize until I came into this particular placement that Rochester had one of the highest rates of teenage pregnancy in the country. This program served the parents, usually the mothers, who were as young as twelve years old, to learn maternal wellness and early childhood development during their pregnancy, birth, and throughout the first few years of their child's life.

The program was designed to help the women get to their prenatal appointments, access good nutrition, health care and supplies for their children, and provide education to support their learning essential skills for parenting and childhood development, while they were at very young ages, themselves. We worked through a curriculum with the whole family, to help them bond with their children and support their growth, physically, emotionally, mentally, and developmentally.

In this role, I learned so much about child development, family systems, and the realities of the inequities and challenges many of these families and children face. I was put into some pretty precarious situations, with bed bugs, domestic abuse, gang violence, and child abuse, along with some instances where my safety was definitely in question.

I also started to notice something about the social work field, being an incredibly hard worker by nature. This was my first experience with a full-time professional salary, including the consistency and promise of a full-time paycheck. I was given what was called a full caseload and managed all of my responsibilities with ease. I noticed, however, that some of my colleagues carried even less work than I did, and they seemed to be out of the office to "manage their caseload" way more than I was. While the work was tough to witness, sometimes, I was able to get done what was required of my job in much less time than I was paid for. I was bored and often looking for more to do.

So, I took on more work. But, at one point, some of my coworkers approached me to ask me to slow down and not make them look bad. They were often doing other things while on the job for their own families or they just wanted to unwind. I had no idea how to handle that request, as someone who was so accustomed to working hard in order to earn my keep. It was always about "doing more to earn more." "Doing less" wasn't in the fabric of my being.

To supplement my employment and expertise, I was also working toward advanced licensure in counseling and held a part-time private counseling practice. For years, I would finish my job and then see patients of my own in the evenings and weekends; concurrently, I pursued the most advanced master's level licensing. What I didn't recognize at the time was that the decision to have a private practice was a *business* decision. I did not even realize until many, many years into the process that I had been a business owner since my social work days! I made the decision to work beyond my employment, sought contracts, private payment, additional supervision, and affiliates, and created partnerships; I even sat on the board for a well-known local counseling collaborative and helped it grow for years. I was always the most business-minded person at the table, which is often why they wanted me around, to help them build, attending to the financials, the strategy, the marketing, and the realities of the business climate.

This entire time, I was building my own business acumen, but I didn't even know it was unfolding. As service professionals, this happens often: we are just doing our work and being paid for our work; we are not business owners. However, that is not true. We are actually business owners and service professionals, and the sooner we can incorporate that into our identity, the sooner our practice can thrive! I held a full part-time practice and probably did that successfully because of some of my natural business acumen, as well as some off-books training from my cousin, who'd owned the franchise when I worked for her, and by working in the restaurant industry.

Also, my training at Columbia had been advanced generalist practice and programming, which was a dual-track program where I learned how to become an effective social worker and counselor, while also learning how to build, develop, and fund programs. I know now, in hindsight, why I chose that track as opposed to a clinical-only track: it helped me learn how businesses and programs are built and maintained. It was my first formal business training, without even knowing it was happening.

Eventually, I moved onto another role in early childhood development from a medical perspective. I was named one of the point maternal and child social workers for our local hospitals, to help mothers get access to supplies, health care, and maternal and pediatric care, as well as basic necessities. During these two roles in particular, I came to more deeply understand the realities of the lowest levels of Maslow's Hierarchy of Needs.

If the women I was supporting didn't have food, diapers, a roof over their head, or formula for their babies, we weren't going to sit down and talk about tummy time or bonding with their child. If their environment was dangerous or abusive, we weren't going to handle proper nutrition, rest, and self-care during their pregnancy. While I'd had my own chaotic upbringing, these positions opened my eyes to the vast and varied realities of people's lives.

I was particularly drawn to working with the families with complex medical diagnoses. There was so much need for these families—logistically, emotionally, mentally, spiritually, medically, etc.—that to be able to help them mobilize quickly to gather resources and support felt like I was making a real difference.

Not only were these families struggling with access to care, but they were also often dealing with real-life limiting circumstances for their children. I wanted to help them in whatever way I could, and the ability to move quickly, work hard, and get things done was welcomed in this particular setting. I became well-known as the social worker who could make things happen for these families, and I thrived in this collaborative environment to support these children.

I found myself called to pursue working in Pediatric Palliative Care on a team of providers, to help children with life-limiting illnesses receive support, treatment, comfort, and care during the most difficult diagnoses. Through this program, the families were often able to live through an amazing healing journey and sometimes even a cure of their illness. This was a miracle to witness, everything anyone could hope as the outcome for these young children.

Unfortunately, this was not always the case; when decline in their health happened, our team would support the families through the child's disease, which sometimes ended in their death, and our support continued then for a few years after those untimely, painful, and life-altering outcomes for their family. These families found themselves with their worst fears being realized and would never have chosen this path, did nothing to create it, and wouldn't wish this reality on anyone.

We bore witness to these families processing the intense, debilitating loss and held space for their grief. There was nothing any of us could do to change the outcome; we could not "fix" the situation. After the loss of a child, these families were forever changed. A piece of their heart was broken, irrevocably. They would always long for what could have been. They would always harbor the "what ifs" and the wishes, the angers, the fears, the doubts, and the worries. They were faced with having to carry on without the physical form of the child they would always deeply love, deeply grieve, and deeply miss.

Some of the families who experienced the loss of a child would rightfully crumble. Some lost themselves completely in the grief, some went completely numb, while some remained forever stuck in the moment of their child's death. Others grieved the loss and *insisted* on leaving a legacy for their child to be remembered forever. They would fight for answers, advocate for a cure, become lawmakers and change-makers, and create foundations, programs, or charities to honor the legacy of their child, in order to help stay connected to them, even in their absence, and to help them make sense of something that could have left anyone questioning life.

I was fascinated by how two families could respond in such different ways and how even each parent in the same family responded in their unique way. Since I moved into business coaching, I have seen this same pattern unfold across personal and business development over and over again. When humans run into a challenge, a problem, a trauma, or a shift in their life or business, they tend to respond in one of these three ways, which I've come to call: Stuck, Sink, and Soar.

About one third will become completely stuck, overwhelmed, lost, or numb to their reality. They will face indecision, analysis paralysis, and not know where to go next. They will repeat various limiting patterns for an extended period and will have an inability to escape the negative feedback loop they find themselves running.

Another third of the people will begin to sink. They fall into self-negating, self-sabotaging, even damaging patterns and continue to make what they are going through increasingly impossible, more challenging, and painful while perhaps begin to feel hopeless or depressed. Some will quit. Some will retreat. And some will hit their own personal version of rock-bottom.

The last third will either reach their rock-bottom or have their own personal pivotal moment and decide that this is the moment to climb, soar, sail, and strive for their potential. All that has been challenging or painful becomes motivation for these achievers to grow, to thrive, and to learn from what they had gone through in the past by making the choice to do whatever is in their power to never feel that way again.

They understand it's not their fault, while it is also their responsibility; they take ownership and make commitments with dedication and drive to make their lives better, in spite of the pain or hardship. They are like the phoenix rising from the ashes. They are on their Hero's Journey and ready to step into all that life has to offer, with a newfound perspective about their life and business that propels them to greater heights. They don't let their lives be run by what happened in the past. They use it as information and choose, instead, to fly.

Everyone responds to the no-good, very-bad situations in life differently. We all have our own path and journey; and we all deserve the freedom to grieve in our own timing, to integrate our life education at will, and to choose what we make of the cards we are dealt. There is absolutely no wrong way, and there is no judgment. We all need to feel and go through the full spectrum of life's richness and the natural human emotions that come into play at different points in our personal version of "life school."

And there is always a choice.

My intention in sharing this observation is only to highlight and offer a reminder of that choice; and in hopes to empower as many people as possible to choose to soar, because you are worthy, worth the effort, and deserve the chance to choose. Those that are on the path to self-actualization must make that choice at different points in their lives and businesses. This choice is to seek personal growth, no matter the personal realities, which is often easier said than done, but always worth it.

These families, these dear children, and the program I had the privilege to be a part of taught me in very deep ways very early in my life and career the power of resilience, compassion, empathy, love, spirituality, the body-mind connection, advocacy, personal development, the importance of support systems, self-care, holistic wellness, and so much more. This put me on a fast track to those very hard questions: "Why God?" "How could the world be so cruel?" "Why them?" "What does it all mean?" "Why can't everyone be saved?"

Professionally, I think about these children and families all of the time, and I am forever grateful. Whether these families know it or not, their legacy in some way lives inside of me, and they are part of my drive to bring this work to the world.

If someone can create beauty out of arguably one of the absolute worst-case scenarios in life, there has to be a way to capture this significant shifting power and bring it to less egregious examples of life: personal and professional development.

One of the deep lessons I learned about myself in this process, something I wasn't aware of until they helped me see myself more clearly, was that I am an empath and a highly sensitive person. Empathy is when we feel *for* someone and put ourselves in their shoes to understand more deeply what they are going through. When someone is an empath, they not only feel *for* others, they also actually *feel what* other people are going through, in their bodies, heart, minds, and souls.

I always knew I was a highly sensitive person, but I didn't understand the depths of this characteristic I possessed until I was put in front of these very, very tough circumstances. There, I started to witness how my *own* body, mind, and soul responded.

Bearing witness to their illnesses, their deaths, their disease, and their pain was extremely hard on my body-mind. At first, I felt weak and less of a person, thinking, *What do I have to complain about? They are the ones going through this right now! Why can't I just deal with it? How can some of these other angelic providers, doctors, and practitioners do this work for decades, while I am falling apart after less than five years?*

Also, I noticed myself wanting to jump into action and fix whatever I could. My team and the families I served benefited often from this skill set, as I was able to make things happen for people, gather resources, rally the troops, find a way, and, as they say in the social-work profession, "ask for forgiveness instead of permission," in order to get what my families needed so they could be as comfortable as possible in an intensely uncomfortable situation.

Except there is nothing to fix in grief. Everyone has their own process, their own path, and their own unique needs in order to go through their own unique journey.

While I *could* hold space for them, it was becoming painful for me as an empath and someone who was naturally skilled at getting everything done quickly and under any conditions.

I remember attending another funeral one afternoon after the loss of a teen with whom I had really connected. When they passed away, I found myself in a scenic gully, sobbing while literally looking at the sky and saying *"Why, God? Are you even out there?"*

I knew, at that moment, something needed to shift for me. I couldn't be as effective for these families if I was taking on their pain. It was their pain, not mine. I needed to learn how to use my skills and strengths in a way that served others *and* my own needs; I had to put the proverbial oxygen mask on myself first, in order to save the rest of the plane.

There needed to be a middle ground between wanting to help others and caring for myself. I also became attuned to the acute reality that it was my responsibility to live life to the fullest, because I had been given another day when these children were not. I was moving up the hierarchy. I had fulfilled the desire to belong on a skilled team and care for the most vulnerable; they ended up teaching me the urgency and importance of leaning into the gift of life and the importance of actualizing your potential as another level of leadership and service.

And so began my journey to holistic business coaching, where I bring everything that I was blessed to learn from these families to all those whom I serve now. And hopefully to inspire you, dear reader, as well.

One of the most important lessons I take with me daily is that life is not guaranteed. Hell, tomorrow isn't guaranteed. You may look right and never be given the chance to look left.

Life is not to be squandered.

This moment is not to be missed or wasted.

It is meant to be savored, honored, witnessed fully, and met with deep gratitude. No matter what position you find yourself in right now, you've been given another minute, and *that* is a blessing.

I take these lessons with me into every day, every experience, every moment with my children, family, clients, and life. Gratitude for life has been the fabric of who I am, thanks to these impactful beings.

Synchronicity

During one particularly challenging loss of a pediatric client, coupled with some internal struggles within a personal, unhealthy relationship at the time, I decided to take some of these lessons into action and follow one of my dreams.

As a child, I had always wanted a tricolored, female Cavalier King Charles Spaniel. My mother, however, had always said they were too expensive. So, in my mind, the Cavalier King Charles became a part of my money story. I decided I was still going to get my Cavalier *and* I was going to find a way to adopt one. Once I made enough money, that was going to be the first thing I did.

I never let this thought go, and when I entered into my first well-paying job, I got more serious about finding the puppy of my dreams. I learned about a group of puppies who needed to be rescued; this still involved a large fee, though, to support the rescuing efforts.

I made the decision to adopt her and brought her home. Within a week, I received a check in the mail from an unknown overpayment for my homeowner's insurance, the amount exact to the penny of the adoption fee for Lady Madonna, my sweet, female, tri-colored Cavalier King Charles Spaniel.

This was one of my first conscious experiments with synchronicity, the phenomenon where an event in the outside world coincides meaningfully with a psychological state of mind. I was just entering into learning more about the universal laws, and this moment set my belief and curiosity on fire. Lady was my first major confirmation that these laws are real. And this opened my eyes and mind to amazing possibilities.

Synchronicity has become one of my favorite parts of the work I do now. When people can start to see those seemingly coincidental experiences as clues or breadcrumbs leading them on their way, or as little gifts from the universe urging them on in their actualization, they are generating the feelings of faith and connection and are taking that leap of faith to believe they are being guided to something greater.

I hear so many astonishing stories from my clients about how synchronicities in their own lives have created great meaning for their journey, like a phone call from someone they had just been thinking about, offering them the precise solution they are looking for in their business. These stories always bring me so much joy in my work, and those miracles always send chills throughout my body.

If you'd like to create your own synchronicity experiment, try asking the universe to show you something like a lime-green car. Take a deep breath, close your eyes, imagine the lime-green car, and say to yourself, "I now manifest a lime-green car." Practice believing that it's possible to see that car. And then, just wait for the universe to deliver!

When you continue to practice this skill, you can begin to manifest whatever you desire in your life and business, too. For example, I make a personal practice to reach out to whomever comes to my consciousness, personally and professionally. If I think of a friend, I reach out. If I think of a client, I check in. If I think of a former client or prospect, I send them a note or pick up the phone and make a call. These little intuitive breadcrumbs have created some of the most beautiful and sometimes magical interactions with my loved ones and clients.

Inevitably, they will exclaim, "Woah! I was just thinking about you! Were your ears ringing?" Or "How do you always know exactly when to reach out?"

These interactions become trust-builders, and my business is a relationship business, where the foundation of trust is paramount to any interaction. By following those little "nudges from the universe," I have been able to foster such an environment of love and care between me, my clients, and many of my close relationships that I have made this a standing business practice!

Strategic synchronicity in client attraction is a fascinating topic. A great resource in order to dive in more fully is the work of Stacey Hall and Jan Brogniez and their book, *Attracting Perfect Customers: The Power of Strategic Synchronicity.*

Lady also came to me at the perfect time to help me pivot away from that very unhealthy relationship. She helped me more fully understand and accept the power of these principles, showed me the value of unconditional love, that I am worthy of that love, and that I am worthy of wealth and riches, now that I could finally afford what I'd previously considered unattainable.

THE INTEGRATED ENTREPRENEUR

I gained confidence through ending my toxic relationship, through the unconditional love from Lady, and from the positive feedback at my work. I started to learn how to listen to my body more and began to see that my empathic nature was not cut out for consistent exposure to the level of pain involved in the social work I was doing.

Holistic Business Coaching

I remember visiting one of my mentors, my uncle, during the death of another young person. We took a walk together, and I cried. We spoke about those deep lessons I was learning, the major "Why God? What's it all mean?" questions I was asking myself and the level of suffering I was taking on through this work.

He said he saw a place for my talents and skills for program development, counseling, and action-taking in his existing business coaching program, as a sales and operations manager.

At first, I was doubtful I could coach people who were running a business, and really, I didn't see myself as a "salesperson." I definitely hadn't adopted the identity of a business owner. I was still "just a social worker and counselor," with the bulk of my training being in pediatrics. Luckily, my mentor helped me understand that sales in this context was just the first point of entry to service. I was able to click that into my brain without too much difficulty.

I took a major leap of faith and started to work some hours with him in his coaching program. I quickly started to see how my skills were, in fact, transferable, and I leaned into the feeling of loving the coaching modality. I went to work finding more business owners to serve and using my counseling skills to help them develop holistic expressions of their lives and businesses. I dropped down to part-time in palliative care, and eventually transitioned completely out of that work to help my uncle build his business and become a full-time coach.

My business coaching practice started with much more emphasis on counseling, and I eventually became trained officially in coaching modalities. I gained vast skill and proficiency over my decade working as an employee in this setting, as I helped my mentor build his business. I was able to support him during its ups and downs, changes of administrative support, marketing challenges, planning and scheduling challenges, office-space challenges, revenue concerns, making contract and proposal decisions, and so many more critical business lessons, all of which I learned first while in the support seat and, eventually, as COO of his business.

I also learned through the eyes of the business owners whom I served. I helped them create a more balanced life and take better care of themselves; I saw how their personal relationships, their teams, their clients, and their business also improved. I helped them build their confidence, self-worth, and belongingness plus heal past traumas or current fears, doubts, and worries. I helped them shift from the scarcity mindset to one of abundance and to leverage the universal laws and principles to see their lives improve and their businesses skyrocket. It was through the inner that we would see the outer respond positively.

As time carried on and my skill set improved, I began gaining more knowledge about particular industries and, equally important, more masculine approaches to business. I developed accountability systems, tracking systems, KPIs, goals, projections, and client-relationship management systems. I began to learn more about marketing, business development, prospecting, the economy and economics, politics, and how the state of the world affects business ownership.

However, it always comes back to how you *feel* about those masculine elements, what you *think* about them, and how you *respond* in relationship to them. This is what affects your outcomes. It is all about your mindset. The more you can do to leverage the universal laws and principles to change your beliefs, thoughts, and emotions, the better aligned your actions will be in all of these areas and the greater likelihood your preferred results will unfold.

And thus was born my holistic coaching practice and philosophy; this is where my expertise lives. It is both the feminine and the masculine; both the inner and the outer, and both the mindset and the strategy.

After about a decade of coaching in this employment setting where I'd started my business-coaching career, I had developed confidence in what I brought to the table. My results were strong, consistent, and reliable. My clients were happy, loyal, and referred generously, and my services were regularly completely tapped out and highly sought-after, while still employed by my former company.

While I was an employee, I was *teaching* entrepreneurship but not living it. As a result, I was creating for someone else, building for someone else, earning for someone else, supporting someone else's mission, vision, values, and ways of being. As an employee, I always answered to someone else and supported the legacy of that someone else. I was guiding others through entrepreneurship in theory but not applying it to myself, in practice.

As a natural and trained employee-minded person, my decision to end my employment didn't come easily and probably resulted in my staying under an employment contract for far longer than was healthy for me. I was beginning to recognize I was not going to be able to actualize my potential. I needed to find my own voice and begin to step into my own power to use my unique abilities in service to more people. It was time for me to take my next risky, courageous entrepreneurial move and open my own coaching business.

The employee-minded person seeks comfort, safety, and consistency above risk, even if it means accepting less reward in the form of a paycheck. They want to support *someone else's* dream and goal; and they enjoy being a bolster to someone else's or some other entity's success, legacy, and vision. They are comfortable when they know how to do their role, when they know exactly what their responsibilities are, and when they can fulfill that role to support someone else's program or business.

Not every employee is a hard-working employee, but those ones who are will go above and beyond, to "water the flowers" or do everything necessary to support the business or program's mission and vision. When an employee is passionately connected to the business's mission, they will work tirelessly to fulfill and support that mission and accept the pay commensurate with and specified for their roles and responsibilities.

The entrepreneur, on the other hand, craves building their own thing and living into their own mission, vision, and values. They set aside the need for consistency or stability in exchange for the risk and reward that is necessary for an entrepreneur on many levels. They are willing to invest in themselves through their time, energy, and currency, and they will do anything they need to do to make their dream business a reality. They thrive in the roller-coaster of the ups and downs, and they see that the market is just offering feedback about their business, to which they get to respond accordingly, swiftly, and with an air of curiosity, exploration, and excitement.

Many entrepreneurs are overflowing with ideas, and many also will start various different ventures, because they understand the value of having a variety of revenue streams in a variety of qualities of business, both passive and active, high-ticket and low-ticket, brick-and-mortar and digital, service-based and/or product-based. They leverage other people's support and their employees in order to get it all done, and they are willing to delegate and invest in the business through hiring that support, because they know they can't do it alone.

To fully step into freedom and autonomy, I needed to step into the full expression of the entrepreneur's mindset: the willingness to create a strategic and calculated risk, take a stand for something I believe in, pivot, and make decisions as often as necessary in alignment with my own personal greater mission, vision, values, and purpose.

The risk of staying in someone else's story, one that was no longer aligned to my personal path, became too risky and outweighed the benefits of staying. I took the leap and trusted my skills, despite the inevitable uncertainty. It was the best decision I could have made for me, my family, my clients, and my future vision.

Soon thereafter, I opened my own holistic business coaching practice, while maintaining my counseling practice as an additional source of income. Nearly all of my clients decided to stay with me as I made the leap into entrepreneurship full time.

My practice stayed full, and referrals came naturally. For months, I maintained a full thirty-five client caseload of coaching clients and an additional twenty in counseling. One of my first lessons as an entrepreneur was going to have to be to learn how to trust in releasing parts of what I used to do in order to scale into something different. So, I raised my coaching rates and released my counseling clients to local trusted sources in an effort to dive fully into growing my coaching practice. Since creating the space in my time and energy, my coaching practice has only continued to grow exponentially, both financially and logistically.

I was uniquely qualified to help my business owner clients understand more deeply how they were showing up in their behavior and mindset, either as employees or entrepreneurs, because I had lived and experienced both worlds in a variety of different settings. I am able to help them sort through the right hires because I know well that being an employee is not at all bad—it's just different! So, we are able to structure compensation, highlight strengths, bolster weaknesses, and put the right people in the right seats on the bus to support wherever they are on the spectrum of employee versus entrepreneur mindset.

My Entrepreneurial Mindset

I used to call myself an "employee-plus," because I was a natural employee with a deep understanding, appreciation, and actionable implementation of the entrepreneurial mindset. Now, I recognize that I have many natural abilities as an entrepreneur and some tendencies, in my money mindset and ways of being, that needed to shift in order to step more fully into the entrepreneurial spirit. I do that work on identity, belief, and mindset to more fully own my CEO status in business, and I use my empathy and my honoring of the employee mindset to guide my business owners and to help them learn how best to relate to, frame, and understand their employees.

My shift from the poverty or scarcity mindset into a prosperity or abundance mindset has been and continues to be an incredible journey. My business-coaching practice has earned multiple six-figures annually for over a decade now, and I have supported myriad business owners achieve six- and seven-figure incomes of their own. Through this, I have seen just how much of an impact the internal money story can have on an entrepreneur's success. Along the way, I have learned many different lessons, along with my own triggers into the lower modes of thinking and being. I have been able to witness these same triggers in the high-achieving, visionary leaders whom I serve.

On paper, I shouldn't be where I am today, given everything that I had stacked against me. But instead of letting my past programming around money limit me, I have been able to grow into a new set of beliefs, experiences, and circumstances that I now use to grow my business into limitless potential, to enjoy life to the fullest, and to support my clients in their doing the same.

For example, now that I've fully settled into what it means to be in business and sales and have witnessed what so many business owners grapple with in their sales process, I understand that part of my own growth around what it means to be in sales can now support other business owners, as well.

So many business owners have strong negative beliefs about what it means to make a sale, to be a salesperson, or to speak freely and openly about sales; just like I did, when I began my entrepreneurial journey. I've met far too many business owners who are afraid to charge for their services at all, and more who are undercharging, discounting, or diminishing their offer in order to avoid speaking about the transaction, the money, or the sale inevitably involved in business. Many people feel it is pushy, sleazy, or manipulative to be a salesperson and want to have nothing to do with selling at all, to avoid being lumped into that category. These belief systems need to be shifted, because business is inextricably tied to money, no matter how tuned into your purpose you may be. Sales doesn't have to be a four-letter word!

What I've learned, instead, is that sales can indeed be viewed as an artful practice, and the artfulness in sales often revolves around effective communication, persuasion, and influence. It involves a combination of emotional intelligence, communication skills, a deep understanding of human psychology, and adaptability.

By understanding and empathizing with customers' needs, concerns, and desires, salespeople can tailor their approach to resonate emotionally, because they recognize that emotions play a significant role in decision-making. Skilled salespeople know how to establish trust and rapport, making customers more inclined to buy and recommend the product or service to others and, more importantly, to cultivate long-term authentic relationships with care. They are often compelling storytellers and able to convey the value and benefits of what they are offering in a way that is relatable and memorable. They often artfully employ various influence techniques, such as reciprocity, social proof, scarcity, and authority, to guide customers toward a favorable decision, ethically and effectively, while focusing more on empathetic listening, compassion, and awareness of where their customers are, and then gently guiding them into their higher self, if their product or service is in the customer's highest best interest. Understanding the customer's needs, concerns, and objections allows the salesperson to respond effectively and tailor their offer accordingly, which requires a combination of intuition, experience, and the ability to read and respond to cues from the customer and often involves overcoming objections and solving problems with unique solutions.

If you are a salesperson who is truly in self-transcendence, then you are there to create the greatest impact for the greatest good of all concerned. Business and sales are about the power to serve and pull someone into their highest potential, not the force to push a faulty product or broken promise for your own benefit. Money is just the energy of exchange, the masculine energy to provide and the feminine energy to receive.

I still sometimes fall into the "lower-self" version of my money story; it is present and becomes triggered in business from time to time. One of the primary ways I have learned to notice when I am falling into my lower self is through the signals in my body and emotions, which are very much physical manifestations of mental thoughts, beliefs, and feeling sets.

I continue to learn how to decode the signals my body gives me, after many, many years of neglecting, ignoring, and avoiding what my body was trying to tell me. We are not taught to listen to our bodies or our intuition, which is one of the superpowers of the divine feminine. Our body is a vessel for our mind in our soul. It is constantly engaging in a miracle set of automatic systems that operate without us even having to think about them, but which keep us alive every single day. We do not have to think in order to breathe, to digest, to move, to circulate, to see, to hear, or to use any of our other senses.

These amazing systems keep us moving in space and become a part of the essence of our humanness, but they are not all of who we are. We have a personality, an emotional intelligence and identity, a genetic code, a human design, cultural programming, a spiritual connection, and so many other pieces that make us who we are completely.

With that said, all of this is changeable; it is subject to neuroplasticity.

The first step is to become aware of all of these different programs we are running, which are either empowering us or disempowering us over and over again. We must decide which ones we are going to release and which ones we are going to hold close to our heart, based on whether they are in alignment with whomever we choose to be in our journey and path toward evolution. Then, we can start crafting a new money story to replace and run in our minds, bodies, and business, moving forward.

Here are some examples of mantras to try that have been shown to improve your relationship with money. Consider each one and notice which one feels aligned. Then, begin reciting it to yourself to help replace some of those old stories. Make a special note of any of them about which you feel internal resistance, because that is usually a good hint that you carry a limiting belief about money that may require some attention:

❖ I choose now to believe that money is a renewable resource and that it flows easily to me and through me, to support me, my business, and my family, along with whatever abundant ways we need or desire at any given time.

❖ I choose prosperity for my own family and for my business, without needing to rely on anyone or anything to make that happen. I need or want something; I have all the acumen and resources to make that happen immediately and indefinitely.

❖ I trust money and money trusts me.

❖ I love money and money loves me.

❖ I am grateful every day for all the amazing experiences and circumstances that money brings into my life, to the lives of my family and clients, and to my business.

❖ I am no longer limited by the stories of money from the past or the stories that some of my close family members continue to carry about me or money. I release those stories, because I am limitless.

❖ I choose to carry some of the useful wisdom passed down by my ancestors and even send those stories to my children, as some of the wisdom will help them grow and evolve, as well; however, this time, with grace, ease, joy, and abundance.

❖ I am so happy and joyful, and money now flows to me in such expansive quantities that surprise me how big they continue to grow.

❖ I am generous and grateful for those abundant resources.

❖ Money is energy; money is love; money is service.

❖ I choose to live in that vibration every day, generating more abundant love and positive energy, as a valuable service I bring to the world, and the fact that it creates more abundant growth for everyone involved.

If we take the principles of manifestation into account, we want to start feeling the feelings we imagine financial freedom will bring us immediately. Then, we have already won, *and* it will be more likely that we achieve that goal due to the Laws of Vibration, Focus, and Attraction.

It is also useful during this process to go back to your past experiences and learn about what limits may exist in the story you are telling yourself about money. Do that work on your money story from the past. Some of the messages you received in your childhood and upbringing, from society and culture, will be supportive of money; and some will be diminishing.

There are impactful timeline meditations you can walk yourself through or receive in a guided coaching or therapy session that can help you really look at different points in your own personal timeline that have impacted your beliefs about money. This can also begin reprogramming what you choose to feel and think and your beliefs about money.

You may need to address some real traumas along the way, and if that is the case, this work is best done in collaboration with a trained trauma specialist. I have found substantial results through Havening to help calm the central nervous system; Emotional Freedom Technique to reprogram the money story; Eye Movement Desensitization and Reprocessing (EMDR) to process deeply held traumas; and somatic psychotherapy to help process those traumas lingering in the body. There are so many different modalities to support you in rewriting your story in the process of creating the financial freedom you crave.

If *freedom* is the operative word in your desired outcome, perhaps this deserves some added exploration. It's quite common for entrepreneurs to seek freedom in a number of ways. Some crave the ability to work for themselves, the flexibility to craft their own hours, pay, or vacation time. Some want to work remotely anywhere in the world, and some want to be able to decide how they run their business or have the freedom to create however they choose. What does freedom look like for you, in your business?

It starts with claiming your new preferred story, then releasing the attachment to the outcome, which we will dive into next. It can be an incredibly helpful process to begin by writing a letter to money, as if it were something you could connect with and address directly.

Money is energy. It's an energy of exchange. And so, we get to direct that energy however we choose. Go through the process of writing out all of your past, present, and future feelings about money, much like I did in this chapter for you. Any experiences that you've had, any cultural or childhood programming, anyone you know who handed stories about money down to you personally and professionally; plus, any beliefs, thoughts, or feelings you still carry about money. And then, begin transitioning into how you *prefer* to feel, think, believe, and engage with money now.

I do encourage you to handwrite this letter, in order to go through the full process of externalizing those thoughts and feelings onto paper, as a part of the process of separating yourself from money and seeing more clearly what you used to think about it versus how you now choose instead to feel, think, and behave around money.

You may also consider naming your "lower self" and your "higher self," to help you decipher who is showing up at any given moment. What distorted feminine and masculine energies show up with your lower self? Where is your lower self often triggered to on the hierarchy? What are those typical negative belief systems, emotions, and the money stories that accompany that lower-self version of you? What is a name you can give that version of yourself?

How about your higher self? What could you call that version of you? What is that version aiming for or looking to achieve? How do they feel about money? What positive, loving, and supportive belief systems do they carry? And what blend of empowering feminine and masculine energies do they carry? Where are they on the hierarchy, and what do they choose now?

I have had clients find significant shifts to take their personal power back by naming their lower and higher selves and going into great detail about the differences between those different versions of themselves. They can visualize how they look, what they tend to wear and drink, what activities they engage in, and how they speak and behave.

One poignant example arose in my work with one client who, throughout our work, had identified that his lower self had a strong distorted feminine ego manifestation. Early in our work, he started to see how his lower self was internally berating, ran a negative inner dialogue of judgment, fear, doubt, and scarcity, and often creeped up when he was trying to evolve or grow beyond his comfort zone. He would have loud, diminishing, and fearful thoughts about money, his business, his value and worth that emerged whenever he was trying something new or stepping into his evolution.

We decided that giving this version of himself a name would be helpful to create some separation between this part of him. He did the work of going within and really getting to know this part of himself. What came from his internal reflection is that his lower self is named "Phyllis." She is this older, crotchety woman who drinks martinis and smokes cigarettes and only has negative things to say about his evolution. She piped in when he was trying to grow and interrupted his progress by shouting negative things about money and his business, encouraging procrastination and avoidance for the sake of self-sabotage, and really was just downright mean to him.

Now, on our coaching calls, Phyllis comes up often. We can both picture this woman clearly when she shows up. We name her, we laugh about it a bit by telling her to sit down and shut up. We hand her a martini and find out what she's trying to protect him from. Then, we take the wisdom and keep moving forward without letting her drive the bus of his life. We have come to develop a fondness for Phyllis. We appreciate her without buying into her antics!

These exercises can be incredibly helpful in creating awareness about who you are being and will allow you to make the choice to release the old stories and step into your chosen version of who you are becoming, instead. To help you along in your process, check out some of the journaling prompts below, which will support your process of sorting through your own personal stories and beliefs about money.

Money Story Integration

Summary: Healing your past, present, and future money stories is essential to step into abundance in life and business.

Resources

Employee vs. Entrepreneur Mindset Quiz:

www.raeannelacatena.com/quiz

Synchronicity Experiment

Have you found your lime-green car yet?

Money Manifestation Mantras

Naming your higher and lower self: Your scarcity self vs. abundant self

Writing your Money Story

❖ Write a letter to Money: In this letter, share with money your desires for your wealth expansion and even your vision for your relationship as you embody your wealthiest self, as well as process and reflect where you developed your past and present experiences, beliefs, and thoughts in relationship to money.

Journal Prompts for Letting Go of Your Lower Self Money Story

❖ What does success mean to you?

❖ Why would you need to avoid success?

❖ What would it say about you when you are successful?

❖ What will it say about you if you are *not* successful? Why is this the safest option? Who taught you these things?

❖ What is *bad* about being successful, having wealth, and being accomplished?

- ❖ What is *good* about being successful, having wealth and being accomplished?
- ❖ What is your relationship with money and wealth?
- ❖ What is your current energetic minimum (earning potential) and your energetic maximum when it comes to money? Where do you desire to be?
- ❖ What lower-level frequency behaviors are you allowing yourself to let go of? How could you shift these behaviors?
- ❖ Where have you been *waiting* for the other shoe to drop, i.e., unexpected debt, bills, or accidents that cost money, etc.?

Chapter Five

Control and Release

"Doubt is resistance, faith is surrender. Worry is resistance, joy is surrender. Control is resistance, allowing is surrender. Ridicule is resistance, believing is surrender."

—Jen Sincero

ON OUR THIRD DATE, my husband and I decided that, on the count of three, we would both call out how many children we would like to have when the time came....

"One.... two.... three.... go.... *Three!*" we both stated enthusiastically at the same time.

My husband's soul purpose is to be a father. He's always dreamed of having a family of his own and is able to be in his greatest expression through all things fatherhood.

We were married in Punta Cana, and on our mini-honeymoon after the wedding, we were floating in the pool after the festivities when we decided we would bring our three children to the resort for our tenth wedding anniversary.

We went to the Greek islands for our honeymoon and to Hawaii on our first wedding anniversary. Then, we decided we were ready to begin trying to build our family.

After months of unsuccessful attempts at becoming pregnant and a lot of disappointment, we decided to seek professional help. We discovered that both my husband and I had some medical complications preventing us from getting pregnant, so we began medical support for both of us to work through those issues. This involved surgery, medication, injections, and even one pregnancy that resulted in miscarriage.

During this season of our lives, we were on a roller-coaster of emotion mixed with the pain of watching our family and friends grow their own families easily and happily. It started to feel like everyone around us was pregnant. Each month brought an additional medical procedure and increased disappointment. Add into the mix a hormonal cocktail from all the medications I was taking, and I was in a very low place.

For me, this time was especially challenging. I coach people all day, every day about how to control what you can actually control and maintain a healthy mindset, but this infertility journey felt impossible to manage. This led me to feel out of integrity with what I was teaching, and I began to question myself.

For example, I have a strong understanding that there is only one thing in the whole wide world that is ever actually in any human being's control: *which thoughts we energize.*

I understood this intellectually, and I'd seen it create magic for people in their lives and business. But this time, around what both my husband and I wanted so deeply, I could not release control. I found myself trying to control everything.

The Western medicine approach to fertility only fed into those control dramas through what became a timed, cold, and devastating time of life for us. The precise timing of different medications and injections and the constantly changing schedule. The foods to avoid eating. How much physical activity and even the restrictions on having sex. There was no more joy, only anticipation, disappointment, fear, and stress.

I tried to control all of this uncertainty by trying to involve anyone who knew anything about fertility, going fully into work mode around this task. I completely lost myself to the delusion that I could control this outcome and that, if I didn't, I was a failure. I couldn't even do the most natural expression of femininity. My body was failing me again.

A small voice in the back of my head did understand I had no control over this outcome, but for almost two years of this rollercoaster, I just couldn't surrender.

There is an important principle called non-attachment, in which attachment can be viewed as a spectrum. On one end of the spectrum, we have *attachment*, which is where we are trying to control anything and everything that is actually outside of our control, creating an environment for stress, anxiety, frustration, and disappointment. I was deeply attached to the outcome of building a family and getting pregnant.

THE SPECTRUM OF NON-ATTACHMENT

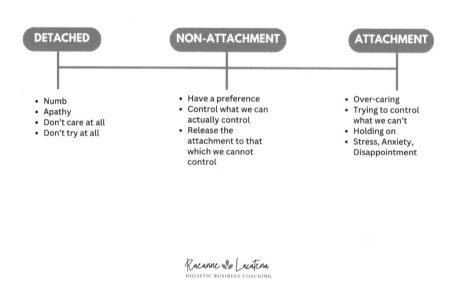

Then, on the opposite side of the spectrum, there is *detachment*, where we don't care about anything at all to a point of apathy and numbness.

We are all human beings having a human experience. The work is not to numb out our natural human feelings. However, we must learn not to create so much angst in our bodies, minds, and ways of being through trying to control that which is outside our control.

The middle point of this spectrum is called non-attachment, where we acknowledge that we are human with preferences. We accept that we control what we can *actually* control, while we release our attachment to the rest.

While my husband and I were on our fertility journey, I understood this principle and taught it every day in my coaching practice, but I just couldn't find a way to let this one go.

Eventually, the pain became so deep and acute, I decided I needed to take a break. I went inward and asked myself, "What do you *actually* want to feel? What do you *actually* want right now?"

The answer came that I deeply wanted to *love* and *nurture*. I wanted to help raise someone to their greatest expression.

So, I asked my higher self, "How could it be possible to feel that right now?"

And... my higher self said, "Get a puppy."

That same day, I noticed that an acquaintance from high school had a litter of puppies who needed homes; they just happened to have been born on our wedding anniversary. (Another synchronicity!) My husband and I talked it over and decided to follow the breadcrumbs and get Lady Madonna a puppy sister. We let her know we would like to adopt one of the puppies when ready, and we decided we were going to take a break from any and all medical intervention, to let our bodies, minds, and spirits heal from the challenges.

When we went to visit the little puppy family periodically, I noticed the warmth start to reenter my body. We decided to name her *Kata*, which is derived from the Japanese name meaning *worthy*. When we brought Kata home, she weighed only one pound. We poured nurturing into all her tiny puppy needs. She was silly, energetic, and required all that puppies require at the beginning of their lives. We started to feel joy again, and our nurturing feelings were being fulfilled.

Within a few short weeks of having her home, Joe and I learned that we had conceived completely naturally. No medication; no procedures; no pain. Just receiving and giving love and nurturing, which were the feelings we'd been chasing so desperately.

This pregnancy was successful, and nine months later, we welcomed our first baby boy into our home.

I firmly believe, when I was able to move the needle back to non-attachment, I was able to conceive naturally. I released control of the outcome, which I now deeply understood was not mine to control, and I focused on what I could actually control, which was: which thoughts I energized, which feelings and emotions I leaned into, and how I responded to those thoughts and feelings.

I know with 100% certainty that finally embracing this teaching within my body, mind, and spirit brought us our beautiful baby boy. And Kata helped, too.

My body had been carrying the stress and, therefore, the inflammation, which absolutely does *not* create favorable conditions for success in pregnancy. The environment in my body was not suitable for a successful pregnancy. That was the cumulative effect of all that I was feeling and thinking. The Western-medicine approach was feeding my need to control and actually limiting the outcome I really wanted.

When I released all of this and gave myself to full-bodied feeling, my body healed and was ready to receive this child we had worked so hard for. I hear stories like this all of the time. I've even heard fertility specialists say, "Get a puppy, and you'll get pregnant." Or I hear of families working hard on their fertility and eventually adopting a child, only to finally become pregnant soon after their adoption is finalized.

This advice is often difficult to share with someone who is in the depth of the darkness and pain that result from not attaining what they truly desire. And it's certainly not always the case, considering some people have much more serious medical diagnoses or complications that are impacting their ability to conceive. This story is not to dismiss their real pain or the need to bring in medical support in order to achieve the outcome you choose.

The real point here is to explore the possibilities of what you can actually control and to lean into those, personally and professionally. It is to more deeply understand the principles that are governing our life, whether we are aware of them or not.

The lesson I learned from my infertility journey was one of the greatest lessons I have learned thus far in my life. It fully locked into my body and mind this understanding, so I can bring this wisdom to others in the service of maximizing their potential.

Non-attachment is a critical ingredient to self-actualization, because there will always be challenges along the way of our journey. We will inevitably and without a doubt go through interruptions in our path, which often feel like setbacks or painful upsets in the moment. If we are able to understand what we prefer, what we can actually control, and then can truly, deeply, and fully release our attachment to the outcomes that are outside of our control, we are more likely to manifest that desired outcome.

One of the most important skills to learn in the journey toward actualizing your potential is to understand the value of the present moment. As human beings, we operate in three time zones: the past, present, and future.

The past is already gone. It already happened, and we cannot change it. When we find ourselves living in the past tense, it often leads to feelings of depression and hopelessness, feeling stuck or frustrated, because the past cannot be shifted.

The future also cannot be changed, because it's not here yet. When a person spends the bulk of their time thinking about the future, it often produces feelings of fear or anxiety, because the future is a fantasy that hasn't happened yet. It can feel unstable and out of control to try to live in the future.

The present moment is the only thing that is actually real. It's the only place where we can effectuate change, because it's right here and right now. It's where we have choice and are able to take action. In the present moment, we can shift our response and feelings about those past events and future concerns into more productive thoughts, emotions, and behaviors.

The art of living in the present moment is a skill that can be learned. One of the most effective approaches to building the muscle to remove ourselves from the past or future is developing the skill of mindfulness. This is an evidence-based practice that helps us focus on what is happening right here and right now without judgment.

There are many protocols and approaches to mindfulness that can help us practice settling into the present moment, which can make a remarkable difference in our lives. Practicing using our five senses to ground ourselves into the current moment, while we practice releasing thoughts that no longer serve us or that come from the past or future time zones, can become a self-care strategy that develops in impact and ease over time.

This skill becomes incredibly important in the formal thought and feeling work necessary during the journey of self-actualization. We are not our thoughts, but we have thoughts. Those thoughts become feelings and emotions, which become our actions, behaviors, and eventually, results.

So, as a business owner, the art of managing our thoughts and emotions on purpose becomes an essential tool for supporting the well-being of our lives and businesses.

When we tap into the power of doing formal thought and feeling work, we begin to recognize that there is a feeling behind what we are looking to accomplish. Honing the skill of emotion management allows us the capability to choose which feelings we want to feel *now*. We can practice generating those feelings now, instead of waiting for one particular outcome.

Another set of important principles I was taught through my fertility journey are the Laws of Vibration, Attraction, and Focus. The Law of Vibration suggests that everything in the universe, including thoughts, emotions, and physical matter, is in a constant state of vibration. These vibrations emit energy, and different vibrations attract similar vibrations. This concept implies that our thoughts and feelings emit specific frequencies or vibrations that can influence the outcomes and events in our lives. Positive thoughts and emotions are said to emit higher, more harmonious vibrations, while negative thoughts and emotions emit lower, less harmonious vibrations.

SUMMARY OF UNIVERSAL LAWS

LAW OF POLARITY

- Everything in the universe has an opposite or polar counterpart.
- Dualities are inherent aspects of existence, forming a unified whole.
- Emphasizes balance, with harmony between opposites maintaining equilibrium.
- Linked with the Law of Harmony and Law of Rhythm.

LAW OF VIBRATION

- Everything, including thoughts and emotions, is in a constant state of vibration.
- Vibrations emit energy and attract similar vibrations.
- Positive thoughts emit higher, harmonious vibrations; negative thoughts emit lower, less harmonious vibrations.

LAW OF ATTRACTION

- Like attracts like, suggesting that dominant thoughts and emotions attract similar experiences.
- Focusing on positive thoughts and maintaining high vibrations attracts positive circumstances and people.

LAW OF FOCUS

- The more attention and energy dedicated to a goal or task, the higher the likelihood of success.
- Emphasizes concentrated effort, avoiding distractions, and prioritizing important objectives.
- Concentrating thoughts, time, and effort on specific goals leads to significant progress and desired outcomes.

Raeanne Lacatena
HOLISTIC BUSINESS COACHING

The Law of Attraction is based on the idea that like attracts like. It posits that we attract into our lives the experiences, people, and situations that resonate with our dominant thoughts, emotions, and vibrations. In other words, if you focus on positive thoughts and maintain a high vibrational frequency, you are more likely to attract positive opportunities, circumstances, and people into your life. Conversely, dwelling on negativity and low vibrational thoughts may attract unfavorable conditions.

If you are moving in the direction of the greatest expression of who you choose to be, these principles help us understand the importance of the fact that the energy you emit through your thoughts and emotions can significantly impact your journey toward self-actualization.

When you focus on positive thoughts, emotions, and intentions, you are more likely to attract opportunities, people, and experiences that support your personal growth and self-actualization. Maintaining a high vibrational frequency can create a more favorable environment for your self-improvement efforts. By consciously directing your thoughts and emotions toward your self-actualization goals, you can harness the power of these laws to manifest your desired outcomes.

Self-actualization often involves gaining a deeper understanding of yourself and your values. The Law of Vibration and the Law of Attraction can help you recognize the impact of your thought patterns and emotions on your life, as it helps you gain a deeper understanding of yourself and your values. The Law of Focus suggests that the more attention and energy you dedicate to a particular goal, task, or area of your life, the more likely you are to achieve success in that area. It emphasizes the power of concentrated effort and the idea that what you focus on expands.

In essence, this concept underscores that, by concentrating your efforts and resources on a specific objective, you can make significant progress and achieve your desired outcomes. It encourages you to avoid distractions and prioritize what truly matters to you. In practice, the Law of Focus promotes the idea that when you concentrate your thoughts, time, and effort on what's most important to you, you are more likely to achieve your goals and undergo personal and professional growth. It can be a valuable concept for those seeking to enhance their effectiveness and accomplish their objectives.

With all of this in mind, what energy you are vibrating and what you are focusing on will become more of what you attract in life. I was focusing so deeply on the *absence* of pregnancy and a baby that I was repeatedly attracting more of that to me. The laws cannot interpret the nuances of feelings; they just read the energy associated with your desires.

Once I was able to shift my perception, focus, and energy, I was able to receive more of what I truly desired. I am so incredibly grateful to have lived through this lesson, as we now have our three gorgeous babies and took them all to Punta Cana for our tenth wedding anniversary, just as we had planned!

This was the first of many lessons that parenting has taught me thus far, and I'm sure more are coming. Now that I've more deeply settled into this understanding, I can more confidently and completely bring this teaching to the clients I serve. Non-attachment, control, and the universal laws impact our business success, as well as our actualization process daily.

Business owners are constantly faced with opportunities to prefer some particular outcome that is really outside of their control. For example, they can't control other people, the market, the economy, their staff, the demands of their family's needs, or whether or not a potential client accepts a proposal, decides to work with them, or pays their invoice. Non-attachment is definitely a central theme to the experience of business ownership. If we hold on too tightly to one particular outcome in business, ruled by attachment, we will push it further away from us. We don't want our customers to feel desperation, push, force, or scarcity coming from us during their decision-making process. In sales, this is called "commission breath."

In the mental health field, we use the word "rumination," which can be defined as thinking about something over and over again to the point where it increases our stress and anxiety. What often happens when someone is overthinking in this way, in relation to these laws and principles discussed in this chapter, is we focus so acutely on those topics causing us stress and anxiety that those are what we end up manifesting. That very thing you would actually prefer to avoid becomes a reality, because you are looking for evidence that it's going to happen by sending your brain a constant reminder. Your brain does what it's told and sets out to look for those clues that your worst fears are coming true.

I see business owners ruminate about where their ideal clients are coming from, how their revenue or production is going this year, whether they are hitting their goals, whether a client will sign a contract, call them back, or make a referral and so much more. In the act of obsessing over those outcomes, they inevitably push them further away.

One pertinent example of this was with a prospective client with whom I had spoken once a year, every year, for about six years in a row. Each year, he asked for a check-in call because he knew, somewhere in his heart, that we were meant to work together. Every year, when he came to the call, he had been in about the same place: barely making it in his business, struggling to pay his bills, and frustrated, while deeply in scarcity, fear, and doubt about whether he could make it. Each year, he hadn't made the choice to invest in himself for coaching due to these ruminating thoughts about his value and worth.

Clients weren't responding to his follow-up requests, and he constantly felt like there was a bottleneck of opportunities that just wouldn't open. He always felt like he was on the verge of something big. During our check-in calls, I was able to help him see that by not being willing to invest in himself, not trusting that he could return the investment, receive the support, and be coachable enough to make a massive difference in his life, how could he possibly expect those results from his clients and business?

Well, the last time, the teaching finally clicked for him. The *day* after he invested in our coaching work together and bet on himself, he closed the biggest six-figure client opportunity of his career. He interrupted the patterns that were holding him back, shifted his behavior, and trusted his worth and value, and the dollars followed that value. He believed and focused fully on a different outcome for the first time in his business, and that outcome delivered.

These principles can also be intertwined with other personal development ideas, such as goal-setting, time management, and productivity. They highlight the value of setting clear goals, staying committed to them, avoiding spreading your attention too thinly across various tasks or objectives, or getting stuck on one particular outcome's going one particular way. We see this shine through in client-relationship management, team management, and leadership skills. Who we are being becomes a reflection of the success of our teams and other business relationships.

When we are able to control what is actually in our control and have a known preference without attempting to control that which is outside of our control, we are able to become happier, healthier, and wealthier in all areas of our lives and businesses. Instead of using force to try to bend life our own way or try to make something a particular way that suits you and your definition of success, you are embracing your personal power, knowing who you are, what is actually in your control, and then authentically moving in accordance with those realities.

I also know the pain and challenges that come with this concept, which is sometimes easy to talk about, however very, very difficult to fully enact in real time.

All of this takes practice, time, compassion, and support. All of which you deserve.

First, remember that you are whole. You have everything you need to be successful inside of you, right here and right now.

You are worth the effort it takes to grow.

And your personal experiences are happening *for* you, not *to* you.

It's not your fault that what you are going through is hard, but it is your responsibility, especially if you are choosing the path of your highest expression and potential.

And who you are everywhere is who you are anywhere. So, you can glean wisdom from what you've gone through to foster business and personal growth across all realms of your life.

You can also have it all.

And what "having it all" means comes from inside of you, personally, and is unique only to you.

The art of self-awareness can help you discover what that means to you. These philosophies, laws, and principles can help guide you up the stairway to actualization.

Now that you understand the principles of the Laws of Vibration, Attraction, and Focus, you can appreciate the importance of having the power of emotion at your fingertips. Mindfulness helps you be here now, notice your thoughts, and choose which ones to energize into feeling at the present moment and which ones to let float right on by.

This skill becomes paramount to tap into those universal laws, which inevitably helps the actualizing of your potential become far more enjoyable, efficient, and fulfilling.

Control and Release Integration

Summary: Non-attachment is when you have a preference and practice that creates favorable conditions for success through controlling what you actually have control over, and by learning to release the outcome to that which is outside of your control.

Resources

Non-attachment

Mindfulness

Universal Laws

Universal Laws Exercises

❖ Law of Polarity - Finding Balance:

Identify an aspect of your life with opposing elements (e.g., work-life balance).

Reflect on how you can integrate and harmonize these opposites for a balanced approach.

Implement small changes to align with the Law of Harmony.

❖ Law of Vibration - Conscious Emotion Monitoring:

Throughout the day, pay attention to your emotions and thoughts.

Notice the vibrational frequency associated with positive and negative feelings.

Consciously shift toward positive thoughts and emotions to align with higher vibrations.

❖ Law of Attraction - Visualization Exercise:

Choose a specific goal or desire you want to manifest.

Create a vivid mental image of achieving that goal, focusing on positive emotions.

Regularly visualize this scenario to enhance the alignment with the Law of Attraction.

❖ Law of Focus - Priority Setting:

List your current goals or tasks in your personal and professional life.

Identify the top priority, and allocate dedicated time and energy to it.

Avoid distractions and commit to concentrated effort to see and feel the Law of Focus in action.

Integration Exercise - Holistic Practice:

Combine elements from all laws in a holistic approach.

Choose a specific area of your life (e.g., relationships, career), and apply the principles of balance, vibration, attraction, and focus simultaneously.

Reflect on how these laws interact and amplify one another for a comprehensive impact.

Chapter Six

Repeat Lessons

"If you're climbing the ladder of life, you go rung by rung, one step at a time. Don't look too far up, set your goals high, but take one step at a time. Sometimes, you don't think you're progressing until you step back and see how high you've really gone."

—Donny Osmond

AFTER MY EXTENDED experience of infertility, when I'd started to unlearn my tendency to strive to control that which is outside of my control and to practice the lesson of surrender, releasing more deeply in my body, I noticed myself falling back into the pattern again during my first pregnancy.

Unfortunately, I was diagnosed with gestational diabetes, an illness caused when the placenta interrupts the mother's ability to produce appropriate amounts of insulin to support her food digestion and blood sugar regulation; it often occurs in women who have polycystic ovarian syndrome, which was an unfortunate reality of my health profile.

I was told I could work at "controlling" gestational diabetes through food and exercise but needed increased monitoring for me and the baby. As a result, I had regular blood sugar checks, increased ultrasounds, and various stress tests to make sure my little one's development was on track. Asking someone recovering from control issues to control something that was actually very much outside of my control was a recipe for a trip into a repeat pattern.

As human beings, we all have an intricate system of neurons and synapses connected in our brains that creates patterns and programs to help govern our bodies, systems, and mind. These patterns in our brain allow us to run on autopilot for things that we've learned and mastered over time. For example, we tend to be hypervigilant and lack skill when we are first learning to drive; but at some point, we can drive from work back home without even really remembering the drive at all! These autopilot modes are very useful and incredibly supportive to the human condition, including self-referential thought, mental imagery, memory retrieval, attention, decision-making, and emotional regulation.

Simultaneously, it can be incredibly limiting, if we are unaware and running a default that is no longer useful. Part of the work of actualizing our potential requires *un*-learning a series of patterns that are deeply held in our thoughts right down to our neurons and synapses, as well as in our body and muscle memory. It's not as simple as stopping thinking one particular way, feeling some type of feeling, or behaving in a way that's not in alignment with what we want. There are a lot of deeply held patterns that live functionally in our brains and bodies that support us but often also end up limiting us until we begin the work of pruning those old ways of being, thinking, feeling, and believing.

I fell into my old control-and-perfection patterns when diagnosed with gestational diabetes. I became obsessed with managing my diet and exercise. I wanted to protect this baby I had fought so hard for, and I wanted to create the healthiest and most natural environment possible for the little one's growth, development, and birth.

This led me to actually create a lot of additional stress during my pregnancy, which was already highly difficult; the new stress most certainly added inflammation into my already changing body. On top of that, my medical team fed into this need to check, alarm, and manage my medical condition.

At one point toward the end of the pregnancy, I was at one of my routine stress tests, and the baby didn't have much fetal activity. The nursing team sent me in for an urgent ultrasound to monitor the baby, but by the time I was in the ultrasound room, the baby was having a little dance party again in my womb. The nurse smiled, saying it was a relief, and told me that the baby had probably been taking a nap during my stress test. She told me not to worry, that there was nothing to fear.

She needed to get a doctor to sign off on the results of my ultrasound, so she called in my own OB, whom I deeply trusted and respected and who had been an ally in my care. My OB signed off on my release, and I was packing up ready to go.

Before I knew it, though, the maternal-fetal medical director was in my ultrasound room and aggressively advised me that *today* was the day I was delivering my baby. She said, with my diagnosis, the stress test, and how far along I was in the pregnancy, she was recommending an emergency medical induction of the baby.

I told her that the baby had shown great movement in the ultrasound, that he had probably been napping, and that I knew my baby and body weren't ready. He was very high up in my abdomen, and I wasn't ready to deliver.

She said I couldn't possibly know all this, as a first-time mother, and that I "needed to stop being selfish and start acting like a mother." She threatened, if I left without being admitted immediately, I would have to sign an AMA refusing medical treatment and confirming that I was putting my baby at risk to die, which would be irresponsible and dangerous.

Through sobbing tears, I tried to tell her I felt certain that I wasn't ready, but she held her ground. I called my husband and reluctantly went in to be admitted.

We did our best to shift the energy to a feeling of excitement that our baby would be joining us that day. I was admitted to the hospital and began the medical induction process. Nothing happened with the first attempt at induction on that first day; but I was on continued medical observation (which was *quite* uncomfortable for mom, but the baby seemed to be happy as a clam and quite cozy in my womb!).

I also was administered a treatment for a condition called GBS, which happens with some women; except I had a documented negative reaction to the antibiotic they proactively treated the condition with. When I asked for an alternative, they didn't provide an option. Every four hours, I was given this antibiotic, which felt like fire in my veins. I tried to request another treatment, and they denied.

I was in labor and receiving this intense burning through my veins for about five days before my baby came. I had medical contractions plus every single medical intervention they could throw at me and continuous observation. I slept a few hours over those many days and probably met every labor and delivery nurse who worked in the hospital. The nurses were rooting for me; they would leave their shifts and come in the next day, still seeing my name on the board for patients in active delivery.

I saw couples come into the hospital for their labor and leave with their babies without my making any movement toward the outcome I was so ready for.

I had told my family with excitement that the baby was coming, but then, out of exhaustion and frustration, I started to resent everyone checking in with me. Everyone was worried.

My OB visited me once but couldn't even look me in the eyes. She knew what I knew: I had been right. I knew my body. I knew we weren't ready to labor. And she knew I wasn't listened to. They offered me a C-section a number of times; and I was permitted to refuse as long as the baby was healthy and thriving during monitoring, which he continued to be throughout.

They offered me pain medication and an epidural, which I declined. I labored for four days without much sleep and without pain medication, because I was trying to create as natural a birth as possible for my baby, knowing that all of my other wishes had been ignored by the medical team.

I was trying to control what was left for me to control. Still, I knew, somewhere in my mind and heart, that this was outside of my control and that I needed to release.

I finally listened to the nursing staff, who recommended an epidural for the sake of a nap. They told me I was going to need some rest to deliver, when the baby was finally ready to come. I finally gave in out of pure exhaustion and allowed myself a nap.

That rest and releasing of control led to the final safe delivery of my charming baby boy.

Another lesson I had to learn on control. Another lesson about the beauty of release.

Another new lesson on the need to listen to my body and advocate for myself and my family.

In life, we often circle back to lessons over and over again. More spiral learning.

With enough awareness, attention, presence, and practice, we can spiral upward in our personal development to grow, even if we have to repeat a lesson in order to move through a pattern and give our default network a new pattern, to replace of the one that no longer serves us.

The brain is a fascinating, malleable organ. The ability to change those patterns and evolve and grow through even the stickiest habits and pathways is one of the body's most empowering realities, if we allow it to be.

Once I became aware of this lesson again, I was able to make a series of decisions about how I wanted to proceed. I crafted a new aligned medical team and created some proactive changes in my health and wellness to support my healing and future pregnancies. I interviewed and brought into my life a craniosacral therapist to support my body's new changes as a mother who had been through a birth trauma; the person also became my doula for both of my future pregnancies. She was there to support my ability to advocate for myself and to decode whatever the future pregnancies brought my way; so I could make appropriate aligned decisions in my birthing plan.

My next two pregnancies and deliveries were so much more peaceful and self-guided. They were far healthier and both without any recurrence of gestational diabetes.

I increased my internal advocacy and built the necessary mothering muscle to be able to make choices for me and my family, based on what is right for us, not what is convenient for traditional Western and often broken medical systems, which ignore the feminine wisdom and internal body awareness and intuition that most women possess naturally.

I also learned the value of rest through this whole experience, and in a much deeper way than I had been able to accept before. The high achiever will often sacrifice rest, thinking that getting more done, pushing, forcing, and doing more are the ways to get everything done. During this lesson, I felt and became aware in real time that rest is actually active. It is necessary. It is productive to rest, sleep, breathe, and relax. I had only really valued hard work, and even had undervalued sleep. Now that I'd seen just how important rest was, I could begin to implement what that might look like in other areas of my life, as well.

This has increased my confidence, my wellness, my health, and my understanding of my body, mind, and spirit. I am a better parent and a better wife. I am happier, healthier, and wealthier in all realms as a result of it.

I have been able to test this theory in business, too. When I begin feeling tired or burned out in whatever I was doing in work or life, I've stopped to listen to my body and mind and tried to *rest*, instead of push or force. As a result of taking that time for myself, I actually got a more positive outcome. Not only is the quality of my work better, but I also get the results I desire with greater effectiveness and efficiency.

At one point in my business, I was feeling exhausted, so I decided to take a nap and woke up to an additional $10,000 in my bank account that wasn't expected in my monthly recurring revenue! When my clients tap into this wisdom, they are able to live a happier, healthier, and wealthier life, too.

That said, spiral learning can very easily go in the opposite direction. If we become aware of a repeat pattern and choose to ignore, replay, or do the same thing over and over again but expect a different result, that is what Albert Einstein called the definition of insanity.

The plasticity of our brains and the abilities of humans to learn, grow, evolve, and shift our minds, bodies, and experiences can either be the most empowering or the most limiting of our lives.

Each human gets to choose, and you *always* have a choice.

I know that these deep lessons around control now live in my body. I have grown, and I have evolved.

I know that control is a tendency embedded in the default network in my brain, so there will be times when I fall into that spiral in order to learn something again.

With the awareness and the commitment to grow, however, I can now quickly recognize the pattern and then spiral up to my higher self, where I have the ability to control what is *actually* in my control and can release the rest. This allows me to close the gap between my lower and higher learning with greater ease and efficiency.

I will fall back into the pattern, and I will continue to climb. That's what humans *get* to do. We *get* to choose to climb, which allows us to exercise our autonomy.

The freedom to choose, instead of being told what to do, is a necessary ingredient in self-actualization, because each person has a different definition of what self-actualization means to them. We can say that it's possible to "have it all," but we need to acknowledge that having it all means vastly different things for different people. If we only do what other people tell us we should do, only believe what other people tell us to believe about ourselves and the world, and only operate or behave the way we are expected to, we will never be able to learn what having it all or being free to live our authentic truths really means to us. The freedom to think, feel, believe, and behave as our authentic selves is imperative on this journey.

In every spiritual teaching across every religion, it's one of the primary mechanisms to support getting closer to God, the universe, or whatever you consider your higher power.

When we hold onto something that wasn't meant to be controlled, we are actually giving our power away. The art of learning how to surrender or to let go is easy to talk about, but sometimes difficult to do.

We all have our internal struggles between what we hold onto and what we are willing to release.

One simple, easily implementable tool that helps with the process of practicing releasing is called a "pattern interrupt." You pick a short word, phrase, or physical reminder to help trigger your brain into a new story whenever you begin telling yourself an old story, engage in an old undesirable behavior or habit, or whenever your body or mind begins looping into an old pattern of thinking or feeling.

This pattern-interrupt word or phrase may be something as simple as "Stop it!" Simply a quick trigger phrase or word to quickly reset your brain and body and let them know we are no longer going down that path of control or looping that negative understanding. I've had families come up with words or phrases to help send a signal to interrupt a pattern within the entire family, something like a code word they can all resonate with, to help break the pattern.

I still remember the example from my counseling days, when I was supporting a family struggling with big feelings, arguments, and aggression at home. During one session when I was going over the concept of the pattern interrupt, the sweet little four-year-old shouted, "*Bacon!*" to break up the tension, which made everyone laugh. They unanimously decided that *bacon* would be their pattern interrupt, because they all found this so silly, it would be impossible not to smile when someone shouted it, no matter the circumstance. The introduction of this small shift to change the state of being in the moment made a huge difference for the recovery of this family's communication and interactions.

We might also then couple this verbal pattern interrupt with some physical support, such as a reminder token from the teachings of cognitive behavioral therapy; like a necklace, ring, or bracelet to remind us that we are moving in a new process, or even a rubber band on our wrist to "snap us out of it," when we are going down the wrong path.

A more spiritual approach to releasing and letting go is the art of forgiveness, which is also found in many spiritual teachings across a variety of religions and belief sets. After we become aware of something that is limiting us, we can practice forgiveness: self-forgiveness, when we understand that we ourselves are the entity who is self-limiting; or forgiveness of another person or incident.

An impactful forgiveness exercise is to practice writing out everything you are controlling or wherever you are holding guilt, a grudge, shame, or any other feeling or belief set about yourself or others.

Then, go through each part and parcel of the situation and send forgiveness, whether it is forgiveness to yourself for judging yourself, forgiveness to another person for how they treated you, or forgiveness for that which is causing you upset or helping you to hold onto limiting patterns.

Once you identify what piece you are holding, you can simply say:

"I forgive myself for judging myself for _____."

(e.g., *I forgive myself for judging myself for submitting that task past its deadline.*)

Or, for example:

"I forgive myself for judging {{this person}} for {{this circumstance}}."

(e.g., *I forgive myself for judging Susan for consistently showing up late for work.*)

Notice, in both of these examples, we are forgiving *ourselves* for judging either ourselves or the other person, because in life we can only control ourselves and our response to other people. Forgiving someone else is more for yourself than for the other person, because, if you carry that upset, it will only affect you internally and negatively, not so much the other person.

Gautama Buddha said, "Holding onto anger is like drinking poison and expecting the other person to die." This became a core Buddhist teaching.

So many people struggle with forgiveness because they think, in order to effectively forgive, they also need to forget what someone has done to hurt or harm them, which may even mean what feels like condoning the behavior. Instead, where we focus is on working on what we can *actually* control, which is releasing the negative feeling set that we are holding within our own bodies and experiences, so it no longer creates that poisonous effect in us.

Anger, fear, doubt, worry, shame, and blame are all very low-vibration emotions and can create inflammation inside our bodies. If someone else has done something *to* us or *against* us, that is on them to clean up. In the meantime, doing the work to clear what is being held in your own body is all the change we can actually effectuate, until the other person wakes up to what they need to do in their own personal development journey.

One business owner who found a significant shift in his life through the implementation of a forgiveness practice was an entrepreneur who was also an active minister in a church and a father of three amazing daughters. This business owner was naturally a man of service and was able to artfully integrate his love of service with his commitment to his mission in all areas of his life. However, one area that came to light in our work together was becoming a challenge to overlook.

As a minister in this church, he found himself looking away at some of the ways he felt misaligned with some of the teachings that ostracized certain groups of people, specifically in the LGBTQ+ populations. When one of his daughters courageously came out to him as gay, that misalignment came to a head.

He suddenly felt intense anger and frustration with his church community, some of their accepted teachings, what he imagined his daughter's impression must have been, and at himself for being the leader of this church, when his daughter must have been suffering. Our work became focused on first forgiving himself, his God, his church, and church community, as well as the necessary conversation with his daughter to seek her forgiveness.

Going through these stages opened up a new pathway for this business owner's life in totality. The peace that came from his active forgiveness allowed him to see his chosen path and to resign as a minister, focusing on his family first and on his business more fully. This resulted in a deepening relationship with his daughter, an accelerated course of his business's success, and a more aligned way of living his life in general. His success in all spheres of life was fueled by the forgiveness he showed himself and others.

Another more masculine and highly effective approach to unlearning old patterns that are no longer useful is called habit stacking, which is a concept introduced by James Clear in his book, *Atomic Habits*. It involves linking a new habit to an existing one by "stacking" them on top of each other. The idea is that, by piggybacking a new habit onto an existing one, it becomes easier to remember and more likely to stick.

To use habit stacking, you first need to identify a current habit, something you do consistently, like brushing your teeth in the morning. Next, you identify the new habit you want to establish, such as doing ten pushups. You then link the two habits together by performing the new habit immediately after the current one. So, after you brush your teeth, you would immediately do your ten pushups.

The key to making habit stacking work is to choose habits that are simple and easy to perform. You want to create a chain of habits that you can complete without thinking too much about it. As you become more comfortable with the new habit, you can add more challenging habits to the chain.

Habit stacking is a powerful tool for building new habits because it leverages the power of existing habits to create momentum. It also helps to eliminate decision fatigue, or the difficulty of making new decisions when you are faced with the need to make them frequently, which is especially common with business owners who are parents. By pre-deciding when and where you will perform a new habit, you remove the need to decide in the moment, making it more likely that you will follow through eventually and removing a common barrier to creating new habits.

There are so many different ways to work with your brain and body to create new beliefs and new patterns of thinking, coupled with new synaptic connections to support new feeling sets and, eventually, new behaviors. Eventually, those repeated efforts through repeated practice will allow us to unlearn those no longer desirable habits, traits, and patterns that we all fall into with our bodies, minds, and behaviors.

You can very much reprogram the default network, and even though there are 100 billion neurons and over 100 trillion synaptic connections in the brain, the really amazing news is that you don't need to have trillions of repetitions to create new patterns in the brain and body. The intricate network that produces these patterns can become a domino effect in the brain. So, when you shift one set of synaptic connections, there are countless bundles of connections reprogrammed and affected by your reintroduction, integration, and practice of that new belief and habit.

You never know how many repetitions of these different supports will create a completely different way of being and allow a new default way of behaving to settle in naturally. Either way, you are worth the effort!

Putting one foot in front of the other and creating small pivots and shifts over time can culminate in massive transformation. These incremental, one-degree changes toward finding your right-fit routines, right-fit self-care mechanisms, right-fit support structures, and right-fit approaches to creating new habits and beliefs all come together to walk you one step closer to transcendence. It is rarely zero-to-60 mph; however, those step-by-step encounters accumulate to create lasting change in those deeply held negating patterns and beliefs.

You will soon look back at how far you've come and be astonished about the progress you've made. The deeply held patterns will shed away as if they never existed.

Repeat Lessons Integration

Summary: In life and business, we will spiral back to and repeat lessons during our evolution, growth, and development. It's natural and expected, and we get to choose how long we spiral downward or upward in our grasping of those lessons.

Resources

Habit Stacking

Pattern Interrupt

Forgiveness Exercise

❖ An impactful forgiveness exercise is to practice writing out everything you are controlling or where you are holding guilt, grudge, shame, or any other feeling or belief set about yourself or others.

❖ Then, go through each part and parcel of the situation and send forgiveness, whether that means forgiving yourself for judging yourself; forgiving another person for how they treated you; or forgiving that which is causing you upset or enabling you to hold onto limiting patterns.

❖ Once you identify what piece you are holding, you can simply say:

"I forgive myself for judging myself for _____."
(e.g., *I forgive myself for judging myself for submitting that task past its deadline.*)

Or, for example:
"I forgive myself for judging {{this person}} for {{this circumstance}}."
(e.g., *I forgive myself for judging Susan for consistently showing up late for work.*)

Chapter Seven

Competing Responsibilities

"The price of greatness is responsibility."

—Winston Churchill

MY CHILDREN (AND THE many children I've had the privilege to love, know, and serve!) have become my greatest spiritual teachers.

They are my why, my most loved and deeply motivating sources of inspiration daily. My mission to help people become the greatest expression of who they choose to be starts first with my children. I am here to help the planet heal for *them.* I know, if I can use my unique ability to help as many people actualize their potential, lean into their higher selves, and remove any barriers to success, they will be more likely to help more people in turn.

The ripple effect continues and comes back, ultimately, to positively impact my children. The more people in the world who have what they need to be the greatest expressions of who they choose to be, the better the world becomes.

I also believe that these beautiful souls are pure of heart, and they come to remind me of so many of the spiritual principles that are often programmed out of us over time.

As a Reiki master and highly empathic being, I am very attuned to other people's energy, emotions, intentions, and behavior. Over my lifetime, I've had to learn how to manage that superpower, and I can already see the ways that my children have inherited some of these skills. All three are attuned to level 1 Reiki, which basically just opens their channels to receive and perceive more love, the highest vibration of my intention in life and in business for them, myself, and the people I encounter.

It's unbelievable to me that so many people don't even know what Reiki is because it is everywhere. Reiki is energy. It is healing. It applies energy healing to someone's body, mind, and spirit to help them heal, grow, shift, and love.

One of my favorite stories is, when my sweet little niece, Adele, was five years old, she asked me what I did for a living. I told her about coaching and Reiki. Like many people, she had no clue what Reiki meant.

I asked her to hold out her little hands, and I covered them with mine, to give her some Reiki right then and there. After a few moments, I asked her what she felt. She said, "Aunt RaeRae, it feels like love." In just under a minute, she had captured the meaning of something that can be so difficult to understand. *Reiki is love.*

I use Reiki for personal self-development, for my family, and for my clients, when they are interested in that kind of healing. Reiki is a part of how I offer holistic care to my clients. Either from a distance or in a shared space, I can use this extraordinary healing form to serve my clients and loved ones, to help them ground, expand, or heal through the energy of love.

A child's closeness to the universal principles still shines through in their interactions with me on a regular basis. One of the key ways this is true is through the beginner's mind, which occurs naturally in a child. Everything is new. Everything is fascinating. Everything is bewildering and exciting and amazing. There is always something new to learn and to try and some challenge to dive into with an open heart and a willingness to grow.

Daily, they remind me that this mode of being is available to all humans. It's just a choice.

As adults, we like to think we know it all and understand it all, but that pressure is too big a burden to be true.

If, instead, we approach life with a beginner's mind, through curiosity, wonder, and adventure, we lean more into the divine feminine and can live life through a lens of growth, learning, and exploration that never ends. This instead of a "need to know" and "know it all."

I know my little ones will turn anything into an adventure, and whenever we engage with them in this way, things go so much better for the whole family. If we simply say, "We get to go on an adventure to find some groceries, and we are going to play a game," versus "We need to go to the store to get groceries," it can make the difference between a joyful visit to the grocery store versus a terrible time filled with tantrums and frustration on everyone's part.

Children seek comfort, rest, and nourishment. They strive to meet their basic needs straight through their mental and spiritual needs with such ease and grace. Finding our own routine around rest, healthy food, and water to nourish our bodies and exercise to keep us strong is incredibly important for any human form, not just the child. As we've seen, if our bodies are not healthy, how can our business and life be healthy?

Another natural state of the child is love. They are only seeking love, comfort, and nourishment from the beginning. They only interpret the energy of love as the baseline, and even the most precarious of situations are interpreted through the lens of love. They freely express love and receive love and continue to seek love, no matter the circumstance. They transcend and actualize just by being who they are, which is available to us as adults, as well.

The value of creativity, imagination, and play is an oft-overlooked approach to life and business that children engage in naturally. Play and imagination for the sake of just enjoyment of that process is something adults rarely allow themselves to engage in freely. When we take the lead from these tiny spiritual teachers and reintegrate those natural feminine states back into our lives, life and business become much more joyful and easeful.

For me, I began my journey thinking that music was my purpose. What I've learned in the process is that music is still, in fact, a part of my purpose; however, now I understand that creativity for the sake of creativity, singing, playing, and engaging in music are what balance and inspire me to be in my higher self.

I have noticed that, when I am in the best mood, I am singing. I have now reverse-engineered that reality, and I sing to help elevate my mood and inspire creativity. Even in the act of writing this book, I often started my creative juices flowing by doing some singing, playing, and/or listening to music. The bulk of the book was written with high-level musical frequencies and songs playing during my many, many writing sessions, to keep me in that high frequency of creation.

I have borrowed that strategy and applied it to my business, as well. I incorporate as much creativity, art, and music into the creative process of growing my business as I can. The more I balance in that right brain and feminine genius, the easier it is to tap into the left brain and masculine traits, as well as to integrate the two worlds in service to my highest possible outcome.

When we consider imagination more deeply in the context of business ownership, we are able to see how valuable it can truly be. Have you ever seen an Olympic slalom skier at the top of the mountain, before they go down their track to compete in a race? I've witnessed many times how these prodigious athletes have their eyes closed, take a deep breath, and imagine themselves going down that particular mountain track in their *mind* successfully, to envision winning that race. Athletes of all kinds are taught to use their mind as a part of their training. Outside of their physical training, they are taught to practice their sport and competition over and over again, to rehearse the ideal outcome or to imagine that ideal outcome coming to fruition. With thousands of repetitions in their mind, in combination with their physical training, they are showing their full system their potential success path.

The mind doesn't know the full difference between imagined play, rehearsal, and actual performance, when you are able to create a realistic picture in your mind, accompanied by feelings that support the preferred outcome.

Right now, ask yourself:

❖ Are you rehearsing and imagining success in your business? Or are you letting your brain think over and over again about how things are going poorly?

❖ Are you envisioning abundance and prosperity in your results or preparing yourself for inevitable scarcity and lack?

❖ Are you visualizing what it feels and looks like to achieve your ideal goals and outcomes as if they are here now? Or are you letting your brain run rampant with all of the ways you can possibly fail?

Choosing to focus on imagining and visualizing that positive outcome is a skill you can practice for your business right now. Modeling that childlike wonder, create the picture in your mind and match the authentic feeling in your body, and you will be more likely to have that outcome come to fruition. As a business owner, bringing all of these systems of imagination, creativity, play, visualization, and adventure into your daily life can be the pathway to freedom and joy that you seek. Simply being. Simply experiencing the moment that you are in now with as much joy as possible.

One of the most healing ways that this childlike wonder shows up is through encounters with nature. Again, we want to pay attention to this education from children, as well. Being in nature is a critical factor in human health and wellness. A child craves being outdoors. You will see them jump in any puddle, revel in the beauty of a butterfly or flower, laugh and jump in the waves, play for hours in the sand or mud, and become deeply curious about any animals, bugs, and wildlife they come in contact with while outdoors. Nature brings out that natural curiosity.

This connection with the natural world has essential healing properties. We need sunlight, water, fresh air, and grounding in the sea, sand, or grass in order to heal. With modern technology and first-world delights like comfortable homes and accommodations, many of us are stuck inside, behind a computer or device, and rarely make it outdoors. That is incredibly detrimental to our health, our body, our minds, and therefore our business. Making an effort to be outdoors and revel in nature becomes an entire education and healing process, if we allow it!

Here are a few more high-level spiritual lessons we can learn from children to consider:

- ❖ We can also get excited about any learning process, instead of harshly judging ourselves for not knowing.

- ❖ We can ask questions, instead of being the expert, always telling or advising.

- ❖ We can see learning as neutral and natural, instead of a "have to" or "need to." We can make it a reflection of our goodness or wholeness or worthiness.

- ❖ We can approach life through play and imagination, instead of force, drive, grind, or hustle.

- ❖ We can laugh through the process, both at ourselves and our circumstances, and ask ourselves, "What's next?" Instead of making perfection the goal or becoming overwhelmed with the need to know the outcome.

- ❖ We can collaborate with others and know we don't have to do it all or be it all.

- ❖ We can proudly own our strengths and abilities, without harshly criticizing anything we haven't come to learn or without seeing it as a shortcoming.

At times, I will definitely fall out of these states of being, as a culturally programmed adult, even with my kids right there as constant loving reminders of these possibilities.

As a business owner, children keep me connected to my mission and allow me to better enjoy the process.

This doesn't come without challenges, of course. As a mother of three children and two dogs, and as a business owner, there are constant demands and pressures on my time.

With this strong connection to mission and values, I am able to make decisions that are in alignment with them, and I create boundaries that support that alignment. My kids remind me of what is important, while also showing me where I need to make adjustments to stay on course from this higher perspective.

I am able to be in harmony with the masculine and feminine to meet my children's needs, equal parts nurture and provide for, offer comfort and structure, adventure, and logic.

Doing this also helps me to be a better business owner, as it is necessary to do all of this for my business and in service to my clients as well, without losing the integrity of my values, where I'm committed first to support my family authentically and lovingly.

Being a parent, of course, is not without triggers. Sometimes the business-owner parent can feel pulled in a million directions, that they are failing everywhere and are unsupported and isolated, plus have unrealistic and unattainable expectations from themselves and society.

My childhood programming and a lifetime's worth of happenings can be triggered during my parenting journey. I find myself getting overwhelmed with the chaos of all the noise and moving parts. But instead of judging myself, I do my best to let that be a guide for all the areas where I can continue to practice self-compassion and grow.

I see how the journey affects my money story, and I choose to continue to rewrite it along the way with a more abundant lens.

I see how parenting affects my body, and I choose to practice self-love and gratitude for all that it's overcome and all that it's provided me, and I am reminded through the faces of my lovely babies.

I see how it's shifted my relationship with my husband, and I choose to let it be a deepening of the expression of love and appreciation I have for my partner on his soul's path; to be in awe of his patience and providing and grateful for his support to my soul's path and our family's growth, safety, and well-being.

I notice how it shows me my own upbringing, and I continue to allow myself to process the past; to reframe and reprogram in order to create better relationships now and in the future.

I live my life with urgency for my children. I cherish life because of them. I set better boundaries in service to them. I insist on self-actualization to create a path for them to do the same. I am so grateful that they chose me as their mother and my husband as their father. They are my greatest accomplishment and my highest mission.

That said, I'm often asked by my clients "How do you do it all?"

Many of the clients I serve are working parents and business owners who also want to be a loving presence in the lives of their families, marriages, and to their children. They want to be involved in their development and want to nurture their relationships. However, they also want to be able to actualize their potential in their careers and in their business, as well. If they aren't parents, they often have competing responsibilities, priorities, and interests in their lives outside of business, such as caretaking their elder parents or loved ones, volunteerism, passions, hobbies, or multiple projects or businesses running at the same time.

So much of the traditional business ownership diatribe reinforces the push, force, hustle, grind, dog-eat-dog mentality that leaves these business owners uncertain about how to make it all work together. If they want to have more for their families, provide for their children, and be present, they are left scratching their heads about how to get it all done, because it has been drilled into them that, in order to have more, they need to do more; in order to be successful, they need to give their business their total, complete full attention and need to be working or thinking about working 24/7.

They see models of successful business owners in the marketplace who are consistently out in the field, grinding to create new opportunities, and they make assumptions that they, too, need to behave that way. They are also told by some of these counterparts quite literally and directly, that they just need to "make more calls," show up ten to fifteen times a day on social media on every platform, block out more time, and even "make their business their favorite child."

This way of being is something many of the entrepreneurs who come to me have tried or will try, but it ends up feeling like an ill-fitting suit. They try to push more and force more business, but what ends up happening is one major area of their life or business falters, or they feel like they are failing everywhere. Some of these business owners will see the financial success but feel guilty for missing out on the lives and relationships with their children. Or they feel like their business is unsuccessful, so now they can see their kids and partner more.

Some business owners are very successful in the push-and-force model of business; there is no denying it. There are plenty of examples of business mentors and gurus telling people to do more and who really show through their behavior that it is a viable path to success in their business. However, some of those business owners are "broke millionaires" with nobody to share their wealth with, nobody to celebrate their successes; they feel a sense of emptiness and loneliness and therefore a lack of fulfillment.

The way to "have it all" in business starts first with the willingness to go within and to decide what having it all actually means to you as an individual.

For example, "presence" to your children looks very different for every person. This can range from full involvement with and care of your children with no additional support to full-time childcare, personal assistance, laundry services, cleaning services, and more! What does having it all in parenting mean to you?

What does having it all in marriage or relationship mean to you? You'll also want to get clear about what your ideal relationship looks like, so you can best decide how you want to behave in your relationships.

What does success in your business mean to you? You must know what this means to you personally, in order to be successful. Sometimes, the ideas of what success looks like are implanted in us by outside forces drilling you into the force-and-push mentality. Is that next echelon of achievement what success really looks like for you personally? Or is that something that ultimately doesn't matter to you? Are multimillions your goal or someone else's goal? Perhaps, providing for your family means very different things to you than it does to someone else.

This work will also require you to do some "shedding" of certain internal and external messages, internal thoughts, emotions, and feelings, as well as the past patterned and imagined behaviors that you *used* to engage in. When I say *imagined behaviors*, these are the behaviors you have been thinking you "should" do, because other people do them to be successful; you've been "trying" to do them, but something keeps getting in the way of the follow through.

For example, being on social media ten to fifteen times a day might be something you think you should do, but it never gets done. Waking up at 4:30 a.m. to get started with your day might be good for some, but it might not be a great fit for you, personally. Or exercising twice a day for seventy-five minutes might be an option that supports one human, but that option might not be good for your body and wellness.

This is an exercise of sorting through what is outside pressure, what is aligned with you, and what feels right and works for you, personally and professionally. This will require the implementation of boundaries that support the new way of being, feeling, thinking, and behaving.

Boundaries

First, there are internal boundaries, which help you to create new patterns for yourself in your beliefs, thinking, and feeling. For example, you may want to come up with a series of pattern interrupts to help you stay in awareness about those beliefs, thoughts, emotions, and behaviors that no longer serve you, so you can clear the default patterns and move into a more productive, supportive set of beliefs, thoughts, feelings, and actions.

When those old patterns arise, if you have a pattern interrupt in place, you can stop those negative or unhelpful patterns of thinking in their tracks by using a reminder phrase, like "No thank you!" or "Stop it!" or "Cancel. Error. Thought." Then, you can replace or anchor in a new set of beliefs, thoughts, emotions, and behaviors that are supportive of your desired results. You can set up a series of positive affirmations to replace the old behaviors and encourage yourself to stay in that new line of thinking and feeling. Or you can craft an entire intention statement that reminds you throughout the day of how you intend to behave, feel, and think, moving forward.

Another valuable place to pause and reflect is around energy boundaries. You may have heard the phrase "energy vampires," referring to people who drain the life out of a room and out of you, when you are in their presence.

There are various people or circumstances that just simply don't align with your energy or take away from what you could be using elsewhere. You need to remove these from your life. Yes, this may be certain people who no longer get access to your energy; the boundary is up to you and what you can tolerate from that particular person. If you can no longer keep them in your life for whatever reason, perhaps your boundary is a "love at a distance" boundary, where you continue to want what is good for them in their life and wish them well, but no longer at the expense of your own personal peace, so they are no longer someone you keep in close relationship or proximity.

If possible, love them at a distance, so they don't "live rent free in your brain" or take up more of your power or energy by maintaining a negative hold over your mind, thoughts, or emotions. If you are no longer keeping this person in your life, release them and maintain internal and external boundaries to support your inner peace. If you choose to keep this person in your life, perhaps you can try creating an energetic "love bubble" of protection in your energy field, to help keep their negative energy out of your space.

There are a lot of other elements that may need to be considered when it comes to energy management beyond just those draining people. For example, I have very firm boundaries around watching the news in my home. When my husband was growing up, it was common practice in his home to have the television on pretty constantly, often with news playing in the background. For him, it was just background noise. For me, it completely drains my energy, especially when the quality of the news is bleak or disheartening, which it so frequently is.

So, we have an agreement in our home. If he wants to have the background noise on when I'm out of earshot, great! However, when I enter the room, he supports me by shutting off the TV or putting on something lighter, more positive, or musical, instead. What else is draining your internal energy that needs new boundaries in life and business?

You'll want to spend time figuring out what new boundaries you need to set around you, in order to keep you as safe as possible from stress, unfulfilling activities, unhealthy habits, and environments that are not conducive to your well-being. These are *weak-force attractors*. They contrast with *strong-force attractors*, which promote your vitality and improve your energy and well-being, such as supportive relationships, fulfilling work or hobbies, healthy habits, positive environments, and moments of joy or accomplishment. The more you can attend to what supports and uplifts your energy and can insulate yourself from whatever drains and zaps your energy, the happier, healthier, and wealthier you will become.

This will all help you to begin to craft your aligned business plan that helps you to focus on making those goals happen. Except, in this instance, we are not just going to set some financial targets and key performance indicators in order to attain them. Those are important, and they need to be a part of the process. However, they are not the only piece of the puzzle.

You now have a series of supportive thoughts, beliefs, emotions, and results to integrate into your business and personal understanding of life, along with a number of ways to stay the course during the process of implementation. You will now be armed with internal boundaries to manage your own inner world, and you'll also want to create some external boundaries to minimize the "noise" or external pressures that tend to send you off track. For example:

- ❖ What distractions can you minimize to mitigate the risk of time-wasting?

- ❖ What ways do you gain motivation, inspiration, or energy that you can have at your fingertips, to keep you in a healthy state?

- ❖ And what areas that drain your energy can you minimize access to?

- ❖ What people, places, or circumstances dissuade you from your highest potential to set new modes of communication or connection?

- ❖ Is your physical environment supportive of your growth or is it a deterrent?

- ❖ What are you doing to track your progress?

❖ And what would feel supportive to help you maintain the focus all year long?

❖ What supports, resources, and positive boundaries do you need to put in place to make it all happen, such as additional childcare, administrative or marketing support, home-care support, or internal support structures, like coaching, counseling, or mentorship?

By self-reflecting and deciding on your new set of boundaries, you are creating your own personal success plan. You will no longer be subject to what other people tell you is the right fit, or to external forces that shift you off your own personal version of "having it all." When you go through the process of deep awareness in combination with considering the logistical, emotional, mental, and financial resources necessary to help you actualize your potential, you will set yourself up for the success you crave, now and in the future!

I did this work with one business owner who came to me with the express purpose of better understanding what it was going to be like to become a mother as a highly successful entrepreneur. When we started our work together, she had just become pregnant and was one of the top-producing, most highly motivated, and hardest working financial advisors out there. She loved her work and saw herself easily climbing to the top of the field during her career, but she wasn't sure what introducing motherhood would do for her productivity, and she was afraid it might interrupt her career trajectory.

What she wasn't expecting was the deep love of parenthood that came after delivery of her child and the intense call and desire to be a present mother for her baby. This came in conflict with her love for her business. These two identities lived inside of her: the amazing, hardworking, brilliant, CEO-material business owner was now competing with the authentic and loving desire to be a stay-at-home mother.

Our work has centered around boundary-setting to help her integrate what these two identities mean to her at each stage of parenting. The boundaries needed to shift in her own self-care and awareness, in her marriage, and through the introduction of additional supports, such as counseling, administrative support, personal assistance, and childcare. She needed to add boundaries with her team, her clients, and even with what areas she would allow herself to focus on in business.

The more deeply she aligned with her truth, the further back her boundaries needed to be pulled. With every new baby she brought into her family, the more support she needed to have in place, and the more aligned she chose to become both in business and at home. Now, she has a highly sought-after business model, a remarkable team of support, both personally and professionally, and she is more present than ever before with her children and family.

Every entrepreneur has to master their own boundaries around their *time*. So many entrepreneurs have traded their 9-to-5 employment work only to be consumed with 24/7 business ownership. However, I've never met an entrepreneur who came to business ownership and is excited about being completely consumed with their business, leaving no time for anything else.

Whether you are physically working long hours or constantly thinking or worrying about your business, these boundaries will need to shift to support some rest. There are very effective, more traditionally masculine versions of time boundaries, such as floating time blocks, *The 4-Hour Workweek* by Timothy Ferriss or *The 12 Week Year* by Brian P. Moran and Michael Lennington, to help you organize your time plan.

There are also some amazing more feminine approaches to time and energy management to consider, as you develop your personal plan, such as integrating your menstrual and hormonal cycles or even the phases of the moon into your plan. Women run on completely different hormone cycles than men do, so it makes a lot of sense that our time cycle would also need to be different than the twenty-four-hour cycle. At different phases in the menstrual cycle, energy naturally waxes and wanes. Tuning into your own personal energy can be incredibly useful in the process of learning what time map works for you. Then, find the boundaries that match your energy availability, as well as the natural responsibilities you are managing at this particular season in your life.

Another feminine approach to time management for you to consider and integrate is through understanding that, to fully master your time spent in business, you will also need to master how much time you spend thinking and worrying about your business. Formal and informal thought work, journaling, peer groups, processing with professional support, having a board of directors, and other ways to create community in your life and business are some great ways to externalize your thoughts instead of letting them ruminate.

One important principle you need to consider during the creation of your aligned time-management plan for life and business is the value you place on your time.

Many business owners fall into transactional traps with their business model and end up devaluing their time or even the products or services they are selling, because they are not honoring the full value of their time and what they bring to the marketplace.

There is often some inner work needed to uncover and understand why you are devaluing your time, product, or services. Are you falling into one of the core limiting beliefs? Do you not feel you are worthy of being paid? Not good enough? That you cannot have what you want or don't deserve abundance?

The formal thought work of looking at your money story is also important to this phase of understanding. You cannot gain your time back and make a fulfilling income, if you don't price your services or products in alignment with the true value of your work. You cannot buy yourself more time, if you don't believe you have inherent value. And you won't respect your time boundaries, if you don't understand that your time is actually more valuable than currency.

Time is a non-renewable resource.

Time is not guaranteed, and it's not to be wasted.

Money is a renewable resource, and it's abundantly available.

Not honoring your time resources is a more critical problem in life and business than not having as much money as you desire.

Know your value. Value your time. Create value, and your business boundaries will heal.

Because I have been doing this work for so long, I am able to spot clues and patterns very quickly that are symptoms of time or energy management issues, which are usually more deeply rooted in a limiting core belief system. For example, when a new potential client or existing client frequently cancels at the last minute or no-shows for a call, I know this is a symptom of a boundary issue with time, energy, and/or value. If they are managing their calendar this way, they are likely behaving in this way with their life and business, on some level. And it is interesting when they report being frustrated that the clients whom they serve are also delaying meetings, canceling last minute during an important business cycle, or "ghosting them" for weeks or months on end.

We can only control how we respond to what's happening in our environment. And so, if the business owner is running their time boundaries from a place of fear, doubt, worry, or scarcity, that is the type of result they are bound to receive.

The other, more commonly recognized expression of boundaries is around how to engage in relationships with other people. Boundaries in relationships are ultimately about teaching other people how to behave in relationship to you. However, it's critically important that you are aware of your own personal boundaries and hold themself first. In relationships, the only person in the equation whom you can "control" is yourself. So, knowing your boundaries and sticking to them on your end is all you can ultimately account for. When you set your boundaries in a relationship, it's important to directly communicate them with the other party in the relationship.

If you think you have a boundary but have never communicated what you need from the other person, it is not their fault when they break your preferences. Don't assume the other person knows what your held boundary is. That is an internal fantasy, and if you assume, you make an *ASS* out of *U* and *ME!*

Assumptions are sometimes coupled with blaming or accusing the other person, which can lead to defensiveness, resentment, and further conflict. In reality, the only person to "blame" is yourself, when you don't take the time to let the other person know the rules of the game. Assumptions come into play both in the interpretation of what you think someone else is thinking or feeling, but also through what their body language or tone means in in-person or written communication. This is one of many communication pitfalls that can lead to communication and, therefore, boundary issues in a relationship. Other examples of communication pitfalls include:

❖ Generalizing or stereotypes about a group of people, which can be offensive and can lead to biased judgments and discrimination.

❖ Avoiding difficult conversations, which can lead to unresolved issues, resentment, and loss of trust.

❖ Interrupting someone while they are speaking, which can be disrespectful and can prevent the other person from fully expressing their thoughts and feelings.

❖ Failing to actively listen to the other person, which can result in misunderstandings and missed opportunities to connect and collaborate.

❖ Reacting emotionally to what someone is saying, which can be counterproductive and can prevent effective communication and problem-solving.

❖ Failing to give clear and specific feedback, which can lead to confusion and missed opportunities for improvement.

Part of the dance of learning healthy boundaries in relationships is learning healthy communication. If you do effectively communicate your boundaries and the other person still doesn't respect them, it's important that you do your best to hold your end of the boundary.

I often hear entrepreneurs say they are frustrated with a client, for example, for not showing or canceling an appointment; but then they will reschedule numerous times to accommodate the client's changes of plan, effectively teaching the client that it's okay to devalue their time. It's your responsibility to keep to the boundary around time, and sometimes, that results in consequences.

The Five Ingredients of Communication, found in the integration section below, work like a charm when the stakes are high for a conversation.

The first ingredient of effective communication is called *permission*. In short, asking questions to find out if you even have permission to move forward with this conversation is the first, most important step to healthy communication. Have you ever walked into a room when someone is doing something else, like watching their favorite show or game or heavily working on a project, and then started a difficult conversation with them without notice? How well does that go?

Permission starts with first making sure to slow down and actually ask the other person if the timing is right for that conversation, or perhaps requesting some time more formally via email or a direct ask. For example, "I have some important information to go over with you about the health of our business. Is 1 p.m. on Friday a good time for us to meet and have a conversation? If so, can we put that in our mutual calendars?"

Permission can also look like asking the other person during the difficult conversation if you have permission to be direct with them, or asking them after that conversation if you have permission to help hold them accountable to what you both agreed on. Ultimately, permission is about inviting the other person into the conversation space, instead of just hitting them over the head with something they may not be ready, prepared for, or interested in. Many people skip over this step in communication, and it results in really tumultuous conversations at best, when the other person isn't ready or willing.

The next ingredient to healthy communication is to *acknowledge* overtly and directly that the other person may have *feelings* about what you are about to say. One of the biggest pitfalls in unhealthy communication is that people try to avoid thinking about, discussing, or having empathy for the other person's feelings, which are real and valid and likely even to be expected, during a hard conversation.

Human beings are meant to feel feelings, and if you are having a tough communication with someone, of course they will feel things! Usually, if you are going into a high-stakes conversation with someone, you tend to have some kind of preexisting relationship with them. Therefore, you likely have a pretty good sense of how they may feel based on how they tend to respond. If not, you can at least surmise how they may feel and how you don't want them to feel, as a result of your conversation.

This part of the conversation starts to integrate a noteworthy teaching from the book *Crucial Conversations* by Kerry Patterson, which uses the contrasting statement. To begin, you overtly state what you don't want the other person to feel, as a result of your conversation. For example, "I don't in any way want to make you feel like I am micromanaging you or leave you feeling uncomfortable or frustrated as a result of our time together today."

Then, the contrast comes through the use of the third important ingredient to successful communication: *intention* and, preferably, a shared positive intention between both you and the other person in this conversation. Another major pitfall of communication is when someone launches into a conversation without sharing how the conversation may actually *benefit* both parties, and without stating that intention overtly and with clarity as to how the conversation you are about to initiate is meant to be in positive service to both of you.

In Patterson's contrasting statement, an example of this might sound like, "What we are both here to do is work together to have the healthiest team dynamic possible, so we can serve our clients from our shared mission of providing excellent customer service."

There is usually an intention to have that conversation, but it is often left out of the conversation, which leads to more problems in the delivery. These first few ingredients to success are using the principle where we "slow down to speed up," or where we are as proactive and prepared as possible before entering into the communication, to integrate these critical factors and create favorable outcomes in the conversation. By slowing down to ask permission, acknowledge feelings, and set an intention, we create a smoother landing ground for the rest of the conversation.

All of this can be an example of formal thought work for you to sort through in preparation for this conversation. Suppose, perhaps, you slow down to engage in this thought work, and you uncover that you don't actually have a positive shared intention; but that, instead, you really just have negative feelings and thoughts about someone that you are feeling called to spew on them. How well do you think that conversation will go?

By taking the moment to take a step back and search for the shared positive intention, this forces you to, first, have a heart-to-heart with yourself. Is this conversation really in the best interest of the relationship? Will saying this only make me feel better momentarily, but then make the other person feel terrible? What am I trying to get out of this conversation? And what will the other person gain, as well?

Sometimes, this exercise results in your making the decision to completely forgo the planned conversation. There are times, when we slow down to do this preparation work, that we learn there is really not enough of a benefit to even have the conversation, and other times, when we do our own formal thought work before this conversation, we are able to get to a place of closure, non-attachment, release, and/or peace about the conversation we thought we needed.

In some ways, we have the conversation with ourselves internally and first through thought work, which helps us to gain clarity about whether it's worth it to move forward. If you do go through the process and find your positive intention, permission, and acknowledged feelings for the other person involved, you will have far greater success to implement those steps when it comes time to move forward with the rest of the conversation.

When that time does come, the next most important step is to remember that conversations are a two-way street. They require both productive, proactive speaking to the other person and *listening* actively to the other person. Another pitfall that can occur in unhealthy communication is a whole lot of speaking and not enough real listening, or just giving the other person the chance to speak and hearing them, but waiting for your turn to speak again without really integrating the other person's thoughts, feelings, and body language into the process, too.

You actually want to seek to understand the other person's viewpoint of whatever circumstance led to the need to have this conversation, so pausing to listen and create an open forum of discussion instead of a one-sided conversation is imperative. Patterson's next phase in the framework is to state something along the lines of, "I'm going to share with you some of my thoughts, feelings, and concerns. Then, I want to hear from you, too." This is the first part of the conversation that you can't prepare proactively, because you have another human involved in this interaction. You cannot control how they show up to the dialogue. But you can prepare and create favorable conditions up until that point.

If, for some reason, the other person starts to have a negative response, behavior, reaction to, or feelings about your dialogue, you've already laid down some "life rafts" in the beginning of the conversation. You have your shared positive intention and acknowledged feelings there to fall back on. You can remind the other person of the contrasted feelings and intentions, such as, "Remember, I don't want you to feel frustrated. What we are here to do is to work together toward the same positive mission."

Then, you'll want to incorporate what you mentioned and what you heard from the other person into an *agreement*, which is the final important ingredient for successful communication. Too many times, we have a conversation and then nothing comes from it. When crafting a healthy dialogue, you want to overtly discuss what each person is going to do, what are the next steps, and when are we going to follow through and follow up, as well as potentially sort through what the consequences might be, if that agreement is not respected or upheld.

You want the agreement to respect and honor what the other person brought to the table, in addition to what you had intended to accomplish. It is also often important to bring in some level of accountability during this phase. Accountability is "who is doing what by when." Getting clear about all of these elements will allow you to understand the mutually beneficial next steps for both parties to follow through, in order to make something come from this difficult conversation.

I have taught this tool to hundreds of people throughout my career, ranging from small children to high-level CEOs of major corporations. There have only been a handful of people who came back to our coaching, after their challenging conversation using these tools, to report that it didn't go well. But, after learning these key ingredients, then they promptly shared that they didn't actually use all (or any!) of the elements we'd gone over, for whatever reason, usually due to some heavy unhealthy patterning in the relationship.

This is an important example of how even relationships can be managed and supported by slowing down to do that internal work, too. By focusing on what you can control and setting yourself up properly to avoid pitfalls and incorporate positive communication techniques, you can create favorable conditions for success, even though we cannot control the other person's response. We do what we can to control what we can actually control, and then, we release the rest. Sometimes, that's easier said than done when the circumstances are painful.

As we move further and further into actualizing our potential, what we are willing to tolerate becomes more selective. The boundaries become stronger and clearer and are communicated more intentionally, effectively, and efficiently. As we step into our higher impact, we are also collecting more and more responsibilities.

I have heard so many business owners whom I serve report how they are noticing their relationships shift over time. The more decades that pass, the smaller their circle of friends and even proximity to certain family members becomes. The types of clients we serve starts to shift, the further you climb into transcendence, and you start to see some of those lower-frequency people start to fall away. This can be a painful but necessary part of actualizing your potential. It can be quite challenging to integrate the true loss of a relationship with someone you love, because they are no longer able to see the evolved version of you as you climb.

Some of our oldest and once-closest relationships need to shift, if they are not willing to evolve with you. Your responsibilities will increase over time, therefore you have to reapportion where you spend your time and energy naturally. Your interests and goals shift, and so, likely, you will gravitate toward new circles of people who are engaging in similar activities. Your personality and boundaries have changed. If your first, closest relationships, friendships, or even clients do not see those changes as a gift and can't welcome them fully, they may not be willing to actualize with you or at least support you fully in your process.

I hear stories from clients who say their family still sees them as "Little Johnny" or "Little Susie," and are not willing to see them in a new light. If you continue to be questioned or compared to what you *used* to be, if you are being judged for changing when your intention is to create a bigger impact and step into your higher self, if you are ridiculed, mocked or misunderstood by the people who loved your *lower* self better than your higher self, how could that relationship be healthy and supportive of your evolution?

Do they need to fully understand what you are after? No. Do they need to evolve to the level that you choose or take the same path that you have decided to take? Absolutely not. And anyone who *gets* to be in your life and love you will honor your growth and development, not diminish it. The ones from your past who are healthy in your expansion will be your cheerleaders, your support system, your grounding touch points, and your biggest fans.

It is a natural process for all humans to shift their inner circle as time marches on. Nobody is exempt from the process of relationships shifting over time. It's always astonishing to evaluate how different your life and most trusted relationships look from decade to decade. This natural loss of relationships over time tends to be amplified as you climb the hierarchy.

Some relationships will end with the other person's volition and choice to leave. They will no longer resonate or see you for your true authentic self and will decide to move on. Sometimes, you will have to make that choice for yourself in order to support your continued growth, and without a doubt, that can feel painful.

Business owners will notice this in their client relationships and sometimes be triggered into scarcity. Even in the process of writing this book, which is a metaphor for my own continued growth and evolution in life and in business, I witnessed my inner circle shift, both personally and professionally. I watched as some clients who had been with me in my coaching practice for nearly a decade decide they needed to move on. I watched some friends fall away in closeness. I watched some family members decide that some old traditions we had were no longer worth keeping.

I am a human. This can hurt. *It is* a loss. And there can even be some grief involved. But I understand this principle and witnessed it with curiosity and openness as often as possible, because I also understand that ending certain relationships, personally and professionally, only means that I am growing and evolving. I am also creating the space for new, amazing relationships who are a better fit for the woman I've become and who are in better alignment with who I am becoming, what I stand for, and what impact I am committed to making in the world. The more I trust that reality, the more amazing people will come into my circle. I welcomed the momentary discomfort, because I trust this process fully and understand that the clearing is paving the way for more beauty, joy, love, and abundance, personally and professionally.

I lean *into* the clearing and take it to as many places as I can. It feels amazing to extend this to my environment in my home and office, to clear out as many anchors from the past that no longer serve me. I clear out old belongings that no longer create value for me or that were just taking up space that can now be filled with higher-frequency events and people, or even just be space to create more peace and calm.

This doesn't mean I go in like a bull in a China shop and destroy relationships or chuck out everything in my home (even if I am tempted, from time to time!). Instead, this is using discernment and awareness to make sure I am in alignment as best possible with what my higher self is calling into my world, and that I'm supporting myself in the here now.

What needs to go, and what gets to stay? What is draining my energy, and what is increasing my energy? What is supporting my evolution, actualization, and transcendence, and what is diminishing me or sending me back into the lower modes?

This is an act of love to self *and* others and is a critical part of stepping into your highest expression in business and life.

Can you trust that more of what you choose to be, do, and have can be found on the other side of releasing what no longer serves and supports your growth?

Competing Responsibilities Integration

Summary: We can learn so much from observing and modeling what comes naturally to children, which can make evolving in life and business much more easeful and joyful.

Resources

Visualization

Imagination

Boundaries

Spend the time to figure out what new boundaries you need around you to keep yourself as safe as possible from stress, unfulfilling activities, unhealthy habits, and environments that are not conducive to your well-being.

These are weak-force attractors versus strong-force attractors, which promote your vitality, improve your energy and well-being, which might include supportive relationships, fulfilling work or hobbies, healthy habits, positive environments, and moments of joy or accomplishment.

The more you can attend to what supports and uplifts your energy and insulates you from whatever drains and zaps your energy, the happier, healthier, and wealthier you will become.

Journaling Questions

❖ What distractions to your purpose can you minimize to mitigate the risk of time wasting?

❖ What ways do you gain motivation, inspiration, or energy that you can have at your fingertips to keep you in a high vibrational state, and what areas drain your energy that you can minimize access to?

❖ What people, places, or circumstances dissuade you from your highest potential that you can set new modes of communication, proximity, or connection?

❖ What does your physical environment look like? Is it supportive of your growth or deterrent?

❖ What are you doing to track your progress, and what would feel supportive to help you maintain the focus all year long?

❖ What supports, resources, and positive boundaries do you need to put in place to make it all happen, such as additional childcare, administrative or marketing support, home care support, or internal support structures like coaching, counseling, or mentorship?

Love Bubble/Protection Meditation

5 Ingredients of Effective Communication

1. **Intention**: Are you clear about *why* you need/want to have this conversation? Are you clear about how this conversation is a win/win for both parties?
2. **Acknowledging Feelings:** In communication, people will have feelings about what you say. Spend some time imagining what the other person may feel and what you hope they don't feel, as a result of your talk.
3. **Listening:** Make sure you are willing to listen as much as you speak.
4. **Agreement:** The goal is to work toward a clear, direct, mutually beneficial, and mutually agreed upon plan as a result of the healthy conversation.
5. **Permission:** We want to ask permission when creating a new agreement in service to the relationship, building trust, and supporting one another.

Chapter Eight

The Mental Toll

"The more we learn to let go of thoughts, the more we gain the ability to drop our negative stories. As we continue to practice, we may begin to catch ourselves earlier in the chain—perhaps even noticing dislike at the feeling level and choosing a mindful response rather than automatic reaction."

—Sean Murphy

VERY EARLY IN THEIR MARRIAGE, my mother- and father-in-law, Debbie and Ken, were offered the chance to invest in the family cottage in the Thousand Islands. Ken had such amazing memories there as a child, growing up in their family's cottage, and he had his own dreams of bringing his future children and grandchildren to a cottage by the water to gift them the same. However, as newlyweds just beginning their careers, it felt too early, too risky, and too much of an investment to purchase the family cottage. So, it was sold.

Ken's dream of having this home by the water to share with his family stayed close to his heart for the rest of his adult life, and he often thought back with regret to that decision not to invest in the family home.

To make up for the decision, my in-laws saved heavily and kept their expenses to the absolute minimum for their entire adult life, holding the promise and dream of investing in a home by the water as their retirement plan. They even kept duplicates of furniture, decor, and housewares in their basement, planning to use all of it in their beloved dream home when the timing was right.

Right before my husband and I were married, when Debbie was in her mid-fifties, she started to show some symptoms of confusion, forgetfulness, and uncertainty. Soon after, she was diagnosed with early onset Alzheimer's and had to retire much earlier than anticipated from her job as a teacher, which she loved dearly. Not too much later, my father-in-law also had to retire from his career early, to care for her.

Her disease progressed rapidly in a rare presentation called Capgras syndrome (CS) or frontal-lobe dementia, where her brain could no longer identify the faces of her primary caretakers and mistook them for a threat.

She was no longer safe living in her home with my father-in-law, because she became terrified that he was trying to harm her and thought he was a dangerous stranger.

There was even an instance where the police needed to get involved. Another where the hospital team questioned my father-in-law's intent, and even one time when she tried to get out of a moving car to get away from him, all because of the cruel presentation of this disease. This was heartbreaking to witness, especially for Ken, knowing he was a loving, gentle, loyal, and steadfast caretaker throughout their marriage and her illness.

Her body was so healthy, strong, and vibrant. She had so much living to do, and yet her brain was completely shutting down.

This terrible presentation of the illness resulted in my family having to look into alternate care for my mother-in-law. She ended up moving into a memory care support home called The Cottage Grove.

The support in the Cottages was impeccable. There was a cozy, homelike feel and atmosphere, which helped Debbie stay comfortable for many years and safely got her through the Covid pandemic, which began soon after she moved into the Cottages, resulting in our being isolated from her for months. She was ushered carefully and beautifully through this disease by caretakers called Shahbazim, who are doulas specifically trained to support Alzheimer and dementia patients through their disease process. They truly treat their residents like family and support them with authentic love, compassion, and understanding. For that care, we are forever grateful.

Debbie and Ken's retirement plan to invest in a cottage later in life happened much differently than expected. Instead of memories of their grandchildren laughing and playing in the water, family meals together during the summer, lake views, and boating excursions, my father- and mother-in-law had to live out their retirement dream in a memory care facility called the Cottages, instead.

They put off their dream and ended up having it end in this terrible irony that nobody would have chosen for our dear, sweet Debbie. She would have been the most amazing grandmother; however, she never even got the chance to know my children before her brain started to fail her.

We are grateful for her strong body, and even if our relationship was quite different than we would have preferred, my children still have fond memories of their Meme at the Cottages.

I plan to take this deep lesson to heart in honor of Debbie, to not put off my dreams, not delay my happiness, and not wait on adventures. The deepest lesson Debbie taught us all is that tomorrow is not a guarantee or promise. We never know the hand we are going to be dealt, and it's not a safe plan to put off possibilities, dreams, hopes, or wishes for another day.

In honor of Debbie, my husband and I want to show her grandchildren the world and maybe even get that cottage on the lake, where we can sit by the water and remember her joyful smile, knowing she is right there with us, teaching us the value of living in the moment and of chasing our dreams now, as if our lives depend on it.

That doesn't mean our family doesn't continue to struggle with this loss or continue to integrate what it means to us for the rest of our lives.

I witness this all of the time with my husband. Perhaps he makes the wrong turn on the way home, forgets something at the grocery store, or promises to take care of something that doesn't get handled. These are all minute "mistakes" in the scheme of life, mere incidentals, non-issues, and definitely not problems.

But to my husband, they are cause for concern and create triggers.

Forgetfulness is definitely a part of the human condition, and it's very common for the overwhelmed, exhausted brain of a parent of three small children under the age of six, who has a full-time job and two dogs in the mix, just to keep it interesting. For any given person, this will naturally create an overflow of information and competing responsibilities. The capacity of working memory, which refers to the amount of information a person can hold and manipulate in their mind at any given moment, is limited. The psychologist George A. Miller's research proposed, for example, that the average person can hold about seven items, plus or minus two, in their working memory.

For us, whenever we are out with our whole crew, dogs, kids, and all, we inevitably hear, "Well, you've got your hands full!" Because, at this stage of the game, our physical load is incredibly visible. *Yes, thank you, Karen.* Our hands are definitely full. However, there is an unseen mental and emotional load of a working parent, which is the burden they carry that can't be seen while managing the natural and varying responsibilities of all that falls on their plate.

This mental, emotional, and physical load, both seen and unseen, can definitely have significant implications for a working parent's memory and cognitive functions. The working parent is constantly juggling back and forth between multiple roles and using every available moment to get something done from of their endless list of things to do, for their home, their family, and their work. If Miller's research is, in fact, accurate, seven items is just frankly not a long-enough list. The constant switching between roles can lead to cognitive fatigue, making it challenging to focus on and remember specific tasks.

Multitasking feels like a necessity, but the research is conflicting on how effective it actually is. Heavy multitasking can lead to poor performance (Ophir et al, 2009); and studies also revealed that there is a time cost that comes from moving between all of the different tasks (Rubinstein et al, 2001). There is even some research that showcases how working memory capacity *decreases* during the multitasking process; perhaps even bringing that commonly-cited number, seven, to something much lower (Pashler, 1994).

It makes sense that managing work tasks, coordinating family schedules, and handling unexpected events increases the cognitive load on working parents. We often engage in extensive planning and organization to ensure the smooth running of both our work and home lives. However, such constant thinking ahead and managing various concurrent details can be mentally taxing, which may lead to lapses in memory and forgetfulness.

However, while working on only one task at a time may be an option for some, it may be an impossible approach for working parents. Some may even say that working parents are master multitaskers.

Thankfully, there is also some research that counters this idea that multitasking doesn't work; it says success or failure is more context-dependent. In certain contexts, and with certain levels of difficulty, multitasking *does* work, especially when tasks are relatively simple or routine (Salvucci, D.D. and Taatgen, N.A., 2011). Perhaps that's why a working parent can schedule a doctor's appointment while listening to a zoom meeting for work, or can vacuum the carpet while throwing a load of laundry into the machine and listening to a podcast!

We also want to incorporate the emotional labor involved in all of this, which is, of course, subjective and driven by the context of each human's life, as well. Balancing the emotional needs of children, addressing family issues, and managing work-related stress contribute an additional layer of mental strain. Now, add in the trauma of the loss of a mother, the grief process, and the context that his loss came from a disease that destroyed his mother's cognitive ability, starting with signs in forgetfulness, and it is no surprise that my husband's simply forgetting the bread at the store can lead to an emotional trigger for him, more so than the average human.

When we factor in a working parent's lack of downtime, their disrupted sleep, and the difficulty in creating well-being routines like self-care and exercise, the cumulative effect of this unseen mental, emotional, physical, and relational load can contribute to stress and mental fatigue and can even lead to burnout. The kicker is that this chronic stress can actually lead to memory problems and cognitive decline over time.

The unseen load of being a working parent can certainly take a toll. The first step toward healing and balancing this phenomenon is to become aware that this may be going on, and to normalize the reality. Then, you can start to seek support for these mental, emotional, and logistical burdens, in order to promote your well-being along with your memory function.

Depending on your own unique story, you may also need to seek support to move through whatever grief you are experiencing, whatever trauma you may have endured, or any medical concerns you have about your cognitive abilities or mental health. Then, you can begin to layer in tools like time management, additional supports, and self-care practices, all of which can be incredibly helpful to improve the struggle with juggling all the inevitable aspects of a working parent's life.

Recognize that you can have it all. You can be a successful business owner, entrepreneur, and a present parent. But what "having it all" looks like will unique to your preferences. Having it all does *not* mean doing it all on your own, however. You get to decide how to spend your time, where to pull in supports, what to delegate, and when to release certain expectations, goals, or other people's definitions of a successful working parent. Each definition of success is unique to the individual, and being willing to let go of what other people or society label as success will also be part of the process.

A gift you can give yourself is to go through the process and test the elements that are important to you in parenting and in your business, and then do what you can to divide, conquer, and focus on what you truly love. You still get credit for having it all and getting it all done! Not every parent wants to be home full-time with their small children, while some parents don't want to miss a single game or practice.

It starts with introspection and clarity about your values as a parent and a business owner, and then making sure your behavior matches your innermost values. Coming to the table to have these conversations with any coparent you may have and finding those points of alignment is also an incredibly important part of the process, because it truly does take a village. Some people have that support right in their home, through extended family or friends, while others need to bring in hired caregivers to make it all work.

Getting clear about what that means for you is the first logistical step to success. Then, you implement the necessary support to make it all happen. Of course, there are financial barriers to this reality, at times. However, that doesn't mean you can't create a business plan to match your preferred outcomes and work your way up to that level of support.

If, when you sit down to do this exercise, you notice you are having thoughts that you can't afford this level of support or think "other people" get to have that, but it's not available to you, those are good pieces of evidence to support that there is some formal and informal thought work to be done on your money story to begin building the belief, thoughts, emotions, and actions to help you get there. Just accepting that you can't afford it and that other people are privileged to have that in their lives will keep you stuck in that reality. Go to the corners of your mind and challenge that belief in order to carve out a path that looks, feels, and becomes a different story for you.

Perhaps you notice yourself getting frustrated that you don't have the village you would prefer, that your family doesn't show up for you in the way you crave, or you don't have the support in your workplace. Again, these thoughts and realities are just pieces of information. *You* get to decide what the narrative looks like for you, moving forward. It may be true to you now, but that doesn't mean it needs to be true indefinitely. Let your brain go to work on what could be possible to make the changes and adjustments to create a more preferred outcome and reality for you, your family, and your business.

Throughout life, there are so many naturally occurring transitions that can create intense amounts of stress across all of the realms of our lives, personally and professionally. For example, the loss of a parent or loved one is a transition wrought with grief. It usually requires an entire integration and renegotiation process of what life looks like, now that this key person in your life is gone indefinitely. That transition period is a common time for stress to increase, making it more difficult to manage the typical stressors of life and business.

The mental toll during these transitions is heightened, and so, of course, the grief and loss trickle into all elements of our life. It may be tempting to think you can just compartmentalize that loss and keep your business separate. However, you will find that taking this approach will affect all aspects of your personal and professional life one way or another. Creating the space to feel the full spectrum of human emotions during these very human, albeit challenging, times is critical to your success, happiness, and health.

When there is a change in the family dynamic or team dynamic, a loss, a move, a divorce, or any other major transition in life, it is better to acknowledge that stress as real and valid, rather than try to stuff it or move through it without adequately addressing the reality of the experience. The mental toll only compounds and intensifies when we try to pretend like it doesn't exist. All humans will encounter transitions in their lives, so it is not a matter of *whether* this will affect our business, but *when* it will.

When we are in these moments of transition, that is the time to lean into our support network, not away from them. I will often say, "It takes a village to raise a Raeanne!"

I used to think my need for a comprehensive support team was high-maintenance, and I judged myself for falling apart without it. Now, I ardently and proudly lean on them. I'm so grateful to have found a group of people who genuinely support me in staying as happy and healthy as possible.

At any given moment in life and business, here is a list of whom I regularly connect with: coaches, masterminds, peer supporters, chiropractors, naturopathic physicians, general practitioners, therapists, acupuncturists, Reiki masters, massage therapists, craniosacral therapists, friends, childcare support, team members, administrative support, accountants, graphic designers, colleagues, affiliates, family, and so much more!

I feel so loved, held, and supported by my village, and I know that they have my greatest interest at heart. They are a part of making my dreams a reality. They are there during those tough transitions in life, while also being present to keep me strong, healthy, and vibrant during the day-to-day.

I encourage you to take the time to reflect on this: *Who is in your village of support?*

Mental Toll Integration

Summary: Business requires a lot of mental energy to maintain, coordinate, and excel. Add in the natural life responsibilities and it can feel like a lot to manage!

Resources

Introspection

Reflection

Boundaries:

Complete your free time audit here:

www.raeannelacatena.com/audit

Delegation and Support

❖ "Have it all" Exercise: Visit the expanded free workbook here:

www.raeannelacatena.com/integrationworkbook

❖ Village of Support Exercise: This quick exercise helps business owners identify and appreciate their support network, enhancing personal and professional resilience.

Reflect on Your Journey: Take a moment to think about your business and personal journey—its challenges, triumphs, and key moments. Consider the people who've played a significant role in supporting you.

Identify Key Support Categories: Break down your support network into personal, professional, and emotional categories.

List Your Village Members: Write down names of those who've supported you, specifying their contributions.

Recognize Different Types of Support: Identify the specific ways each person supports you—emotionally, strategically, financially, etc.

Evaluate the Strength of Your Village: Reflect on the overall strength of your support network. Are there areas where you could use more support?

Express Gratitude: Take a moment to thank each person on your list, conveying your appreciation for their role in your journey. This could be face-to-face, handwritten, a text, or phone call; you could even give them a gift to acknowledge your gratitude, a referral to their service, or just send them the energy of gratitude.

Plan for Growth: Identify potential new connections who could further enhance your support network.

Chapter Nine

Malleability of Thought

"Your thoughts will never stop. Just always come back to the breath. As long as you can do that, you're meditating."

—Jon Kabat-Zinn

MY GRANDFATHER WAS AN avid golfer and taught on a course in North Carolina when I was growing up.

Golf has always been an important part of my family's life, so when my grandfather invited me out to the golf course to give me some lessons, I was very excited about joining the family sport. He took me out for a few lessons on the driving range and the putting green, and then even on a few holes of his well-known course in Durham, North Carolina.

Around about the third hole, my grandfather turned to me with a loving smile, and said, "Do you know what else is really fun, sweetie? Driving the golf cart! Why don't you just plan on doing that from now on, instead?" Clearly, it wasn't going very well!

I have never golfed since that day, aside from a few rounds of putt-putt with my kids.

This is not a tragic story. If anything, from what I hear, I have saved myself thousands of hours, thousands of dollars, and a whole lot of heartache by avoiding golf.

I share the story with you as a way to illustrate how one moment in time can create complete identity shifts based on external implanted beliefs. My grandfather was one of my favorite people. I loved him dearly, and he loved me, as well. I didn't feel pain when he told me that day that I was more suited to driving the cart. Instead, when he looked at me with love, I trusted him implicitly: I believed him, and I decided on that day I would never be a golfer. I also decided on that day it was better only to do things I was good at and not even to bother trying things that, when I started them, I showed no natural skill and strength for.

These beliefs, which came from a thought expressed by someone I loved, became a part of my identity for most of my life. I didn't question that belief, because I felt it coming from a place of love from someone who loved me, so I took his coaching and carried on driving the golf cart.

These kinds of beliefs are unwittingly instilled inside of us as young people completely without our knowledge, completely innocently, and sometimes even from a place of love.

This is especially true for the young, very impressionable mind we have while under the age of seven, when our brains are really open to whatever it is we are told. From birth to seven years old, our brains are working at forming and are primarily in what are called theta and delta brain waves.

The four different brain waves support different functions and are present at different times of our lives and at different times in the day. Theta waves are associated with deep relaxation and sleep, as well as creativity, intuition, and meditation; they are thought to play a role in learning and memory formation.

Delta waves are the slowest brain waves and are typically associated with neural development and deep, dreamless sleep. They are also seen in some forms of meditation and can be induced by certain types of sound therapy. In infants, delta waves are more dominant than any other type of brain wave, as infants are still developing their neural connections.

Alpha waves are associated with relaxation and meditation and are more prominent in adults. Beta waves are associated with active thinking and concentration and become more dominant as we age.

Early in our development, we are heavily influenced by theta and delta, which is extremely important for the development of our brains and our identities, because whatever we are told, we believe, and anything that is repeated to us over and over again becomes a part of our identities.

Young people also cannot discern positive intention versus negative intention, especially from their parents and caretakers. It is not until we are older that we develop the alpha, beta, and delta waves in our brain that allow us to discern more about what is true and what is not true; then, we can start taking things a little less literally. That is why we can tend to see children in the most abusive environments still wanting to be with their parents, despite the neglect, abuse, and abandonment they endured. They believe that all this must mean they're not good enough and don't belong in the family, and adopt the understanding of what they went through as data points that feel like facts to their brains.

When deep trauma and abuse was a part of your story as a child, if you want to shift your mindset and beliefs, you will definitely want to go back and heal some of these thought processes that came from very early in your development. Until you take the time to carefully look at where these identity markers could have developed, you may end up running these unfair and non-factual old patterns as a part of your identity for the rest of your life.

This applies to seemingly mundane or inconsequential identity markers, too. Remembering what my grandfather taught me on the golf course, if I'm ever going to decide to go back to the sport again, I get to address that belief instilled in me as a child and choose to think, feel, believe, and behave differently about myself. I get to reprogram my brain, body, and mind that I can, in fact, try new things and that I can try something new for the fun of it, even if I'm not very good, and that I am worth the effort to do so. For now, I will stick with putt-putt.

The good news about theta brain waves is that we still have access to them as adults. It is critically important to the success of our life and business to begin to explore how to access theta brain waves, which are associated with not only deep relaxation and sleep, but also with creativity, intuition, and meditation. We do have the capability of accessing these incredibly impressionable times for our brain, most commonly right before we go to sleep and right at the moment we wake up.

If we are in the business of changing our thoughts, shifting our beliefs and identities, and getting unstuck, one of the most important things we can do for ourselves is to learn how to capture these incredibly impressionable time frames in our day, in order to offer our brains a different way of thinking about things, so we can start to create new patterning and programming that allows us to see ourselves differently.

This is where meditation comes in. If you are still hitting the snooze button five times in the morning, the jury is out! The snooze button is terrible for your health! If you could simply reallocate your snooze time, which is actually a detriment to your sleep, and replace it with five to fifteen minutes of meditation during those prime theta-wave times in the morning, your life is going to change. Witnessing and watching your thoughts and offering them a different way of looking at things is exactly what we're learning how to do here in meditation.

In many ways, meditation is the practice of noticing your thoughts as they arise and choosing which ones to energize. The discernment that comes in the process of choosing which thoughts you allow to settle into your subconscious and conscious mind, while also choosing which ones you allow to float right on by, helps you take back the power and control of your thoughts, feelings, belief systems, and identity.

Human beings, and specifically human brains, are meaning-making machines. The brain wants to know the answer. It doesn't like blank space, and it will do what it needs to do to fill in the gap.

Our brains, thoughts, and emotions will go wild with possible perceived negative and positive versions of what is really neutral. A very important question, one I often ask during my coaching calls with entrepreneurs I serve, is, "What is your brain doing right now?"

First, asking this question helps the listener to pause and *think* about their *thinking* in the present moment. When we take a moment and become self-aware about what our thoughts are doing with the information, we turn on a different processing center in the brain. This helps us to look at our thoughts differently, which is actually part of what is happening during a meditation practice. This active introspection allows us to familiarize ourselves with our thoughts differently.

Second, it helps the listener recognize one fundamental reality: *You are not your thoughts.* You are not your brain. You are not your judgments, opinions, feelings, fears, doubts, or worries.

Your thoughts are happening as a result of stimuli from your external world and your internal response to each stimulus, as well as the default thoughts that your brain has been programmed to think. Thoughts are actually created neurochemically through the interaction of neurons in our brains, which communicate with one another through the release and uptake of neurotransmitters, the chemicals that allow signals to be transmitted from one neuron to another.

When a thought is generated in the brain, a series of electrical and chemical signals are triggered between neurons. Neurotransmitters, such as dopamine, serotonin, and norepinephrine, are released into the synapses, the small gaps between neurons, to facilitate the transmission of signals. Thoughts are basically chemical and electrical signals!

As we've discussed, research has shown that the brain is highly adaptable and capable of changing its structure and function in response to events and environmental stimuli. This process is known as neuroplasticity, and it occurs through the strengthening and weakening of neural connections. We can literally change the makeup of our brains, our minds, and therefore our thoughts.

Sometimes, understanding this science can help us grasp that we are not causing our thoughts, we didn't ask for them, and they aren't our fault; however, they are our responsibility. When we create a separation from what our thoughts are telling us, we are able to recognize that we are so much more than the limits of our thoughts.

We don't have to identify with that voice inside of our head telling us we aren't good enough.

We don't have to carry out a limiting story that our brain keeps telling ourselves over and over again.

We don't want to get into the habit of judging our thoughts. However, it can be helpful, while we sort through what we are working with and what we want to focus on.

We are getting into the habit of noticing our thoughts, which, ultimately, is the practice of meditation. Often, people think meditation is "emptying our brains" and "stopping the thoughts." So many people quit trying to meditate because they find, when they sit down to practice, they have such busy brains and thoughts, and they notice it's so noisy in there, they begin to think they are doing it "wrong," get frustrated, and give up.

Sure, one of the positive byproducts of one type of meditation is that you may experience inner quiet on a more regular basis. But there is so much more to it. There are many different forms of meditation and many more positive byproducts.

Just to name a few, meditation has been shown to: reduce stress and anxiety, improve focus and concentration, boost your immune system, lower blood pressure; enhance emotional wellbeing, stability, and resilience; improve sleep, increase self-awareness, increase empathy and compassion, improve creativity and problem-solving skills, reduce pain, and improve overall wellbeing, leading to a greater sense of happiness, contentment, and fulfillment. If this sounds like I'm trying to convince you to meditate, it's working.

In meditation, we can begin to practice by looking at the quality of our thoughts and really getting a sense for what is happening in our internal dialogue or self-talk. Early in the process, we do want to notice our thoughts to understand the meaning they are giving to whatever we are going through. This is part of the work!

When we slow down and differentiate between the *not-so-useful* and *useful* ways of thinking about something, we open up our minds to possibilities, to reframing, and to different ways of thinking about things. Sometimes, even sorting through these options can make enough of a difference to move you through whatever seems to be limiting you.

Because we can only really control one thing in our life—which thoughts we energize—it is critically important for us, as entrepreneurs and human beings, to find those modalities that help us learn how to effectively do this. In a formal meditation practice, we may sit cross-legged on a bolster with our eyes closed and practice emptying our mind, in the traditional sense of the practice. However, there are so many different ways to engage in meditation.

I like to teach a variety of ways to manage your mind, thoughts, energy, and feelings, until you can find a modality that really suits you, as an individual, because, just like anything else, what works for one person may not work for another, and different modalities will feel better in different seasons of your life.

I personally have a practice I do every single morning. I take a moment and ask myself, "What do I need today to be the greatest expression of who I am meant to be?"

I practice listening to my mind, my body, and my energy. I pay attention to how my sleep was the night before and what I have on the docket for the day. I listen to what I need to set up my day for success.

Sometimes, this looks like a high-energy cardio workout, weightlifting, and a formal meditation practice. On other days, this looks like a very gentle, restorative yoga and Reiki practice. I have given myself a gift of exploring hundreds, if not, thousands of different ways to take care of my mind, body, and spirit in service to being the highest expression of whom I choose to be. I allow myself to pay attention to what I truly need in that moment, to actualize my potential and fulfill my purpose.

I know that other individuals have a very specific routine they enact every single day in the exact same way, and that is what feels supportive to them. In some way, finding your right-fit self-care plan is meditative in and of itself, because you are practicing noticing what you need as a unique individual and releasing the rest.

One helpful meditation hack that I will offer my busy, high-achieving, and masculine-leaning entrepreneurs, to support them in creating a meditation routine, is to encourage them to incorporate it into their workday and even go so far as to make it one of their key performance indicators. I encourage them to add it to their work calendar and give themselves credit in their business tracking for when they honor that commitment to their excellence, just as they would give themselves credit for prospecting, writing, billing, or any other business-related task.

The beginner meditation practice can be as simple as closing your eyes in your natural environment and taking two or three deep breaths, filling your lungs to capacity in through your nose and out through your mouth. It is unbelievable how different you can feel just by introducing some deep breaths into your life and practicing that on a regular basis.

If you want to try something a little more structured, you can try what is called box breathing, where you breath in for the count of four, filling your lungs, then holding your breath for four seconds, before you release your breath to the count of four, and then hold again for four counts. The four-count breaths and holds are visualized in the shape of a box. This style of breathing has been found to be very effective at calming the central nervous system and body.

You might also practice what is called the 5-step grounding practice, where you take a moment in your natural environment to find five things you can see around you, four things you can touch around you, three things you hear, two things you can smell, and one thing you can taste, using your senses to help you get present. This teaching comes from the tradition of mindfulness and is a rapid method to bring you into the present moment, no matter what is happening in your world.

Give a few a try and see what feels right for you!

I would argue that some form of meditation in your daily routine to set your mind up for success is the *most* important task you can be doing for yourself, your business, your family, and everyone you impact. When you do the work to access your higher self daily, everyone you engage with gets a higher version of you that day. Instead of pushing or forcing yourself through your day, take a moment to pause, reflect, release, or just be. This is an essential part of setting yourself up for success to be the greatest expression of who you choose to be as a business owner, family member, team member, and human being.

One of the main benefits that comes from implementing a meditation practice is that it increases what is called your window of tolerance. When we sit down to meditate, we are practicing patience, presence, mindfulness, and intentionality; again, we are working on discernment, deciding which thoughts to energize and which thoughts to let float on by.

In this practice, we get comfortable with extending the amount of time we can sit with our own thoughts and engage in the process of transcending the discomfort and the desire to move, or allowing ourselves to settle into a line of thinking that is unproductive. The more we practice, the more cushion we create between a thought happening and our giving into the temptation to respond to or lean into it. This helps us to create a larger window of tolerance or gap between some sort of stimulus happening and our response to that stimulus.

The cushion this creates in a formal meditation practice is incredibly useful to carry into our daily lives. First and foremost, engaging in some kind of higher fuel resourcing to start or during our day creates favorable conditions for success for us to manifest in our higher selves. As they say, you cannot pour from an empty cup, so taking the time on a very consistent and regular basis to find those modalities that fill up our cup will allow us to be happier, healthier, and more likely to be able to fulfill our purpose, as well as reach financial freedom and wealth in all categories.

Every morning, you may wake up and brush your teeth and take a shower to cleanse your physical self before you start the day. Meditation, tapping, journaling, Reiki, prayer, and other high-level self-care mechanisms are ways we cleanse our minds, emotions, and spirit before we start our day; and again, they create favorable conditions for success in all we choose to be.

Yoga is an excellent resource for developing presence and expanding your window of tolerance. It is a very physical version of meditation, forcing you to be present to the instructions you are being given, the placement of your body on the mat, movement on breath, and attending to what your body needs to stay balanced. It's an excellent way for beginners to practice presence and meditation, a true opportunity for body-mind connection. Pairing your practice with an intention or an affirmation can amplify the power of the practice, as well.

The other really interesting phenomenon that becomes available when we engage in these types of activities, is that the premises can also be used informally throughout our day, including during business hours.

For example, many of the entrepreneurs I serve come to me in hopes of actualizing their potential in their business; they are often looking to find ways to scale from solopreneurship into a more leveraged approach to their business. Oftentimes, that looks like beginning the process of finding additional help to support them in their business, so they can begin to focus on doing more of what they love and more of their unique ability.

Many of these solopreneurs have been doing everything on their own in their business for many years and have had to learn how to manage everything without any help whatsoever. They have developed many patterns around how to keep everything under control; they have a very particular way that they like things done, and they are used to knowing the status of everything, because they are doing it all themselves. When they begin the process of bringing more people into their business, this process can be very difficult for them, at first. They may notice themselves micromanaging their new staff, having a difficult time trusting others, feeling dissatisfied with the quality of work because it is not exactly how they would do it, and they may begin second-guessing whether they should just do it themselves, because they could do it faster and better.

Part of the coaching work we do is to look closely at this resistance and how it is limiting their growth, preventing them from stepping into their self-actualized business, and certainly impeding the impact they could have on other people by freeing themselves up to do more of what they love. We often need to start with some more formal thought-work practice, to understand more deeply where the resistance is coming from and which sets of thoughts, emotions, and actions will better support the hiring, onboarding, training, and retaining the right-fit staff in our business.

One of the exercises we go through during this process is what is called a "drains and gains" exercise, where I have the entrepreneurs slow down and begin to craft a list of everything that they do during their business day, and maybe even during their personal time, for at least a week. They start to document what drains their energy and what gains their energy.

I have them really slow down and pay attention to how they feel, physically and emotionally, what their thoughts are telling them about each of the tasks, whether they have resistance before, during, or after the task (drains), or if they are excited, inspired, motivated, and energized by engaging in the task (gains).

Time Gains	Time Drains
• Coaching	• Messy desk
• Discovery/ Prospecting Calls	• Zoom calls/behind a computer all day
• Writing	• Social Media
• CEO days	• Full email inbox
• Time outside	• Email Marketing
• Exercise	• Technology
• Networking	• News
• High Frequency music	• Billing
• Reading	• Accounting
• Thought work	• Graphic Design

Racanne Lacatena
HOLISTIC BUSINESS COACHING

Then, we work on finding the right-fit supportive roles, for example bookkeeping, administrative support, social media management, a personal assistant, or a client relationship manager, to help them engage in as many of the gains list as possible while finding the role that supports as many of the drains list being delegated off the business owner as their resources support that.

However, because these solopreneurs have been doing everything by themselves for so long, they have deeply rooted patterns on how to get things done, often have control issues, and might struggle with remembering when to delegate, what to delegate, or even knowing how to delegate.

This is where the window of tolerance comes in, and when we have an opportunity to do a more informal meditation or thought-work practice in the moment during our day. I will urge a solopreneur who is looking to bring on more staff and enter into entrepreneurship to leverage their formal meditation practice moment to moment throughout the day. To slow down when anything comes across their desk to get done and ask themselves, "Do I really need to be doing this task right now? Or is there someone else who can help me get this done?" Or, "Does this drain my energy or gain my energy?" Or, "Who can help me achieve this task right now?"

The first step is awareness that there is a new task coming into their field of awareness and then using that window of tolerance to slow down. Instead of responding immediately to do it themselves, because that's what they've always done, they pause, take a breath, and ask themselves these types of questions during this informal awareness exercise, to see if they can create a new pattern of thinking, feeling, and behaving that allows them to engage their business differently in the moment.

Sometimes, the resistance is so strong in the moment, the entrepreneur will have to slow down and find a way to shift their thinking in order to get behind the decision to receive help and support and to trust the people they've hired to get things done. They may need to reframe their thoughts to remind their brain that they've carefully hired the right-fit person. Or maybe they become aware that what they need next in order to feel more comfortable is a standard operating procedure or user manual, some sort of additional technology, or a reminder that this person who was hired to help them can actually do the work more efficiently and effectively. Others will need the reminder that this person they hired is on their soul's purpose, doing what they love, so why not let them live in their purpose, so you can live more fully into your own?

With enough practice, the entrepreneur can teach their brain, body, and business to behave differently, so they can get the desired results of having more time and energy to do more of what they love and produce more revenue and create a greater impact. They are taking meditation out of the laboratory into real life, by using an informal form of meditation within their business in real time.

There are so many different ways that the informal versions of our formal practice can be integrated into our day. For example, intention-setting is a methodology where you clearly state what you want to achieve through your actions. The skill of setting intentions is applicable and useful across all holistic elements of life, personally and professionally. To practice setting intentions in a mindfulness, yoga, or meditation practice can then be translated into setting positive intentions for your day, your business, a challenging conversation, or your year.

Intention setting is powerful. I've had many clients who are now multimillionaire business owners who attribute their success to living out their intentions to the fullest. They decide they are going to achieve something and verbally, internally, externally, and consistently state that intention. They know that, this way, it is more likely to manifest.

To maintain consistency with your intention-setting, you may consider creating a short phrase, paragraph, or even a letter to yourself outlining your intention and reciting it out loud three times a day with your hand on your heart.

You may also consider breathwork, body awareness, and mindfulness exercises. Breathwork involves using the breath to cultivate a sense of calm and focus through deep-breathing exercises or alternate-nostril breathing.

Body awareness involves paying attention to the sensations in the body, noticing areas of tension or discomfort, and releasing them through gentle movement or relaxation techniques.

Mindfulness exercises involve bringing attention into everyday activities, such as eating, walking, or washing dishes, by focusing on the present moment and engaging the senses fully. The informal meditation practice can be as simple as taking a deep breath before responding or taking your shoes off to walk around barefoot in an effort to ground in the grass, sand, or sea, so you can reset your central nervous system.

The exploration to find your right-fit higher-fuel sources can be so much fun and will be a process unique to you. Feel free to download my Self-Care Sandbox at the link below, to begin playing in the sandbox and finding what works for you! Get curious, explore, and have fun!

www.raeannelacatena.com/sandbox

Malleability of Thought Integration

Summary: Learn how to manage your thoughts so they don't manage you!

Resources

❖ Meditation

❖ Box Breathing: Breath in for the count of four, filling your lungs, then hold your breath for four seconds. Release your breath to the count of four, and then hold again for four counts.

❖ 5-Step Grounding Practice

5: Acknowledge _five_ things you see around you. Maybe it is a bird, maybe it is a pencil, maybe it is a spot on the ceiling. However big or small, state five things you see.

4: Acknowledge _four_ things you can touch around you. Maybe this is your hair, hands, ground, grass, pillow, etc. Whatever it may be, list out the four things you can feel.

3: Acknowledge _three_ things you hear. This needs to be external. Do not focus on your thoughts. Maybe you can hear a clock, a car, a dog bark. Or maybe you hear your stomach rumbling; internal noises that make external sounds can count. Whatever four things are audible in the moment is what you list.

2: Acknowledge _two_ things you can smell. This one might be hard, if you are not in a stimulating environment. If you cannot automatically sniff something out, walk nearby to find a scent. Maybe you walk to your bathroom to smell soap or outside to smell anything in nature. It could even be as simple as leaning over and smelling a pillow on the couch or a pencil. Whatever it may be, take in the smells of two things around you.

1. Acknowledge _one_ thing you can taste. What does the inside of your mouth taste like? Gum, coffee, or the sandwich from lunch? Focus on your mouth as the last step, and take in what you can taste.

❖ Self-Care Sandbox:
   www.raeannelacatena.com/sandbox

❖ Drain and Gain Exercises: Spend at least a day, week or even month paying attention to what activities, tasks, events, and people bring you more energy (Gain) vs. what drains your energy.

   Document in a list like the sample below:

Time Gains 〰	Time Drains 🔋

Chapter Ten

Managing Emotions and Feelings

"Only when emotions are truly attended to can they be endured and transformed into useful energies that express our needs and help guide us through life."

—Josh Korda

"STOP CRYING."

"Why are you being so sensitive?"

"Suck it up!"

"Woah, are you hormonal?"

"There is no crying in baseball."

"Leave the emotions out of the board room."

Societal norms for both men and women make it very difficult to express emotions and feelings, because, culturally, we are trained to consider this a sign of weakness. Even when we undergo deeply emotional events, like grief or a loss, people are quick to say things like:

"This, too, shall pass."

"Keep your chin up—it'll get better."

"They are in a better place. Focus on that now."

These messages are often well intended, but they can create an environment of emotional repression, instead of encouraging the healthy expression of held emotion.

Growing up, I always knew that I felt things differently than other people did. Because the idea of the highly sensitive person or the empath didn't become widely known until recently, I was given messaging around "manning up" and taught, overtly and covertly, to suppress my emotions and hide what I was feeling behind closed doors. As a child, I wasn't given tools to manage my emotionality and my highly empathic sense. Instead, I was made to feel that I was different or a problem or didn't belong, so I spent my childhood, teenage years, and well into adulthood hiding the superpower that I now understand has amazing benefits, even though it also has vast responsibilities and requires a fair bit of management.

For those of you who aren't aware, an empath is an individual who has a highly developed ability to feel and understand the emotions and experiences of others. Empaths are acutely attuned to the feelings, needs, and energy of the people around them and may feel these emotions as if they were their own.

Empaths are often deeply compassionate and sensitive individuals, highly skilled at reading nonverbal cues and picking up on subtle emotional shifts in others. They may be able to sense the emotions of others before they are expressed verbally and can often offer support and comfort to those who are struggling.

However, being an empath can also be challenging. Empaths may struggle with setting boundaries and become overwhelmed by the emotions and life events of others. They may also be more susceptible to stress, anxiety, and other negative emotions because of their heightened sensitivity to the world around them.

This is different from *empathy*, which is still an important emotional intelligence scale, but it is not the same as someone who is an *empath*. Empathy is the ability to understand and share the feelings of another person. It involves being able to put oneself in another's shoes and imagine how they might be feeling, without necessarily feeling those emotions oneself. Empathy is a fundamental human trait and an important component of social connections, communication, and building relationships. While empathy is a general human trait, being an empath is a specific personality trait, one that not everyone possesses.

We also hear about highly sensitive people (HSPs) who have a heightened sensitivity to stimuli, including sensory input, emotions, and environmental factors. They may be easily overwhelmed by loud noises, bright lights, or crowded environments, and they, too, may be highly affected by the emotions of others. However, while HSPs are very attuned to the world around them, they do not necessarily feel the emotions of others as if they were their own. Instead, their sensitivity is often more focused on their own internal emotions and reactions to the world around them.

It is important for empaths and HSPs to practice self-care, set boundaries, and develop strategies for managing their emotions in order to maintain their mental and emotional well-being. They may also benefit from developing their own emotional awareness and self-regulation skills, to better understand and manage their own emotions while supporting others.

For the non-empaths and non-HSPs in the world, being aware that there are people around you who feel and move through life differently than you is important. You don't need to fully understand what it's like to be an empath or HSP to, first, believe that this is real, and then to support whoever in your life falls into this category.

It may not make sense to you, for example, why someone you love gets so overstimulated in grocery stores or airports, but you can support them nonetheless by validating their feelings, giving them space, respecting their boundaries, and making their chosen supports available to them with ease. In a business context, an HSP, an empath, and even an introvert may absolutely perform better in a remote setting or outside of the open-concept or bullpen-type office space. Make sure to create a space that is conducive for all different types of energy and emotional needs, so your team can feel like they have what they need to be as supported as possible. Something as simple as a place to isolate may make a major difference in the mental and emotional health and productivity of your team.

Also of note, your clients will need and prefer different environments for their involvement in your care, as well! Make sure to gather information about their preferences when you are engaging in your work with them, especially if your work is sensitive in nature.

This was an important lesson for me, personally, especially in pediatric palliative care work. I found myself taking on the emotions of other people, their pain, their fears, doubts, and worries. Eventually, this started to break down my body and affect my overall wellness. I know now that part of the many gifts given to me during that time was to understand the importance of managing my own empathic ability, so I could better serve others.

When we are climbing the ladder to transcendence, we must first learn how to care for ourselves. As our energy and capacity expands, at every step along the process, we will need to spiral up into deeper and deeper levels of emotion and energy management to prepare for the increasing responsibilities that come as we actualize our potential and purpose. In Maslow's Hierarchy, it's called *self*-actualization, because we are learning how to live in our own personal purpose, and part of that process is learning how to put on our own oxygen mask first. Then, we move into *self*-transcendence, because we need to maintain our self in potential, physical, emotional, safety, belongingness, and other needs, *in order* to create the biggest ripple and impact through living out our purpose in service to others. Integrating this level of emotional intelligence is a healthy approach to your personal and purpose development.

As mentioned earlier, thoughts create feelings through the interaction of the brain and the body. So, our thoughts and interpretations of events directly impact how we feel. Emotions and feelings are often used interchangeably, but there is a subtle difference between the two.

Emotions are automatic, physiological responses to stimuli that are hardwired into our brains and bodies. They are typically associated with a specific set of bodily sensations and changes, such as changes in heart rate, breathing, and muscle tension. Emotions are usually brief and intense, and can be triggered by external events, thoughts, memories, or physical sensations.

Feelings, on the other hand, are conscious experiences that are generated in response to emotions. Feelings are the mental interpretation of our emotions and are shaped by our thoughts, beliefs, memories, and past circumstances. Feelings are more complex and nuanced than emotions; they can involve a range of sensations and qualities, such as pleasantness, intensity, and meaning.

To give an example, imagine you are walking down a dark alley late at night and suddenly hear a loud noise. Your body might react with an automatic fear response, such as increased heart rate, sweating, and tense muscles. This fear response is an *emotion*. Your conscious experience of this fear, such as feeling scared, anxious, or unsafe, is a *feeling*. Your feeling of fear might be influenced by your past memories, beliefs about the safety of dark alleys, and thoughts about what the noise might be.

Another example might be feeling sad after the loss of a loved one. The emotion of grief might manifest in physical symptoms such as crying, feeling heavy in the chest, or having trouble sleeping. Your conscious interpretation of this emotion might involve feelings of sadness, loneliness, emptiness, or despair, which are shaped by your memories of your loved one, your beliefs about death and loss, and your thoughts about the future without them.

Emotions are not only held in our minds; they are also carried in our bodies. Negative incidents, such as stress, anxiety, and trauma, can leave physical imprints on our bodies, while positive events, such as love, joy, and connection, can create sensations of lightness and ease.

Let's explore in more detail how emotions are carried in our bodies:

- ❖ **Stress**: Stress is a common negative emotion that can cause physical tension and discomfort in the body. When we undergo stress, our muscles tense up, our breathing becomes shallow, and our heart rate increases. Chronic stress can lead to headaches, muscle pain, digestive problems, and even cardiovascular disease.

- ❖ **Anxiety**: Anxiety can manifest in physical symptoms such as chest pain, shortness of breath, and a racing heart. Anxiety can also lead to muscle tension, shaking, sweating, and digestive issues.

- ❖ **Trauma**: Traumatic occurrences can leave a lasting imprint on the body, leading to chronic pain, fatigue, and other physical symptoms. Trauma survivors may live through hypervigilance, a heightened state of alertness that can lead to tension and anxiety.

- ❖ **Love**: Positive emotions such as love, compassion, and connection can create sensations of warmth, ease, and lightness in the body. Love can release feel-good hormones like oxytocin, which can lower stress levels and promote relaxation.

- ❖ **Joy:** Joyful encounters can also create physical sensations of lightness and happiness. When we feel joy, we may sense an expansion in the chest, a smile on our face, and a spring in our step.

- ❖ **Gratitude**: Gratitude is another positive emotion that can create physical sensations of warmth and well-being. When we feel grateful, we may have a sensation of fullness in the chest and a relaxed state in the body.

These emotions and feelings trigger different hormones in our bodies, which highlights the importance of managing and attending even to your hormone health in your journey of actualizing your potential. High cortisol levels from stress are incredibly damaging to our bodies and minds, as they create inflammation and, eventually, disease in our bodies. Hormone management is not something that is traditionally taught to individuals, and many people even believe that hormones just are what they are. However, with changes in our coping with stress, attention to our sleep habits, what we are eating, how we are moving our bodies, and how we are paying attention to our natural cycles, we can effectuate significant change in our hormones.

One of the most impactful, efficient, and evidence-based practices that integrates both the psychological and physiological components of emotions, including reduction of cortisol and other stress hormones, came to my attention much later in my career. It is the Emotional Freedom Technique (EFT), also known as "tapping." This is a form of alternative therapy that combines elements of acupuncture and psychology to help individuals release negative emotions, reduce stress, depression, and anxiety, and overcome trauma or physical issues. EFT can be practiced on your own or with the guidance of a trained EFT practitioner, which makes it one of most portable and easily implementable tools to bring all of what we are learning together into one package.

I have had the great privilege of teaching hundreds of people this technique, as a certified Emotional Freedom Technique practitioner, and even so, I am constantly astounded and inspired by its effectiveness. I've taught this tool to high-powered business leaders and seen them respond so well, they choose to bring their whole team and family into the process of learning this skill.

I've taught my own children to use this technique to regulate their emotions during a tantrum or upset, and one of my greatest joys is now seeing them ask for this support when they become aware that they need regulation through tapping for themselves and their siblings. I've personally seen addictions broken, level-ten pain eliminated, fear of flying overcome, and some of the most resistant people come to use tapping in all areas of their life with success.

EFT is based on the concept that negative emotions and circumstances can cause disruptions in the body's energy system, which can lead to physical and emotional symptoms. By tapping on specific points on the body while focusing on the negative emotion or event, the individual can release the emotional energy blockage and reduce its associated symptoms.

Here are the basic steps for EFT:

1. Identify the problem: Begin by identifying the specific negative emotion, traumatic memory, or physical symptom that you want to address.

2. Rate the intensity: Rate the intensity of the emotion or symptom on a scale of 0 to 10, where 0 is no intensity and 10 is the most intense. This is called the Subjective Units of Distress (SUDs), as illustrated below.

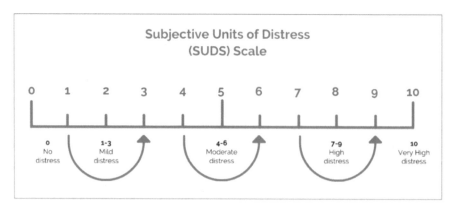

3. Set up the phrase: While tapping on the side of hand point (the fleshy part on the outside of the hand), repeat a set-up phrase that acknowledges the problem and affirms self-acceptance. For example, "Even though I have this (problem/symptom), I deeply and completely accept myself."

4. Tap through the points: Using two fingers, tap each of the following points on one side of the body while repeating a reminder phrase that acknowledges the problem. The points are:

* inner eyebrow

* side of eye

* under eye

* under nose

* chin

* collarbone

* under the arm, and

* top of head.

5. Repeat this sequence three times while focusing on the negative emotion or symptom, and begin talking through some of the negative thoughts you are experiencing, either out loud or to yourself internally.

   Eventually, you can shift the narrative to a more positive version of the reality you are in: pivot your thoughts, feelings, and emotions to a more empowering understanding. If you are unsure of how to shift to a more loving dialogue, that's okay; just continue to use the set-up statement or even a short word or phrase that illustrates your current circumstance.

   For example, if you can't sleep and are tapping to support falling asleep, you can simply repeat to yourself "sleep," and it will work just as well as an elaborate script.

6. Rate the intensity again: After tapping through the points, rate the intensity of the emotion or symptom again on a scale of 0 to 10 using that same SUDs scale from the beginning of the process.

7. Repeat as needed: Repeat the tapping sequence as needed until the intensity of the emotion or symptom is reduced to 0 or a low level, preferably at least about a level two or three.

The Emotional Freedom Technique has become a personal staple in my home and in my business. When I first learned this tool, I wasn't sure it was actually going to help, and I even found it to be a little strange! I resisted it for a while, until I felt the magic in my own body. Now that I've personally adopted and witnessed the effectiveness and efficiency of this tool with so many entrepreneurs, I am joyfully sharing the wisdom with as many people as will listen!

Gratitude

Research on gratitude has shown several positive effects on various aspects of well-being, including emotional, mental, spiritual, relational, and even business well-being. Gratitude has been associated with increased levels of positive emotions such as joy, enthusiasm, and optimism.

Research published in the *Journal of Positive Psychology* suggests that writing letters of gratitude can lead to lasting improvements in mental well-being and life satisfaction. Research published in the *Journal of Applied Psychology* suggests that expressing gratitude in the workplace can enhance employee performance and organizational outcomes.

There is a difference in the positive impact on our mental, emotional, and physical wellness between simply saying, "Thank you," and actually feeling appreciation. There is an even greater difference between feeling grateful and expressing that gratitude directly to another person.

The research shows us that the more we authentically feel that gratitude and, better yet, express that gratitude directly, the greater positive benefits we can come in contact with in our bodies, our minds, and our experiences. Then, we are fully leveraging possibility in the universal laws, such as the Law of Attraction and Focus, because, when we are truly feeling these chosen manifestations, we are vibrating those potentials at the highest frequency, making them far more likely to happen. Again, it's not just think and grow rich; it's think *and* feel and grow rich!

Not to mention, when our team, staff, and colleagues feel truly appreciated, performance and morale increases, company loyalty improves, and internal motivation is enhanced. When our clients feel appreciated and cared for, they are more likely to provide warm personal introductions and become repeat customers themselves.

When we take that time to feel and express gratitude, our business improves, as well! We are better able to shift out of negative mind states, we can problem-solve better, and we have an overarching air of positive connection to what we do, who we serve, what we offer, and the impact we can create.

Gratitude is also *free*. It is one of the easier emotions and feeling states to access, and it can change the trajectory of an entire state of affairs very efficiently and effectively.

It is not a universal panacea, and certainly we don't want to move into toxic positivity by shutting down how other people go through real challenges in life. We don't need to impart "shoulds" onto people or invalidate their feelings if they're not feeling grateful at first. If we are facing challenging times, when we are ready to explore a different outlook or shift those emotions, gratitude can be a great place to start. We can undergo difficult challenges *and* be grateful.

Gratitude is something you can cultivate. It is something that you can practice and a skill you can build over time.

When we look more closely at the outer reward that so many business owners seek, it's often related externally to business development. Many business owners have the same concerns:

- ❖ Where is my next tier-one client coming from?
- ❖ How am I going to grow my business?
- ❖ Where do I find my customers?

When we tap into the power that building a referral culture can create, we begin to understand just how valuable it can be to nurture personal introductions. Gratitude is the #1 most important ingredient to building a successful referral practice. Let's take a deeper look at just how intricately the skill of gratitude plays into the process of building a referral culture.

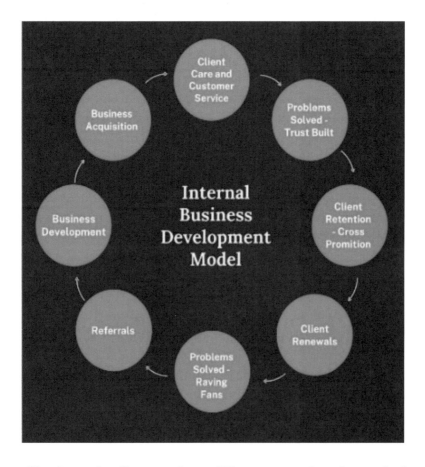

Check out the diagram above. What you see there is a cycle that can help you get a sense for what warm marketing through referral-culture building can do for your practice.

When we introduce gratitude throughout this business cycle, it's extraordinary how the ripple effect manifests into happier clients, more people to serve, and therefore increased revenue! I see this happen all the time in business ownership, after the simple shift of integrating gratitude intentionally and authentically into their business process.

First things first, referral-building is business development. I have been able to create a multiple six-figure-producing practice for over ten years consistently, with referrals as my primary source of new business. That said, it is critically important that you pay attention to the flow of this process, as you begin to learn to successfully create a referral practice.

In short: every step of the way, gratitude comes into play. The first, most obvious way that gratitude is important in the referral process is to be appreciative when you receive a referral. When someone opens their network to your care, that means they trust you, they value what they've accomplished under your care, and they want to share that value with the people who matter most to them by offering a personal introduction. When you receive that high compliment, the first, most critical step is always to express and authentically feel grateful for the chance to provide that care to their network.

Notice that I said *authentically* feel; this is not just about saying thank you for the sake of saying thank you. There's a difference between saying thank you genuinely versus saying thank you with entitlement, desperation, scarcity, or no emotion at all. Your clients will feel the difference. If you want happy clients and the cycle of referrals to continue into a snowball that creates a referral culture, you must truly learn to get in touch with what it means to feel and express gratitude authentically.

If you bring that new client into your care, there are a variety of ways to continue the gratitude throughout the process. For example, when you meet with this prospect who came from a personal introduction, pause to verbally make note in your initial conversations that you recognize and are deeply grateful for the fact that your client made this connection and referral to bring you together today. That creates instant "surrogate trust" and warmth in a relationship, as you are reminding this person that they came from a trusted individual by showcasing gratitude and respect for that relationship.

It is also the first of a variety of referral seeds that will be planted throughout the relationship from an authentic place of gratitude, which will gently show your client:

1. You are grateful.
2. Referrals are welcome here!
3. We are open for business!

Please make note: it is also critically important that you let your clients know you are open to taking referrals and personal introductions. I've heard so many stories where people are hearing things like, "You are so busy, I didn't think you had any space to take anybody else on!"; "I wasn't sure if my friend or family member is a good fit, so I didn't connect you."; or even "I was worried that, if I started referring business to you, I wouldn't be able to keep you as my provider, so I intentionally left you the best kept secret!" The strategic combination of gratitude and direct requests create a healthy business relationship.

You can keep the gratitude chain going by actively listening and thanking your client when they share their deep concerns and fears; by being appreciative when they follow up with any paperwork or next steps you requested during your time together; or by genuinely showing how grateful you are to be able to work with loving, caring people like them in the work that you love so dearly.

Gratitude creates warmth.

Warmth creates trust.

Trust is the foundation of any successful relationship, business or otherwise.

As you can see on closer examination, there is a very good reason to bring awareness to the reality of emotion in business and intentionally learn to steward the emotions and feelings that have been present all along!

Managing Emotions and Feelings Integration

Summary: Emotions are natural and human. Embracing them and learning how to work with them will help you become happier, healthier, and wealthier.

Resources

Gratitude

Building a Referral Culture

Emotional Freedom Technique (EFT)

The Emotional Freedom Technique

Tapping Points

IE — INNER EYEBROW
TOP OF HEAD — TH
SE — SIDE OF EYE
UNDER NOSE — UN
UE — UNDER EYE
UNDER THE LIP ON CHIN — UL
CB — COLLAR BONE
HEART CENTER
UNDER THE ARM — UA
SIDE OF THE HAND — SH

Raeanne Lacatena
HOLISTIC BUSINESS COACHING

Chapter Eleven

Managing Behaviors and Actions

"It is not a question of whether you 'have what it takes,' but of whether you take the gifts you have — they are plenteous — and share them with all the world."

—Neale Donald Walsch

PART OF THE ART OF self-potential is the willingness to step out of your comfort zone into what can sometimes feel like challenging circumstances. In order to expand your risk tolerance, your understanding of what's possible, and your resilience, we must leave our comfort zones.

Actualizing your potential takes effort. You are worth the effort. It takes discipline, commitment, and action. There is work needing to be done to grow into your potential.

It's both:
- ❖ Believe and do.
- ❖ Plan and be spontaneous.
- ❖ Risk and reward.

Intentionally putting yourself into peak performance opportunities can help you stretch and grow those muscles, whether physically, emotionally, mentally, or in some other combination. What is something risky enough to grow your capacity that is safe enough to do now, so you aren't sent into a fight-flight-or-freeze fear response?

My colleague Sean Swarner is a multiple world-record-holder and multiple-time cancer survivor who has built a business under the premise that, by putting in the mental and physical work necessary to climb Mt. Kilimanjaro, you will be better able to take on anything that life brings your way and better set up for success to grow into your potential. He uses many principles—such as core values, awareness, mindset work, and self-development skills—to help people accomplish more than they dreamed imaginable by developing their mental determination and grit in combination with their physical strength in order to accomplish a major, peak-performance goal. And he happens to do so with only one lung!

The phenomenal journey he takes his participants through highlights the need for the internal and external shifts necessary to get those high-level goals accomplished, like gathering the mental and physical fortitude to climb the tallest freestanding mountain in the world.

We've spent some time really learning how to integrate the feminine back into business through managing our thoughts and emotions. These changes can play a huge role in your self-actualization. That said, we must remember that it is *both* the feminine *and* the masculine integration. We need to think, feel, *and* act to truly create the impact we are called to make in the world. We do need the pendulum to swing back and forth in both worlds. It can't be either/or. It needs to be both/and.

This is the premise that comes through in the process of holistic business coaching. Who you are anywhere is who you are everywhere. What you are doing, how you are feeling, who you are being, and what you are thinking in all of the categories of your life are all part of who you are, which invariably affects your business. Beliefs become thoughts, thoughts become emotions, and the energy in emotion becomes action, which then produces our results.

For example, when entrepreneurs go into their process of business planning, many of us tend to focus on the type of goal-setting that highlights the numbers, the financial elements, the KPIs, and strategies that will help us get to the financial outcomes we desire for our business.

This is a critical part of business planning that deserves attention, no question. As entrepreneurs, it is imperative that we are aware of where we are headed, how we are going to get there, what we need to do to achieve the results we desire, and how strategically to move toward those results we seek.

More masculine models, like the SMART method of goal-setting, are very useful for paying attention to the most important pieces of goal-setting. This method helps sort through goals in the following format:

This process is very useful in creating actionable clarity and generating a pathway to success. If this is where you stop your goal-setting process, however, you are leaving so much potential on the table. There are critical factors and categories to attend to that are more feminine in nature.

If we only attend to the numbers, financials, and what we are *doing*, we miss the most important parts of the success process: who we are *being*, what we are *thinking*, how we are *feeling*, and *why* we are doing all of this anyway.

I encourage you to slow down and back up to get clear about why you are engaging in your business to begin with, internally and externally, front stage and back. When we have a clear understanding of our "why" or our mission, it helps us to stay grounded and focused no matter what life or business throws your way.

A mission statement is a concise and specific statement that describes an organization's fundamental purpose and reason for existence. It outlines what the organization does, who it serves, and how it goes about achieving its goals. For example, a nonprofit organization might have a mission statement that reads: "To provide education and support to underprivileged children in developing countries."

Then, spend some time exploring who you want to be, think, and feel in your business.

❖ What type of business owner do you choose to be?

❖ How do you want your customers, clients, and prospects to feel, when they are in your presence?

❖ What do you stand for in your business?

❖ What are your values, and what is your purpose?

❖ What do you want to feel because of achieving your goals?

❖ What do you choose to believe about your business? What thoughts would best support those beliefs?

❖ What would be *amazing* in your business this year?

We want to start with the end in mind, and we want to practice feeling and living those realities now.

For example, I've seen many business owners and teams take the step to develop a loose mission and vision statement, with the guidance of a marketing team, for their website. They might look up how to do this online and treat it like a box to check in the process of building out their social media, website, and business process. However, I've seen those same business owners lose sight of their true aligned mission and values to the detriment of their business success, their team growth, their revenue and production, and frankly, their happiness.

We don't want to create a mission for the sake of creating a mission. We want to live into those missions and values every single day and practice generating feelings, thoughts, beliefs, and actions that create aligned results, in order to be a beacon for that mission.

To fully actualize our potential, it is wise to also consider where we are headed, who we want to be, and what that means for us as an individual. Begin thinking about your vision statement, which is a statement that describes the organization's desired future state. It articulates what the organization wants to achieve in the long term and provides a clear and inspiring picture of what success looks like.

A well-crafted vision statement can inspire and motivate employees and stakeholders to work toward a common goal. For example, a technology company might have a vision statement that reads: "To become the global leader in innovative technology solutions that transform lives and businesses."

Take this process a step further by going more deeply into the full expression of your life, and set some targets and/or engage in some journaling to explore your ideal being, thinking, feeling, and doing in all of the following categories and any others that matter to you:

- ❖ Relationships
- ❖ Time
- ❖ Parenting
- ❖ Physical Well-Being
- ❖ Mental and Emotional Health
- ❖ Spiritual Evolution
- ❖ Charitable Giving
- ❖ Travel and Recreation
- ❖ Education

Then, the work is to begin "chunking down" even further to what specific activities or tasks you as an individual and your team need to perform in order to achieve each particular goal or objective. Key performance indicators, or KPIs, are an important part of the goal-setting process, as they help to break down the overall goal into actionable steps that can be measured and tracked.

When setting goals, it's essential to identify the KPIs or those key actions, behaviors, and activities that will help to achieve the desired outcome. For example, if the goal is to increase sales revenue by twenty percent in the next quarter, the KPIs might include:

- ❖ Conducting market research to identify new target audiences.
- ❖ Developing a new marketing campaign to attract new customers.
- ❖ Training staff to improve customer service and product knowledge.
- ❖ Creating incentives to encourage staff to reach their targets.
- ❖ Analyzing data to identify trends and opportunities for improvement.

By identifying the KPIs that will contribute to the overall goal, it becomes easier to monitor progress and adjust as needed. KPIs provide a clear roadmap for achieving the goal, and they allow for better tracking and measurement of performance, especially when you add in the details of the SMART attributes to make each KPI as specific, measurable, attainable, relevant, and time-bound as possible.

It's also important to prioritize the KPIs based on their impact on the overall goal. Some KPIs may have a greater impact than others, so it's essential to focus on the ones that will make the most significant difference. This can help to ensure that time and resources are allocated effectively to achieve the desired outcome.

Once your goals and KPIs are defined, develop a project plan that outlines the specific steps you need to take to achieve your goals. This plan should include timelines, milestones, and any necessary resources or personnel. Then, clearly define who will be responsible for each aspect of the project, and make sure everyone understands their roles and responsibilities.

You will want to then monitor progress regularly toward your goals and KPIs, and adjust as needed to keep your project on track. This may include revising your project plan, reassigning responsibilities, or setting up systems and processes to track your progress through technology, and a clear, scheduled meeting plan to review your progress on a regular basis. Now that you have put a plan together, complete with your mission, vision, values, and KPIs, it's time to implement that plan through supportive accountability and action.

An important note: often, business owners will come to coaching asking for "someone to hold them accountable." Accountability is an *inside* job. Nobody can really hold you accountable because nobody can control your behavior except yourself. You can certainly receive support, feedback, or direct challenges to any behaviors, thoughts, or feelings that are no longer in alignment with your ultimate goals, your purpose, and the impact you are looking to create. However, at the end of the day, accountability needs to come from within. If you are struggling with accountability, that is internal work; we explore it by diving deeply and understanding the root of the resistance to your achievement and goal-focused internal self-direction.

Then, it's time to enact your plan, while evaluating throughout the process. One key ingredient to successful entrepreneurship is the willingness to move forward, no matter the outcome. Remember, business ownership is an inherently creative process. The marketplace, your customers, prospects, social media, your sales process—all of it is *information* and *feedback*.

Entrepreneurs who can approach their business, their planning, implementation, and evaluation of their business with this neutral approach are often the most successful and, frankly, the happiest business owners. They see something happen in their business, reflect with curiosity on what the information and feedback is trying to tell them, and then pivot. It's a joyful process, instead of one that creates suffering.

We hear the adage "the market doesn't lie." There is some truth to that thought, but too many business owners interpret a "failure," a missed opportunity, a lost sale, or a lapsed customer as a problem or evidence that the market is telling them that their business, service, or product is failing or not worthy. Instead, what we want to do here is notice that incoming information as feedback, first by becoming aware, and then getting curious: "Hmm, that's interesting. What could the market be trying to tell me? And how can I take that information and move forward?" It's this energy of: "Okay, here we are. What's next?" Or even better: "Fascinating! What do we get to do *next*?"

So far, we've handled the "why" in our business through our mission and; "what" we are going to do to get there. Now, let's also talk about, "Who can we serve and how?"

In marketing, we see a formula that helps us to become clearer about who we serve and how it can be helpful to them:

> *I help _____ people so that they can_____.*

In the process of actualizing your potential, another incredible opportunity is to get clear about this very fact: How are you helping others? And in what ways can you be of service?

To get out of our heads and into the hearts of others can be a fantastic higher-fuel source and guiding light during the process of accessing your own potential.

When we come from a place of "how does this benefit me?" or "what do I want to accomplish for me, about me?" we can often be limited in our ability to see the greater scope, potential, or possibilities. The self-focused entrepreneur can also be narcissistic, driven by ego or pride, and can become incredibly controlling, selfish or greedy.

When you come to your life or business from a place of "what's in it for me?" instead of "how can I serve the greater good?" you are seeing the scope of possibility through a limited lens and with singular focus. To settle into the exponential power of service, get creative about how you can create win/win/win/win/win experiences: a win for you, a win for the other, a win for the larger stakeholders, a win for the community, and even a win for the world at large. In so doing, you will operate from a leveraged place.

This will not only help your marketing, messaging, and scalability, as a business owner, it will also help you more deeply connect to your mission, vision, and what's possible on a grander scale. Then, it's time to take all those components of your holistic plan, internally and externally, and integrate the feminine and masculine. This allows you to go out into the world to make an impact by creating value.

Value can sometimes feel like a buzzword in business. It is often used but rarely understood and even more challenging to grasp for some business owners.

We hear advice delivered about social media, for example, that encourages people to offer "value-based posts" or to make sure your offer or product is "jam-packed with value." However, there is rarely any further explanation about what this even really means or looks like in real time.

While there is certainly some truth and merit to this guidance, there is more to the understanding of the principles and internal-versus-external value that needs to be explored by the entrepreneur, in order to truly grasp what value means to them and their market. The idea of value, like everything else we've gone over in this book, is subject to the reality that we need to go inward to get the external results.

On the surface, people believe that value speaks to what something is worth. This is a very slippery slope in business, especially for the business owner, when we understand the principles of going inward to go outward. When someone classifies something has value tied to its worth, and the offer is a professional service or related to something that you created as an artist, for example, the business owner runs the risk of falling into some negative core-belief systems when their product or service is not flying off the shelves for whatever reason. If they have the deeply held belief that they are not worthy, that they aren't important enough, that they don't have what it takes, that they are not deserving, or any other closely held negating belief where they are making value about worth, they run the risk of making their sales about their own inherent value or worthiness as a human being. "No sales" quickly then becomes "no worth."

This is to preclude the idea that the work starts with internal beliefs around value and worth, not so much the external natural and expected fluctuations in the business. Instead of letting a down month be the beginning of the end, when someone comes from an abundance mindset, with a confident belief in the value of their product or service, they can stay neutral and/or positive about their business, no matter what is happening. Because they believe they are worthy, they do not question the value of their offer, the potential of their business, or their own personal intentions. Any shakiness in that truth is just another opportunity for internal self-development, which will open the door to possibilities to create more value and roll with the market with more joy, flow, ease, creativity and grace.

Another internal shift that is necessary when it comes to integrating the full expression of value is to recognize that value isn't just reflected in that one moment in time, that one call offered to a client, that singular proposal you are inviting someone to participate in, or that one product sale. So many business owners fall into a transactional understanding of their business, offer, service, and/or product, and they end up being pushed into a scarcity-based conversation, which further devalues the offer at hand.

Value encompasses all that you are, all that you've done, all the training and mastery and expertise you've accumulated over your lifetime, career, and business, all that you've read, studied, and practiced; all the successes and failures, all of the time you've put in, all of the trials and tribulations that your customer gets to avoid, and all the expertise you bring to the table in your invitation, product, or offer. Value is all of you, and you deserve to be remunerated at the level of value that is found in all that you are and all that you've done to deliver at the level of mastery you've accomplished up until that point. All that *gets* to be included in your value proposition.

When you fall in the trap of the transaction, trading time for money or discounting what you are offering, this is a symptom of a deeper issue: that you don't fully honor your mastery and/or are carrying one or more versions of a limiting belief that is not allowing you to own your power.

The most frequent way that I see this manifest is when business owners go to create their offers or to price their products and services. I worked with a career changer who came to our work thinking he couldn't charge anything at all for his coaching services, even though he had nearly four decades of experience with coaching in a variety of capacities in a corporate setting. He was so focused on the change of the model in how he was going to be offering care, through business ownership, that he couldn't even see the vast skill and value he brought to the table for his coaching clients.

When we are used to trading time for money, instead of living into the full value that we create in the world, we set ourselves up to be underpaid, underappreciated, and eventually resentful to our business, when it doesn't produce in the way we would prefer. You aren't just trading an hour for what you bring to the table. The value you create encompasses all that you are and all that you've become. It takes some unlearning of the transactional approach in order to fully honor your value and set your offers and pricing appropriately. When you step into the full expression of your value, that's when you can truly be remunerated appropriately for your time.

The next step is to become aware of what limiting beliefs you are carrying about yourself into your business, and then to find that path from awareness into reprogramming those diminishing beliefs, using whatever modality supports you in doing so. Remember, it's natural to spiral back to our deep core beliefs at every stage of our evolution. This work is a life's work. When you notice something pulling you into the lower modes, it is just another opportunity to further evolve. Instead of getting frustrated if there is a part of your life or segment of your brain that tends to fall back into the lower modes, the seeker of transcendence just notices, becomes aware that there are more areas where they can continue to grow, through doing the inner work, in order to create a bigger impact and ripple effect.

All human beings have challenging events in life that trigger us back to our earliest wounds. I have seen business leaders carry out the wound that "they didn't belong" for their entire career; it spirals them right back to when they didn't get picked for a team for flag football or weren't accepted in the "cool club." To the developing brain, this might have been the worst day of a young person's life and, if not addressed, could continue to cycle through the entrepreneur's life and business.

Perhaps, when they don't hit their goals, don't receive the public recognition, or don't get invited to the company awards ceremony, it might send them right back to those core feelings from that early memory in childhood, and thus they spiral down to their belongingness wound or down Maslow's Hierarchy to their esteem needs. If they continue to carry out that story, they may face self-doubt, self-judgment, anger, frustration, or embarrassment, which are incredibly low-vibration emotions to try to run your business from.

These low vibration emotions are distracting at best; however, they also lead to results that might create self-sabotaging behaviors, judgment of others, harsh comparison of self to others, or avoidance of the activities necessary to help us get out of that self-negating loop.

The work-around is to create awareness of our triggers and limiting beliefs or realities and then heal those wounds. This allows us to become aware of when we are being sent into a downward spiral and practice closing the gap between the time we are triggered, the moving through of those feelings, and then the choice to patch the wound, so as to be able to spiral back up again. If we keep repeating the story on the flag football field, we will consistently be stuck in the lower modes. However, when we become aware and heal, we can notice those feelings and climb out of the old wounds into the higher modes, which makes us more likely to be happier, healthier, and wealthier in our personal and professional pursuits.

Practices like the Havening Technique (where you cross your arms at your collar bones and gently stroke down your shoulders, arms, forearms, and palms), Emotional Freedom Technique (tapping), or formal thought-work tools are my modalities of choice when the fear-brain kicks. These help me to calm the central nervous system and open myself up to another way of thinking about what I am feeling and experiencing in those moments of resistance, fear, overwhelm, anxiety, etc.

Once you are thinking more calmly and creatively about your circumstances, and once you have remembered your higher self's preferred thoughts, emotions, beliefs, and actions and done any necessary reprogramming, you can start to go to the external to look at value differently.

Caveat: The external is important and necessary in business. The point here is not to vilify marketing or business strategy, tactics, KPIs, studying the market trends, appropriately pricing your offer and products, etc. However, when that is the only thing you attempt to shift in your business, you are leaving so much on the table, and you will bump up against the same thing repeatedly, expecting a different result. (Again: insanity!)

One external take to really consider from a high-level transcendent state in your business is thinking about value in terms of impacting the *other*. With value, we want to recognize that it is, in part, how we feel internally about our innate value, our business worth, etc.; however, it is also what the customer, client, and prospect feels about the value we are providing. Just like your internal value lives inside of you, the perceived value of your offer lives inside of the *client.*

As a business owner, you do need to do the work to understand the market, your ideal client, your customer avatars, and competitors. There is value in studying the trends and fluctuations, and in understanding the fears, doubts, worries, problems, and desires of your customers and how your product or service might solve those needs and wants. It is both. Settle into your own core value *and* understand what your client values.

It can be incredibly helpful to dive into a values exercise, starting with your own internal value system and your business value system, and then make sure that those values are aligned with your ideal client and your value proposition.

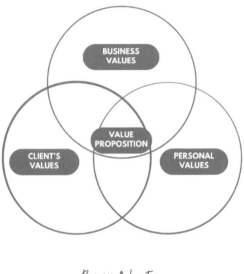

Racanne ❧ Lacatena
HOLISTIC BUSINESS COACHING

Business owners who understand this idea that value lives in the mind of the other, after they also have cleared any limits to what value means to themselves internally, are able to stand confidently in the value they offer. They can then invite the right-fit client into their offer with an air of non-attachment, knowing and trusting that they have created favorable conditions for success in the areas that they can control and have released that which they cannot control.

Sometimes, this may result in not moving forward with a client or having to let go of a contract, when you discover a misalignment. Non-attachment helps us to understand that we are looking to work with the right-fit clients, and that, if we take on the wrong-fit clients, it takes away the time, space, and energy for the right people to come into our life and business.

This is when the magic happens and the business takes off to the new heights that the business owner has been craving. They are living their authentic truth, they are actualizing their potential, owning their value, understanding the value of those they serve, and are committed to making a positive impact in the lives of their ideal customers and/or the world at large.

Their business model is transcendent.

They are at the pinnacle expression of their values, and they know there is only more to explore, they get to unearth more growth and development, and they are creating a lasting ripple effect, now and in the future legacy of their business.

One of the most frustrating trends I see in the world of business coaching is the consistent recommendations to enroll in one course using one particular framework to build your business in one particular way. It's all too common to see coaches and consultants speak as if their way is the only way to be successful; and that their "tried and tested methods" will be universally applicable to anyone who just invests in their course or program.

This claim doesn't consider that every human being is unique, and will therefore need different approaches to support their business. Of course, there is value in particular tools and techniques, if they are used as a *part* of the process, and if they are tested to the *individual* for success, instead of the masses.

I encourage business owners to practice learning how to tap into their own internal wisdom to explore what works best for them. To actualize your potential in life and business, you must learn who you are, so that you can be true to yourself in all aspects of your life and business, authentically and in an aligned fashion. Part of the practice is understanding deeply what your own core values and beliefs are internally and what they are also for your business.

By slowing down to understand these core principles, they can become your guardrails and anchor points to help you make more aligned decisions more efficiently and effectively, and you will be better grounded when the inevitable challenge occurs in your life and business.

Experienced entrepreneurs who are looking at the legacy path for their business can greatly enhance the *value* of their business by doing this deep work, as well. When they have a deep understanding of their mission, vision, values, culture, and purpose, they can create a path that is in alignment with how they see the legacy of their business unfolding, and eventually, they can align with the right-fit buyer to carry on that legacy in whatever way feels right for them.

When we get to the stage of business leadership where we are considering our legacy, the level of impact that we are looking to create is directly related to how willing we are to transcend ourselves. All too often, I hear stories of business leaders who are so self-involved that their legacy plan is only about finding an exact replica of themselves to take over the business. For example, one of the amazing business leaders whom I have supported came to me in preparation for legacy planning for the firm where she was a lead partner.

She has an amazing talent for connecting with people, creating warmth and trust in a relationship, and using her empathic sense to support, nurture, and care for the people in her firm. She also clearly sees the short- and long-term strategy to take the skills, talents, and strengths of the people at her firm and move them toward a tactical strategic outcome that creates more opportunity, more revenue, more retention, and more connection for everyone involved.

Despite my client's being such a valuable asset to everyone she encounters, the CEO at the helm of this firm is stuck in his view of her, based on his traditional-male-ego distortion. He has used many masculine approaches to build his business and been positively reinforced for his behavior for his entire lifetime, because he is, in fact, brilliant and has created stunning success in his conglomerate of agencies. Except, in the process of doing so, his approach has resulted in a firm that lacks warmth and leaves people feeling disconnected in the absence of productivity. People have become numbers and revenue, and they either produce and are highly revered (especially if they are men), or they don't produce and are disrespected or released.

As a result, my client holds a title that in no way reflects the value she brings to the table and is grossly undervalued, underpaid and disrespected in the ways she is spoken to and treated at the firm. While she holds the key to the future success of the firm and is qualified to be the legacy plan to bring the business into the future, she is instead doubted and disrespected.

It is hard for her. Because she develops such care and nurturing for her people, she does genuinely love and care about this CEO, and she sees the greatness he brings to the table. It's especially complicated because he does, on some level, see the value that she brings, too. He just doesn't respect it in the same way as he respects the bottom line or any man doing the job. The future of this industry and, in particular, this firm, is dependent on the key missing ingredients that she brings to the table: empathy and warmth. Unfortunately, *warmth* is not in his vocabulary; *results* are his language and focus. Empathy is not a superpower; it's a weakness.

Even so, she holds the middle road: *both* the strategic vision of the firm *and* the empathy to support and build the people in it *while* producing tremendous results. She has what it takes to lead the firm to even further greatness, because she can create, envision, strategize, produce results, and create a culture of connection. Instead of looking for an exact replica of himself to take over the business, the CEO needs to recognize the changes in the market and the resources available to him right here and right now, while also embracing the changes necessary to be successful in the future.

Our work has been helping this business leader own her personal power first, and then learn how to step into that power and effectively communicate her needs from a place of non-attachment. She now knows that what she does is valuable, that she is worth not only a seat at the table, but more than likely a seat at the head of the table. She is now aware that she is either going to do this work here or somewhere else.

As she steps into her power, either the firm will rise to the occasion and join the reality of the fact that she can carry out and enhance the legacy of this business, or she will bring her brilliance elsewhere. Her confidence is protected, and she is at ease with whatever the outcome.

To transcend, we must let go of what we did to get to where we are in service to the greater good. We need to embrace that the world is changing and that business is changing, and that this is an opportunity not a problem. When we instead use an integrated approach to our leadership, where we can see the skills and abilities of our employees and colleagues, that will help carve a path to a positive future. If legacy is about a lasting impact, suspending the ego and sense of self is a necessary step to the success and longevity of our pursuits. It's not just about the business outliving us; it is about leaving behind a legacy of transformational impact on the lives of those we've served.

Legacy and business exit-planning start internally. You cannot achieve legacy without knowing what legacy means to you personally, and you cannot achieve legacy if your thoughts, beliefs, feelings, and behaviors are not in alignment with that meaning you've assigned. It's not just a balanced book or spreadsheet with numbers. When the business owner craves legacy, they crave impact. They want what they've built to outlive them in a variety of ways. So, getting to the core and heart of it all is where to start. Then, the plan can unfold with the supportive core and foundation in place to help facilitate the decisions, agreements, and next steps to enact that goal of legacy.

In the words of the epic Oprah Winfrey:

> *You're nothing if you're not the truth. The biggest reward is not financial benefit... You can get a lot of great shoes. Nothing wrong with great shoes. But those of you who have a lot of great shoes know that having a closet full of shoes or cars or houses or square footage doesn't fill up your life. It doesn't.*

But living a life of substance can; substance through your service, your offering of your whole self. The baseline for how you live a life of substance is the truth for you. What do you stand for?

When I had finished my school in South Africa, I went to Maya (Angelou) and said, "That school's going to be my greatest legacy."

And Maya said, "You have no idea what your legacy will be. Your legacy is never one thing. It is every life you've touched."

Feel everything with love because, every moment, you are building your legacy.

Managing Behaviors and Actions Integration

Summary: Bring your purpose to the world and make a bigger impact through inspired and aligned action.

Resources

❖ KPIs

❖ Marketing Framework: In marketing, we see a formula that helps us to become clearer about who we serve and how it can be helpful to them.

I help _____ people so that they can_____.

How are you helping others? And in what ways can you be of service?

❖ Know your Value

❖ Value Proposition

❖ SMART Goals

Chapter Twelve

STEAR Clear and Anchor:

A Final Integration

"'Finding yourself' is not really how it works. You aren't a ten-dollar bill in last winter's coat pocket. You are also not lost. Your true self is right there, buried under cultural conditioning, other people's opinions, and inaccurate conclusions you drew as a kid that became your beliefs about who you are. 'Finding yourself' is actually returning to yourself. An unlearning, an excavation, a remembering who you were before the world got its hands on you."

—Emily McDowell

IF WE TAKE ALL THIS wisdom into consideration, we can start to tap into our highest potential.

We are looking to strike the balance between both the feminine and the masculine by feeling into our thoughts and emotions *and* taking action. The emotions we feel become E-Motion or energy in motion. The vibration of the thought is amplified by the feeling, which creates movement, which creates results.

There are plenty of teachers and gurus out there who tout that if you just create a vision board with your internal desires and external preferences and then focus on that vision board, it will manifest. There are even teachers who say that just by speaking it into existence, you are claiming it and therefore it is so. There are definitely instances where this can be true, and I've witnessed that in my own life.

There are far more instances where this is not the case, where waiting for our idea to manifest and not seeing the results creates a negative energy or belief behind what we prefer; then, we actually end up pushing that desired result further away from us.

This is not to knock the vision board or say it's ineffective. I still make a vision board or at least write a letter to my future self every year, to help me focus on what I intend to create in my year ahead and in as much living color and detail as possible. It's unbelievable to witness those goals, intentions, and visions come to life in real time. I definitely recommend spending the time to create your vision in any way that supports you getting those creative juices flowing and helps you to visualize more clearly what you set out to create and achieve. It's powerful.

But we don't stop there. We then need to manage our attachment to those outcomes and make sure we are crafting the full picture, not just in living color, but also in thought, belief, word, emotion, feeling, action, and behavior, too.

Over my last twenty years working in personal development, I have created a tool called STEAR Clear and Anchor. Through this evidence-based framework, I help my clients process and reframe their *Situation* to identify alternatives to their current *Thoughts*, *Emotions*, and *Actions* that will aid in achieving their desired *Results*. Then, I lead them through exercises to *Clear* the negative and *Anchor* in the positive.

At the core of STEAR Clear and Anchor, there are several psychological, evidenced-based practices supporting the process, many of which we have already reviewed in this book. This includes free-association journaling, cognitive reframing, emotional regulation, mindfulness and relaxation techniques, positive psychology, affirmations, self-coaching, and self-reflection. These tried, tested, and proven techniques are seamlessly woven through the framework. They have improved overall well-being and relationships, enhanced decision-making, increased resilience and self-awareness, improved relationships and communication, decreased stress, and increased emotional intelligence, creativity, and personal development.

This framework can completely change the trajectory of entrepreneurs' businesses and lives. There will always be challenges to be dealt with personally and professionally, and this tool has proven effective for all my clients, from new to seasoned entrepreneurs, striving to achieve greater levels of success. The secret? The strategy remains consistent, no matter what the challenge at hand is.

When we take the time to critically think about which behaviors will support our outcome versus deter our outcome, these honest, conscious, and empowering conversations with ourselves can become our reality.

Instead of blaming others, our current conditions, our past, or ourselves, we take control of what we can actually control, which thoughts and feelings we choose to energize. How we respond in action to our present reality is really the only thing we actually have control over. So, when we give that control over to default patterns, blaming, shaming, or unsupportive behaviors, we are letting go of the only areas in our lives where we can effectuate change.

Which thoughts we choose to energize into action is where the power lives.

From a business perspective, this is also where the more masculine energy can be integrated back into the feminine energy, where we are settling into strategies, tactics, attention to numbers, results, outcomes, and key performance indicators. These things matter, and they become matter. When we integrate both the masculine and feminine into the process, we are creating favorable conditions for success.

For example, personally, when it came time to open my own business and step out as an entrepreneur, I knew I needed to create a more robust stream of potential clients to serve, so I started to dabble in different approaches to marketing outside of relying primarily on referrals from existing clients.

I settled on looking at organic marketing through social media outlets like LinkedIn, Instagram, and Facebook, but I had no idea how to make this work as a business owner. I quickly discovered that I had a whole host of limiting beliefs about whether this would be possible or effective or even, frankly, worth the time, energy, and effort.

Thankfully, I had these tools at my disposal and went to work on those beliefs to discover some of what my thoughts and limiting beliefs were trying to show me.

I noticed limiting beliefs about the logistics and thoughts about how much time and energy it would take to build a social media presence. I did the work to decide how much time and energy were aligned with my boundaries, goals, availability, and mental health to put into social media, and I stuck to those boundaries. As the boundaries and my responsibilities change over time, I continue to adjust based on what is right in the moment.

I witnessed my own limiting beliefs about whether I could even be good at marketing at all and quickly recognized, through these tools, that creating a referral and personal introduction culture in my business is, in fact, marketing. And so many business owners crave to create a referral practice! Now, I give myself credit for this as a primary part of my marketing strategy.

I felt fears, doubts, and worries about visibility, being seen, or putting myself out there vulnerably in a more public setting. As a trained mental health therapist charged with protecting the confidentiality of my clients and as a mother charged with protecting my children, this was (and has been) a tough one for me.

I practice gently pulling back the layers of my fears of visibility and moving forward with simple and easily implementable changes to support forward motion. I give myself permission to step out of my comfort zone in phases that feel safe enough and stretchy enough to grow. This has allowed me to grow my social media presence and now has given me the courage to open up enough to share what is written here in this book!

As a result of my willingness to step out of my comfort zone and out of my limiting beliefs about social media, I have met some of the most amazing people all over the world who are doing amazing work in service to a higher mission. I would never have had the chance to connect with these individuals, if I hadn't been courageous and willing to act in alignment with a new set of thoughts and feelings, and aware enough to make different choices in my actions to get these results.

As I built momentum with my social media presence, I also noticed that it became a heavy pull on my time. I started to swing the pendulum in the other direction, from leaning too heavily into the masculine, chasing the algorithm, and getting too rigid in my own expectations of how to build the direction of the organic online marketing; I noticed too much drive and push-myself energy around how to get it done. When I noticed these feelings and thoughts arise, it was time for a reevaluation of the strategy!

This produced two new results for my business. First, I recognized that I needed and deserved more support in my business, so I did the work to find some right values-aligned support to bolster my presence and delegate, in order to regain some of my time and energy, especially as I became more focused on writing this book.

Second, I recognized that this masculine focus was starting to affect my energy, so I went to work on how to create a more feminine approach. As a result, I now practice writing through inspiration in my posts, connecting and communicating with my ideal client through energetics before I even sit down to write. I practice visualization and home in on the feeling I'd like to feel as a result of my efforts on social media, by bringing them into focus as if they are already here now and practicing amplifying that feeling in my body and beyond. I find ways to have more fun, be more vulnerable, and connect more deeply to my mission in relationship with my personal brand, to take into consideration that inner wisdom and collective consciousness, through the art of building a social media presence.

STEAR Clear and Anchor became my primary processing tool to help me navigate all the changes in marketing, visibility, and social media. It all comes back to the integration of all these moving parts in service to what we are building and growing in our business and lives and through to our potential. If you believe, think, feel, and behave in alignment with our highest preferred outcome, then what you seek will seek you.

That doesn't mean everything is going to be a straight-forward, simple path of all success all the time. In business, such as in life, there will always be opportunities in the moment to practice using tools like STEAR Clear and Anchor to get through some of the unavoidable and inevitable dramas on the roller-coaster that business can sometimes be.

Not too long ago in my business, I lived through what I lovingly call my "Tech Tornado." My website had been built and continued to grow for several years of business, and it was tied into client relationship management systems, course-creation sites, landing pages, funnels, email marketing and social media pages. I had done the work to build quite a hefty "tech stack" that was a culmination of a number of different interwoven parts to support my business; they were all layered together to create a client and new customer journey. The whole thing was a bit of a Frankenstein.

I have never felt particularly savvy when it comes to technology and sometimes find myself feeling a little lost or frustrated with tech, because of my lack of knowledge and understanding, especially when coding or development was involved. I know my limits well enough to have brought a number of support structures into my business to help run these elements, as I understand that the more I can focus on my unique ability of coaching, the happier and healthier I am, then the people I serve are better taken care of, and my business runs more smoothly.

At one point, for example, I started to see some outages in my website periodically. Every once in a while, someone would reach out to me to let me know my site was down. I also started to get some feedback from my clients that the number of resources and tech involved in my process would benefit from a new one-stop approach, and I began logging that feedback.

One day, the site went down again, so I reached out to one of my support team and asked them to investigate it. I had been feeling quite sick that day, so I thought it best for someone else to look into it while I rested.

My team member let me know that they had discovered through my web hosting that my site was down, the backups were lost, and the account was in default of payment. He stayed in close contact with customer service as they tried to sort through it all and figure out why my auto payment had not been processed properly.

Soon after my site went down, my email went down, and then my social sites started to come down, my client relationship management system stopped working, and the other sites started to tumble down, as well. I was quite ill at the time, so I decided this was a sign for me to take a step back and let the folks in tech figure it out. There was nothing that I'd done and nothing I could do but let the people who understood these programs try to sort through the rubble.

A few days later, I started to feel better, but the mess only continued to grow. I decided at that point to reach out to customer service myself and escalate the case. Through many, many hours with customer service, weeks of being without a site, needing to create temporary access to my emails, and countless lost opportunity costs, plus hours spent on hold and about five escalations of the case, I finally learned that my site had been subject to a random tech glitch, where my autopay didn't process. It had been lost in tech space for around ten months. The hosting company hadn't been paid, I hadn't been notified, and the site kept running with nobody the wiser. Once this finally came to light, my site was completely missing, and backups were completely gone.

During this roller-coaster period, I had a whole gamut of thoughts and feelings. On the next page is a real excerpt from a STEAR Clear and Anchor that I completed during my Tech Tornado.

As you can see through this example, it could have gone either way! The results could have been very different if I'd leaned into the negative story. Instead of blowing up on an innocent customer service agent or just throwing up my hands and giving up, I instead practiced gratitude, worked on my patience, reached out for support, and knew my limits. I found ways to keep myself grounded, while also being honest with myself about what was outside of my control.

This drama carried on for over a month, and even after I thought it was resolved, it kicked back up again and the sites again went down a few weeks later. I certainly didn't behave perfectly: sometimes I lost my patience; I found myself frustrated and fearful at times. But I did the work to continue to move the needle forward to a positive result.

Now I have a new site, a new client relationship management system, a new team, and more confidence in my tech stack, all of which were important and necessary steps in preparation for launching this book!

I can serve more people, reach more people, and provide better care to my existing and future clients.

I can be grateful for the loud nudge from the universe to move forward in correcting a wobbly tech stack before bringing many more people into my world.

STEAR Clear and Anchor

EXAMPLE

SITUATION	
Website and tech stack are down	

THOUGHTS	
• "Why does this always happen to me?" • "Why can't everything be easy?" • "They better fix this; I'm going to get an attorney" • "Why can't this company figure this out? This is what they are supposed to do for people and my site is just gone" • "I can't handle this now" • "I don't have any time to deal with this" • "This isn't fair" • "I have to figure this out by myself" • "What will my clients think?" • "What business opportunities am I missing out on?"	• "There must be a reasonable explanation for this" • "I'm going to figure this out" • "I trust that this will be resolved soon" • "I have what it takes to get through this" • "I am just going to put this down to come back to it; the most competent people for the job are handing it" • "I trust there is a lesson here" • "I know for sure that I need additional tech support and a new tech stack, now I can mobilize"

EMOTIONS	
Fear, doubt, worry, anger, frustration, alone, scarcity	Gratitude, trust, confidence, calm, focused, supported, abundance

ACTIONS	
Panic, could have been rude, could have approached from a legal perspective, could have jumped the gun and bought a new site, could have made a decision based in fear, could have frozen, could have given up	Stepped away completely to rest, let the experts deal with it, persistent but kind, collaborative, mobilized to change my team and find the right fit support and tech stack

RESULTS	
Out thousands of dollars, faced with creating a new site at a critical time in my business	Saved my site, keep what's good and enhance the rest, improved customer experience, improved team, better prepared for the amazing things that are coming

Raeanne Lacatena
HOLISTIC BUSINESS COACHING

I knew an up-level was coming, but my tech tornado forced me to find the time and the right team to usher me into the next level of my business.

For that, I am grateful.

I also see this as an impactful example of the masculine and feminine blend in a business context. I needed the structure to support my unique ability. I needed to receive support to give more love and service to the world. I needed to destroy it to create a new one. Business can be a series of deaths and rebirths. Destruction *for* creation.

Embracing both sides of the coin can help us weather what sometimes feels like a storm in a more grounded, positive, and welcoming expression of the growth that's coming, instead of resisting or throwing more fuel on the fire.

The STEAR Clear and Anchor Model

This is where the new model comes in: STEAR Clear and Anchor, which can incorporate both informal and formal modes of processing what we are going through psychologically, with personal development, neuroscience, and even energy work. Let's look more closely at this method together.

The STEAR Method is a practical critical-thinking tool that helps us organize our thoughts and create new relationships with whatever is happening in our lives. The method involves breaking down your current reality into its various components, including the facts, thoughts, emotions, actions, and potential results, such as found on the next page. By doing so, we can identify any negative or unproductive thoughts and emotions and reframe them into more useful and positive ones.

The "S" stands for the situation—the facts about the event that lead you to want to process your current set of circumstances. These are just the facts of what's going on right now.

The "T" stands for thought(s)—what thoughts or beliefs are coming up when you think about what you are going through. In this step, we explore all the thoughts that aren't very useful, loving, or productive. This could include thoughts about yourself, others, events, your past, present, future, or anything else that your mind tries to tell you about the facts of what is going on right now.

Raeanne 🍃 Lacatena
HOLISTIC BUSINESS COACHING

BRAIN DUMP: **STEAR Clear and Anchor**

	Perceived Negative Unproductive - Limiting	Perceived Positive Productive - Empowering
S		
T		
E		
A		
R		

CLEAR	
ANCHOR	

The "E" stands for emotion(s)—all the emotions and feelings that come up when you think about those not-so-useful or less-than-loving thoughts. Let yourself explore how it feels to think those thoughts.

The "A" is for action(s)—all the actions that tend to come, have already come, or might come as a result of leaning into those negative or non-useful thoughts or feelings. How would you behave or how have you already behaved because of the way you are thinking and feeling about the event?

The "R" stands for result(s)—imagine the results that could come from engaging those thoughts, feelings, and actions that are not very helpful. If you continue down this road, what could happen?

What are Clearing and Anchoring?

Clearing and anchoring are techniques that can be used to help us release and shift any negative or unproductive thoughts and emotions that we may be holding onto. Clearing involves acknowledging and releasing negative thoughts and emotions from our body and mind, while anchoring involves creating a positive and productive physical, emotional and mental state to reinforce those changes.

When we combine these two practices, we can create a powerful tool to support us in moving forward with our desired outcomes. We are combining formal thought-work, personal development, neuroscience, and some higher-fuel practices, such as spiritual practices or energy work, to fire on all cylinders, change that internal programming, get to the root cause, and create a completely new relationship with that root in order to create completely new patterns, thoughts, emotions, behaviors, and results in our lives.

I encourage the entrepreneurs I serve to create both a formal and informal thought-work practice into their daily lives, to support managing all of what we have gone over through the body of our coaching work together. Formal thought-work typically involves a structured process, often using worksheets or written prompts, to help individuals identify negative or unhelpful thoughts and beliefs and to reframe them into more positive and realistic ones. This process often includes steps such as identifying the trigger, examining the thoughts and beliefs that arise, and challenging or disputing them with evidence or alternative perspectives. Formal thought-work can be a useful tool for individuals who struggle with persistent negative thinking patterns or distorted beliefs; it can help them develop more adaptive thought patterns over time.

Informal thought-work, on the other hand, is more of an ongoing process that can be practiced throughout the day. This involves paying attention to one's thoughts and noticing when negative or unhelpful thoughts arise, then actively working to reframe them in the moment. This might involve questioning the evidence for a thought or belief, considering alternative perspectives, or simply redirecting one's attention to a more positive or productive thought. Informal thought-work can be a useful strategy for individuals who want to develop greater awareness of their thoughts and the impact they have on their emotions and behaviors; it can help them cultivate a more positive and resilient mindset over time.

In the beginning of this framework, or while we are investigating the situation we are in currently, we are really getting present to what is happening right here and right now. So many times, when we attempt to get present, what we end up doing is looping between the three time zones we explored earlier: the past, the present, and the future.

We often take past information and incorporate it into what's going on right here and right now, in order to make an assessment, a judgment, or an excuse. The brain really does want to have all the answers, so it quickly fills in the blanks, based on past information, events, or circumstances. We do this both consciously and subconsciously, so there is a lot to overcome, even in the present moment.

As best possible, the goal is to peel back enough of the onion to really identify what one single, simple, neutral thing is actually happening right here and right now. It's like a still frame or single snapshot in time.

In the next set of phases, we go into the thoughts, emotions, and actions that are creating results around how we are giving the situation meaning. For right now, however, we just focus on attending to what we have in front of us.

Even the art of getting as neutral as possible and pinpointing what's going on right here and right now can be a challenge for some people.

Let's think back to the idea of trauma. Remember: trauma interrupts the typical processing in our brain in such an extreme way that the memory cannot be stored properly, in the "past." That's why trauma affects our present. The brain's whole job is to filter, connect, and integrate information to make sure that our bodies stay healthy, safe, and operating as effectively as possible.

There's a system in the brain called the reticular activating system (RAS). The system's entire job is to take the information coming in from our senses, and filter into it whatever we need to pay attention to in order to keep us safe.

So, when the brain undergoes a trauma, it takes that no-good, very-bad situation and turns it into information about what to avoid for the purposes of keeping us safe; we then watch for anything that looks, smells, or seems to be like that trauma. When the brain notices a warning sign, it triggers a flight-or-fight mechanism, telling us to run, hide, freeze, or fawn because something isn't right, and this will keep us safe.

Whether we like it or not, every single moment the brain unconsciously takes in information through the senses and the RAS, and it filters it through what we already know and want, based on past memories, events, feelings, and circumstances.

Unless we make a concerted effort to overcome this, the RAS will filter in information to keep us safe, but it will also leave out information that could be an opportunity. That is why, as discussed earlier, we work to "reprogram" our default or old patterning.

Here's an example: imagine that, when you were in the third grade and just starting to take standardized tests, you had a teacher whom you really admired and looked up to because they reminded you of your father.

Before you went in to take one test, this teacher told you, "Don't worry about how you're going to do. I don't imagine you'll do very well anyway. You aren't a very good test-taker." And then, they sent you on your way to take a test that you inevitably failed. And that belief became embedded in your brain.

As a very young child, your brain is incredibly impressionable to the feedback given to you about identity, so, if you're told something by someone you respect, whether they are a positive or negative person in your life, you will likely integrate that information as a part of your identity.

Very often, when someone has been given this kind of information about who they are as an individual, they integrate that information and then create self-sabotaging behaviors or self-fulfilling prophecies that reinforce that identity over and over. And so, when they're about to take a test, they don't study or stay up late the night before their test, or they change their answers to the questions a dozen times, because they are so filled with uncertainty about the right answer. And, therefore, they fail.

The brain wants to be right, and so, if the belief lives inside of you that you are a poor test-taker, it will fulfill that request. The more this particular behavior is reinforced, the deeper the belief becomes, and the longer it stays with you. I've had so many business owners come to understand this limiting belief in themselves, when it comes time to get advanced certifications, licensure, or even in continuing education. When these types of limiting beliefs are embedded in their brains as a child, it becomes very difficult to step back into the learning process and successfully pass a test or certification.

In the example here, instead of letting the past voices take over and interrupt your identity as a test-taker, you want to get as clear as possible and as neutral as possible about what is happening right here and right now. Instead of becoming paralyzed, anxious, letting default settings run programs, or overthinking all the possible negative outcomes that might result from taking this test, which is all based in the future, we want to bring it into the present moment. The past is also done. That teacher is no longer here, telling you that you won't succeed.

Right here and right now, you may just be faced with the need to take a test and absorb a set of study material. It is neither positive nor negative, and it currently has nothing to do with what happened before or what's going to happen in the future. It is just a test, and these are just test materials. That is the *Situation* in STEAR Clear and Anchor. For right now, we just want to get to what is actually in front of us right here and right now.

One of the best, most immediately actionable ways to sort through this is to do a free association brain dump or journaling exercise, where we just let our brains dump out anything we are feeling, thinking, being, doing, judging, and are noticing about the set of circumstances. Processing on paper allows us to get it all out there in the open, so we can honor how we're feeling, acknowledge what we are going through, and see it in living color right in front of us. Just this exercise of journaling alone can be incredibly effective to start to move through some of the drama that's happening in the back-and-forth of our mind through all the different time zones: past, present, and future.

Sometimes, this looks like one or two sentences, and sometimes, this looks like a novel. Give yourself enough time to really process it. That is the first step of this process, getting as much as you can out of your brain and onto paper, to externalize what you've been through. When we write down our current conditions with pen and paper, we are signaling to our brain that we are externalizing this challenging event. It's no longer happening. It's a story in our mind that has so much meaning. However, the actual episode is complete for now. This act alone initializes the brain and body to start moving through the upset.

Once you have completed your free association or brain dump, the work now is to go through what you have written down and see if you can discern and derive the actual *facts*. Either get out a colored highlighter or simply circle on the page the actual neutral facts until you can clearly see what is happening in front of you right here and right now. Those facts are the context of what you are going through right now. That is what goes in the "S" line or the Situation at hand.

When we get really good at this exercise, sometimes going through these first two steps, the brain dump and identifying the facts, is enough to move us through whatever is in front of us right now. Journaling can be enough to move on and create a different set of beliefs, thoughts, and behaviors, as well as a new path to positive results. Other times, and more often than not, the rest of the framework is necessary to fully move through any negative or limiting thoughts, emotions, and actions, so we can come to a more positive, loving, and useful version of whatever you're up against right now.

The next step in the process is to separate those facts or current events apart from what you are making them mean through your thoughts. In the STEAR framework, this is the "T" or Thought line. The goal in this step is to practice separating our thoughts into two different categories.

Here are some options to play with. See which feels like the right verbiage for you:

- ❖ Not-So-Useful vs. Useful
- ❖ Negative vs. Positive
- ❖ Bad vs. Good
- ❖ What's not working vs. What's working
- ❖ Problems vs. Opportunities
- ❖ Barriers vs. Options

Start with documenting what thought(s) or beliefs come up when you think about what you are going through right now. In this step, write down all of the thoughts that aren't very useful, loving, or productive. This could include thoughts about self, others, the event, your past, present, future, or anything else that your mind tries to tell you or make this situation mean. Write that down.

Then, the "E" or emotion(s) section is where you write down all the emotions and feelings that come up when you think about those not-so-useful or less-than-loving thoughts. Let yourself explore how it feels to think those thoughts.

On the next page, you will see an Emotions Wheel, to help you practice teasing out how you are feeling versus what you are thinking.

The "A" line is where you document all the actions that tend to come, have already come, or might come as a result of a response and through leaning into those negative or non-useful thoughts or feelings. How would you behave or how have you already behaved because of the way you are thinking and feeling about the event?

"R" is where you can begin to imagine the results that could come from engaging those unhelpful thoughts, feelings, and actions. If you continue down this road, what could happen?

Now, write "S-T-E-A-R" down the page again. Go through this method again and document the same situation, except this time, practice reframing what possible and actual thoughts, emotions/feelings, and actions could produce more loving, useful, and productive results. You may want to start with filling in the desired result and then back-filling the helpful thoughts, feelings, and actions, if you get stuck. Sometimes going through this process will show us a lot of different layers. If so, you can take the time to unpack each one individually in a unique processing and new model of the formal thought-work.

Emotions/ Feelings Wheel

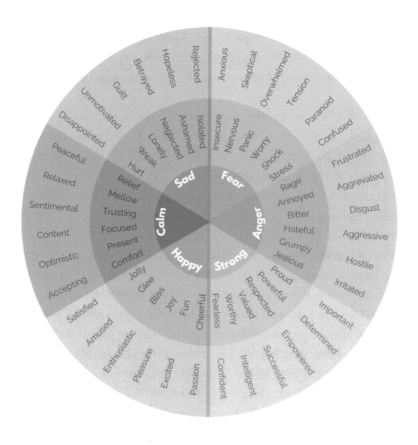

Racanne ❧ Lacatena
HOLISTIC BUSINESS COACHING

Throughout this book, you have explored a variety of resources to help you take what you did in the steps starting with STEAR and really integrate them into your mind, body, life and business. It is incredibly helpful, from the mental realm, to go through this exercise and practice this formal thought-work. If you then take the extra steps to feel the new feelings, to actually clear the old thoughts from the mind, and to embody the new reality through a variety of methodologies, resources, tools, and techniques, you will be firing on all cylinders!

Pulling together body, mind, spirit, and lived experience through slowing down to really clear and anchor is what's next. There are thousands of ways to practice, many of which are scientifically sound and evidence-based.

Clearing exercises are specifically designed to help move the old patterns out of our body, mind, and circumstances. This can be as simple as "shaking it off," calling a friend, or moving our body, or it can be as involved as Reiki or energy work with a practitioner.

Anchoring exercises are then about implanting the new pattern into our body, mind, and experience and grounding in the new reality, here in the present moment. Some examples of anchoring can look like breathing, gratitude, or visualization exercises.

Many of these exercises can serve as both, if you are feeling the positive effects of moving through the old and bringing in the new. For example, the Emotional Freedom Technique integrates body, mind, and spirit, is evidence-based, and helps you clear the old and replace it with the new.

Part of your work is to practice different methods, in order to find which ones resonate best with your personality, your preference, and what fits into your life now. Feel free to download the free resource at the link in the Integration section called the "Self-Care Sandbox," which will help get you started with some ideas of what you could be doing to clear and anchor. This is really a life's work, and it can change from season to season over time. The work now is to get started, see what fits, and begin practicing!

There are also plenty of ways to integrate this inner work directly into your business plan. For example, if you were to use STEAR Clear and Anchor as a business-planning tool, you can tease out what you *don't* want your year to look like and how you *do* want your year to manifest, by carefully considering what thoughts, emotions, and actions you need in order to produce that outcome. Then, it's not only the key performance indicators that need attention; it's also the thoughts and emotions that you are allowing to run throughout your year, which is all we can really control in life to begin with.

You can also use the STEAR Clear and Anchor as a "postmortem" assessment, whether something in your business went well or not the way you would have preferred. To slow down and take the time to process and reflect on how a presentation went to a group or how a proposal landed with a client is a standard business practice that is often skipped over, especially by solopreneurs. The tool allows you to really tease out on a deeper level what worked and what didn't work, what thoughts and emotions led to the success or perceived failure, and what you can do differently next time; it can also give you an implementation roadmap, as well, to take with you on your journey forward.

You can also use it proactively, before you go into a business meeting, critical conversation, or high-stakes environment, to help you sort through what you are feeling and thinking and how you want to behave during the upcoming event, instead of just letting it swirl around in your head, carrying a lot of negativity, fear, doubt, or worry into whatever you need to accomplish.

We can also use the STEAR Clear and Anchor method to set meaningful goals and tap into our vision. For example, you can use the "S," or Situation line, to speak to where you are right now and the "R," or Results line, to reflect where you are headed. Then, sort through the empowering versus disempowering, useful versus not-so-useful, or productive versus unproductive thoughts, emotions, and actions that will either support or limit those particular outcomes.

One side of the page can reflect what you *don't* want to be, do, have, feel, or think, and the other can be the roadmap to success, internally or externally. You can add in the more masculine approach with something like SMART goals, while also incorporating STEAR's more feminine approach to sorting through your internal presentation of goal-setting, as well.

To integrate both worlds in your goal-setting practice will create favorable conditions for success from a place of non-attachment, where you understand your preference and what you can actually control (which thoughts you can energize into emotion and action), while understanding more clearly where *not* to devote your energy of thought, feeling, or action.

The Polaroid

One of my favorite implementations of the STEAR Clear and Anchor model is through what I call the Polaroid method. A Polaroid is a photo that gives us physical evidence of a specific moment in time, one we want to capture and then retain a memory of with a paper snapshot. This is how we use the STEAR Clear and Anchor method through a Polaroid, as well!

There is always something to learn from whatever we are going through in life, and there is *always* something to capture in a moment, as a successful result. When you have a particularly positive outcome, personally and/or professionally, it can be incredibly valuable to slow down and capture all the clues to success that happened during that positive event.

This time, set your STEAR model up by writing it vertically down the page once. Begin by writing in the Situation line what you are celebrating and what went well in life or business. Then, go to work to extrapolate as many of the Thoughts, Emotions, and Actions you used to make that Result happen.

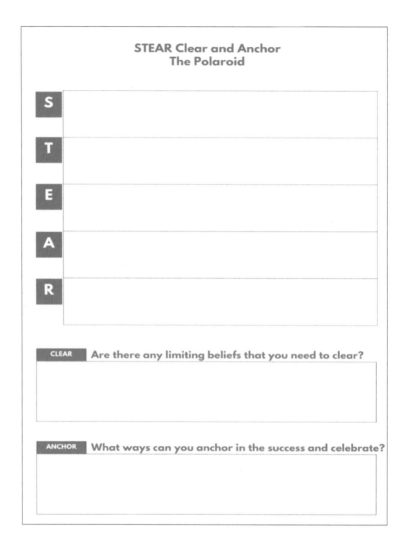

Slow down and capture all those clues to success, so you can replicate them and borrow them in other ways in your life and business! Whatever you did to make that successful experience happen is loaded with clues and evidence, so slowing down to take that snapshot can be very useful for understanding what sorts of thoughts, emotions, and actions helped to make you successful. Then, you can apply them to other possibilities in life and business, as well!

When you do reach a major milestone in our journey, in addition to every small positive step along the way, my encouragement to you is to practice celebrating the successes you've created during the process. Celebration and pausing to honor what you've accomplished is an all-too-often skipped overstep for the high achiever. Entrepreneurs are looking for what they need to do so often, intently that they forget to savor the moment, the feeling, and what is happening right here in the present moment.

Entrepreneurs will also downplay or feel uncomfortable sharing or speaking openly about how much they've accomplished in their lives, due to cultural or gender programming, the desire to remain humble, or a distaste for what feels like flagrant arrogance that they've witnessed from others. As a result, many high achievers avoid celebrating at all, which limits their success.

When we don't take the time to truly honor our accomplishments, we teach our minds, brains, and bodies that we are after the struggle, scarcity, and some of those lower-vibration emotions and events, instead of what we truly want. If we can't own our awesomeness, how can we possibly leverage the Laws of Vibration, Attraction, and Focus to bring more of what we prefer to us?

Celebrating our successes and wins is not something to be glossed over. The positive brain- and body-changing chemicals, such as dopamine, serotonin, endorphins, oxytocin, and even adrenaline, which are released when we truly feel proud, satisfied, excited, relieved, honored, or any other life- and success-affirming emotion, are so important to our healing and continued evolution. These emotions and neurochemicals are high-fuel sources we can pull from to propel us forward. However, they are also what we are really after anyway!

When we've successfully completed or overcome something, all we are truly striving for is to feel these sets of positive emotions and feelings. The recognition, fame, money, or accolades are positive bonuses, of course, but the *feeling* is what we are after. So, when you have a naturally occurring win, lean into the celebration and let the emotions flow, to teach your brain, body, and experience that these emotions are welcomed, safe, and present in the moment. Don't miss the opportunity to truly live into what you've accomplished!

As a practice now, I invite you to write yourself a letter to really explore what you've accomplished so far in your life. Here's a letter format to borrow to get you started:

Dear _____ (your name here),

I am grateful for....

I am so in awe of you for...

You amaze me by...

You inspire me by ....

Thank you for ....

Let the acknowledgement and honoring of yourself flow! I will also have business owners craft a list of a hundred ways that they are awesome, to help them own their greatness. Then, I invite them to read it and add to it when they need a reminder of just how amazing they are!

* * *

We started our journey together with the common goal of financial freedom. When we take a deeper look at entrepreneurship, we begin to understand that we aren't only discussing how to make our lives and businesses financially successful. More importantly, we are discussing how to be happier and healthier humans who have richer relationships and conversations. We are discussing internal satisfaction and fulfillment in answering our higher calling, loving life, loving people, and unconditionally loving ourselves.

The STEAR Clear and Anchor framework creates an easily implementable path for this to be your reality.

We can process the deeply personal through STEAR Clear and Anchor, and it can also help with the more strategic, tactical side of business by sorting through financial and business plans and establishing goals and initiatives. This tool can be used to define a strategy for working toward a TedTalk or landing a book deal or speaking tour. It helps to highlight and celebrate financial accomplishment, become a more present parent or spouse in balance with our business responsibilities, and gain clarity about the legacy of our business. It helps to determine what we value and how to lead a life of fulfillment and significance, as well as many more goals the entrepreneurs I work with come to explore.

It can be challenging, complex, and often stressful to build a business and choose the entrepreneurial path, no matter who you are. It is all too common for business owners to face frequent setbacks filled with uncertainties, frustration, and obstacles that can impact their confidence, decision-making, and overall well-being. A tool like STEAR Clear and Anchor offers a very easily implementable technique to discover the most effective path to the happiest, healthiest, and wealthiest life and business possible. It can help to keep us on our path to self-actualization and continue to show us the path even to transcend ourselves in service to the greater good of all concerned.

STEAR Clear & Anchor: A Final Integration

Summary: Beliefs about the Situation you are currently in will become your Thoughts, which will become your Emotions, which will generate motion into Action, and your Results will follow. Choose wisely by Clearing old, patterns that don't serve you and Anchoring in new, more productive, and loving ones!

Resources

- ❖ STEAR Clear and Anchor

- ❖ Brain Dump or Free Association Journaling

- ❖ The Polaroid

- ❖ Self-Care Sandbox:

    www.raeannelacatena.com/sandbox

- ❖ Celebration: 100 ways that I'm Awesome List

- ❖ Letter to Myself:

Dear _____ (Your name here),

I am grateful for….

I am so in awe of you for…

You amaze me by…

You inspire me by ….

Thank you for ….

Chapter Thirteen

Harmony: Choosing your Results

"Self-transcendence gives us joy in boundless measure. When we transcend ourselves, we do not compete with others. We do not compete with the rest of the world, but at every moment, we compete with ourselves. We compete only with our previous achievements. And each time we surpass our previous achievements, we get joy."

—Sri Chinmoy

YOU'VE DECIDED WHAT having it all looks like for you, and you've committed to doing the work to climb the ladder into actualization and transcendence. You're managing your basic needs and self-aware enough to notice when you are spiraling downward into the lower modes. You are creating harmony in your feminine and masculine energy blend and leveraging the universal laws to manifest, attract, and generate all that you choose to see in your life and business.

You've crafted an aligned money story filled with abundance and freedom, and you recognize that this work is a life's work, no matter what responsibilities you have collected over time. You are actively managing your thoughts, emotions, and actions, learning how to set better boundaries with your time, energy, and resources, and you have become a master communicator. You've committed to practicing the spiral upward daily through formal and informal thought, emotion, and energy work that aligns with what you need each day.

Your business reflects your internal world, and you are starting to see both non-linear and linear results come through in your experience.

This path is available to you now.

I've seen other people's path to transcendence through business reveal themselves during my career, and it's been one of the greatest joys of my life. This is the act of artful living, where we are living with a sense of purpose, meaning, and intention. This is where you know your roots and culture and are open to living authentically into who you truly are, appreciating your uniqueness, remaining humbly in service to others, and therefore feeling an innate sense of belonging. This looks different for every person, and that artfulness of the individual is so much a part of the beauty of this work of actualizing your potential in service to the greater good through your business.

For example, I've witnessed career-changers spend years, even decades in a corporate experience, trying to fit in with what "they" are telling them is the "right" way to live their lives and fulfill their potential. Eventually, they take the leap of faith into entrepreneurship, after wanting to find the courage for years, which finally results in stunning wealth, recovered health, and inner peace after engaging in the shift that was always aligned to them.

I've witnessed a bestselling author, actor, and producer who balanced her masculine and feminine energies in business to own her identity as a business owner and thought leader, in order to lead her life and business from love. In the process, she landed one of the most highly sought-after opportunities in Hollywood, to adapt her book for television and have exciting production roles in the future.

I've witnessed a retired all-star athlete who remembered that all her excellence in her athletic abilities were still a part of her future, and who leveraged that genius to carve a perfectly aligned path to live into her entrepreneurship and create a dream career and business in the next phase of her life.

I've witnessed some of the most distorted masculine egos, men who have abused their families verbally, used their position of power to take advantage of their female staff sexually and destroy every relationship they've ever had, come to recognize that something needed to give. I've witnessed their incredible brilliance in business, which was initially to the detriment of their personal relationships, shift to create a new life by integrating the forgotten feminine.

I've witnessed mothers, who have put off their dream of building a business in order to be of service to their children, come to this work with deep limiting beliefs about being good enough, worthy enough, or able enough to build their dream business at a later stage in their life. Stepping into their own personal power, healing that internal voice, and finding a right-fit strategy to support their evolution has led to successful business *and* continued presence to their family.

There are the great spiritual teachers, ministers, rabbis, and pastors who come to this work to integrate their faith and spiritual selves into their business ownership and to learn how to transcend even further in service to their God through business. They've learned how to speak confidently in their truth, expand their reach, and step more into alignment with who they are in order to create more concrete results in business as a reflection of service in the marketplace, *while* honoring and deepening their faith.

I've seen business leaders of all different industries at the top of their success and the height of their career, who become aware that they are miserable internally, unfulfilled, and unsatisfied with their career trajectory, and have the courage to go within to learn their purpose and then dive headfirst into a change in their career, in order to create a business that is a true reflection of their higher calling. They bravely chose purpose and impact and are now happier, healthier, and wealthier than they have ever been before.

The magic that happens when we put all these pieces together doesn't surprise me, but it never ceases to amaze and inspire me. The phenomenal energy and momentum that I witness, as these business leaders choose to spiral up to their purpose and transcend the self in service to others, creates such a far-reaching impact that I can feel the power and importance of this work over and over again through their remarkable experiences and successes.

This is deep soul work. It is often challenging and incredibly rewarding. We never "arrive" when we choose to transcend, because the possibilities are limitless. As any true entrepreneur in this work will say, when they reach what they thought was their goal, "Okay—here we are! What's next?"

The curiosity, creativity, and evolution remain ever-present. The expansion, rewards, and evolution are boundless. And the impact that the choice to live this path creates is far-reaching.

For me, what started as a teenage dream to become a famous singer has morphed, over time, through all these personal, professional, and developmental experiences, which have been sometimes traumatic and sometimes easeful and anywhere in between.

I am now grateful for the experience that happened so many years ago on graduation day: it was a major teacher and has shifted my journey in so many remarkable ways over the years.

The mask of perfection needed to be lifted; it was always an illusion and a completely unrealistic, unattainable goal. I was going to be "found out" at some point in my life. To learn that lesson early and so publicly helped me to shift, adjust, and really grow. I became committed to moving beyond those stories, paradigms, and experiences that had been given to me as a child and in my natural genetic programming.

As a result of these experiences, I have been able to shed what is no longer mine and continue to reveal my authentic self in potential. With that said, I still spiral back to these tendencies from time to time in my own personal development. That will always be a part of my journey. Except now, I am aware of those tendencies and continue to work on closing the gap between the time I fall into the lower modes and when I decide to spiral back up again.

I also now know that, while music is a deep love, a healing force, and a self-care mechanism for me, fame is not a goal of mine, and I don't believe I would have felt fulfilled or been able to actualize my true potential if I'd "made it big" in music anyway.

I continue to use music in my daily life to support my wellness and to enjoy life to the fullest. It fuels me, fills me, and inspires me in so many ways. I am in awe of music and musical ability in other people. For now, my song comes through me as a way to sing to my children and see them receive my voice with pure, deep, connected, and soul-filling love; and occasionally, even a well-placed lyric or song to support my clients! Each time I sat down to write this book, I started by calling in inspiration through song and each time I wrote, I listened to highly creative frequencies, songs, and tones to help keep my creativity at its height. For me, music is a spiritual experience.

I am still living a life that is based on the foundation of harmony and creativity.

Business is an inherently creative process that is held in harmony with all that we are and all we can be and choose to be, as humans. I see the creation of a business as a symphony that is meant to be in harmony with our authentic selves, our current set of real human realities, our identities, our traumas, our personalities, our relationships, and our dreams. You, as the business owner, can be the conductor or the lead musician or even the backstage helping hand, depending on what suits you at this moment of your life.

The journey from singing on stage in my teenage years to now has taught me one of my core beliefs: that purpose is not a singular destination; it's a journey and a path that evolves over time. When we look back on our path, we can begin to see that our past happened *for* us, not *to* us, and we can begin to integrate, heal, and even leverage what we've been through to support who we are becoming and who we are meant to be in this world.

This integration process is part of the harmony to come back to the middle, where we are respectful of the balance in our natural dualistic expression of the masculine and feminine. That core human essence of who we are allows us to step outside of ourselves and transcend even the self in service to a greater purpose and mission on the planet.

We become fulfilled and in alignment with our true selves.

We discover how we can heal ourselves first, as a reflection of the deep, inextricable connection we have to the greater good, the universe, and all things. That personal and spiritual development work is a process and a journey, not a final destination. We *get* to have a lifetime of experiences and opportunities to continue to climb, grow, evolve, shift, and pivot, as life continues to show us more parts of ourselves that deserve more attention: more trauma to heal, more limiting beliefs to shift, new responsibilities, repeating patterns, and whatever else life throws in our direction.

By healing our past, aligning with our authentic selves in the present, and actualizing and transcending our potential in the future—we can heal the planet. Because we are one.

Evolve then into the understanding that your personal harmony and the symphony you create in your business will reverberate to everyone you interact with: your family, your clients, your colleagues and coworkers, your employees and staff, your friends, and your community. That impact you are making by choosing to live into your purpose and by continuing to evolve, to grow, and to transcend yourself in service to others makes an immeasurable difference in the world.

This work is critical—our lives and planet depend on it.

If you are feeling the call, it is your responsibility to answer it.

You do have what it takes, and you are already whole. Let this be a journey. Recognize that you can have it all, because you *are* "it all."

Harmony: Choosing your Results Integration

Summary: Your business is a symphony of all of who you have been, who you are now, and all that you are becoming!

Resources

Embrace your wholeness and the beautiful harmony of who you truly are to actualize your potential and transcend yourself through your business!

Acknowledgments

THERE IS NO WAY I could have fully known what I was getting myself into when I decided to write *The Integrated Entrepreneur*. I answered the call and followed the breadcrumbs along the way, and it is certainly a culmination of everything I've seen, witnessed, and experienced in my life thus far. This book brings together so many intersecting perspectives, people, and principles that I have gathered throughout my life, from my family, through my upbringing and my experience of the world, my mentors, coaches, guides, teachers, and my clients. It turns out, it takes a village to write a book, too!

First, it's important for me to acknowledge all the clients I have served along the way, who have so greatly influenced the thoughts and teachings that landed in the book. You have each been a teacher to me and made such an incredible impact on my life. I feel honored for the opportunity to be a small part of your world. Being able to support you all in the process of making a ripple in your journey to transcendence has been and continues to be one of the greatest joys of my life. Witnessing your journeys has taught me more about business and life than I could have imagined possible, and I am in awe of what you create!

I am especially grateful for the courage and willingness of the clients who raised their hand in service to the greater good and who have been brave enough to share a part of their story in these pages. Your experiences create a legacy. Your stories will play a part in the journeys of future entrepreneurs on their own paths of personal and professional development, growth, and transformation. Thank you for your bravery.

To my many mentors, coaches, counselors, and guides: I am endlessly grateful for your contribution to this text. As we say, you can't read the label from inside the bottle. Thank you for seeing me more clearly than sometimes I see myself and for guiding me through my own journey to transcendence. The education, support, unconditional love, inspiration, guidance, and sometimes swift kick in the behind has made a massive impact on me on every level, holistically.

To my village of supportive caretakers: thank you for your wisdom, your care, your expertise, and for sharing your unique abilities in the service of helping me be as happy and healthy as possible. You know who you are, and I honor you.

To my team past and present, thank you for standing by my side in service to this greater mission. You each have a unique offering to the world, and I am so grateful to have you in my sphere of support to help make this all possible. To Lauren, thank you for the fantastic graphics and for your limitless cheerleading! You are a kind and caring soul, and I'm so grateful to have your expertise supporting the business.

To my family: the beautiful family forest that makes up all of who you are near and far. You are my first and closest teachers. I am who I am thanks to you. Thank you to my parents for your love and support and to my siblings for your presence and encouragement. To my chosen family, those friends who love me for me and maintain closeness no matter the time or space between our visits, I appreciate you and your support.

Last but most certainly not least, to my little, lovely family unit: you are the driving force behind it all. Joe, you are how all of this works for me, personally and professionally. Thank you for the unconditional acceptance, love, and support you offer to all of who I am and all that I do. I know this process has been challenging at times, and that sometimes I come up with some pretty crazy ideas. Your willingness to step in to provide in such a steadfast and loving way for our home, our children, our future, and for this greater mission is not overlooked. I love you. I am grateful for you every moment. I couldn't have written this book without you. To my babies, you are my inspiration every day. The ripple and impact I insist on making is for you first. I'm going to do whatever I can to help make the world a better place for you. Thank you for choosing me as your momma.

About the Author

RAEANNE LACATENA is a Certified Professional Coach who helps busy professionals and entrepreneurs actualize their highest selves and most fulfilling lives. She achieves this by leveraging her expertise as a Reiki Master, Licensed Registered Mental Health Counselor, and Emotional Freedom Technique practitioner, complemented by her acute empathic abilities and communication skills. Raeanne studied psychology, music, and French at Ithaca College and earned a master's degree in advanced generalist practice and programming from Columbia University.

As an International Bestselling Author endorsed by Tony Robbins, with twenty years of experience as a counselor and over a decade's experience as a business coach, Raeanne empowers her clients to harness their unique talents, curate personalized self-care toolkits, and address any obstacles hindering them from achieving their ideal lives. She currently operates as a Holistic Business Coach, bringing together business management and strategic planning with her ability to unlock hidden potential. This equips her to guide clients past hurdles and toward success and contentment in various aspects of life, including relationships, finances, communication, health, and wellness.

Raeanne's client base spans the United States and is expanding internationally, serving diverse entrepreneurs as they ascend to higher levels of leadership in their respective industries. Among the business owners she serves are restaurateurs, brick-and-mortar offices like those of physicians and therapists, teams, leaders of major corporations, and online businesses for authors, artists, speakers, thought leaders, and coaches. She works with experienced mission-driven and purpose-driven entrepreneurs who are ready to take their business to a transcendent place in service to the greater good.

Raeanne resides in picturesque western New York with her husband, her three young children who are her "why," and two small dogs. She and her family share a passion for travel, music, culinary adventures, basking in the sun, and spending cherished moments by the water.

References

Chapman, G. (2015). *The 5 love languages: The secret to love that lasts.* Northfield Publishing.

Clear, J. (2018). *Atomic habits: An easy & proven way to build good habits & break bad ones.* Avery.

Ferriss, T. (2007). *The 4-hour workweek: Escape 9-5, live anywhere, and join the new rich.* Harmony Books.

Hall, S. and Brogniez, J. (1965). *Attracting Perfect Customers: The Power of Strategic Synchronicity.* Berrett-Koehler Publishers, Inc.

Maslow, A. H. (1971). *The farther reaches of human nature.* New York: Arkana/Penguin Books.

Miller, G. A. (1956). "The magical number seven, plus or minus two: Some limits on our capacity for processing information." *Psychological Review,* 63(2), 81–97.

Moran, B. P., & Lennington, M. (2013). *The 12-week year: Get more done in 12 weeks than others do in 12 months.* John Wiley & Sons.

Ophir, E., Nass, C., & Wagner, A. D. (2009). "Cognitive control in media multitaskers." *Proceedings of the National Academy of Sciences,* 106(37), 15583–15587.

Pashler, H. (1994). "Dual-task interference in simple tasks: Data and theory." *Psychological Bulletin,* 116(2), 220–244.

Reed, P. (2003). "A nursing theory of self-transcendence." (pp. 145-166). In M.J. Smith & P. Liehr (Eds.), *Middle range theory for advanced practice nursing.* New York, NY, US: Springer.

Rubinstein, J. S., Meyer, D. E., & Evans, J. E. (2001). "Executive control of cognitive processes in task switching." *Journal of Experimental Psychology: Human Perception and Performance*, 27(4), 763–797.

Salvucci, D. D., & Taatgen, N. A. (2011). *The Multitasking Mind.* Oxford University Press.

Made in the USA
Columbia, SC
25 September 2024